Trickster and Hero

Trickster and Hero

*Two Characters in the Oral and
Written Traditions of the World*

Harold Scheub

THE UNIVERSITY OF WISCONSIN PRESS

The University of Wisconsin Press
1930 Monroe Street, 3rd Floor
Madison, Wisconsin 53711-2059
uwpress.wisc.edu

3 Henrietta Street
London WC2E 8LU, England
eurospanbookstore.com

Printed in the United States of America

Library of Congress Cataloging-in-Publication Data
Scheub, Harold.
Trickster and hero : two characters in the oral and written traditions
of the world / Harold Scheub.
p. cm.
Includes bibliographical references and index.
ISBN 978-0-299-29074-0 (pbk. : alk. paper) —
ISBN 978-0-299-29073-3 (e-book)
1. Tricksters—Cross-cultural studies. 2. Tricksters in literature.
3. Heroes—Folklore. 4. Heroes in literature. I. Title.
GR524.S37 2012
809´93352—dc23
2012013283

HERO AND TRICKSTER

HEAVEN
THE CREATOR GOD
The perfect time, when all was in harmony. A time before differentiation.
Gods, humans, animals: all are the same. Then the Creator God begins the
work of creation. . . .

↕

THE UNDIFFERENTIATED ENERGY OF THE COSMOS
THE DIVINE TRICKSTER
In the divine trickster can be found the perfection of the gods and the villainy of
the nether forces. He comes to embody a period of chaos, upheaval, change.

↕

THE AGE OF DIFFERENTIATION
THE CULTURE HERO
The Age of Differentiation is embodied in the character of the Culture Hero:
he is both god (the perfect time) and human (the flawed world that we now know),
a combination of hero and trickster. He mediates between gods and humans, and
is therefore himself composed of both. His growing knowledge of his own limits
suggests his movement from the golden time to the contemporary age: his
movement is toward his humanity and away from godliness.

↕

MEDIATING HEAVEN AND EARTH
THE EPIC HERO
He is revolutionary: he creates a culture. This sometimes involves a move from
the old culture (equivalent to a biological state) to the new.

↕

THE UNDIFFERENTIATED ENERGY OF THE EARTH
THE PROFANE TRICKSTER
Untamed energy; feeds appetites at the expense of all else. Amoral; largely
indifferent to human culture.

EARTH
THE TALE CHARACTER
The tale character is conservative: s/he supports the culture that s/he has
inherited; an emphasis in stories having to do with the tale character: changes from
a biological to a cultural being, hence the emphasis in tales on rites of passage.
But the tale character is rarely revolutionary.

Contents

Trickster and Hero

Prologue

The eternal moment, the moment of transition, the trickster moment: Why is this important? Because during that moment, we are out of ourselves. We are broken into parts: we are man and woman, god and human, hero and villain; all of the possibilities of life are there, and we select them and participate in our own re-creation. We are taken apart and rebuilt. It is for that reason that the moment revitalizes us, freshens us. That is a major reason for our love of storytelling: we allow it to dissect us and to remodel us. The trickster is the alpha and the omega of the movement, at once the force of the movement and its end. In the trickster is the hero, like a magnificent butterfly struggling to free itself of the cocoon.

We are present at our dismemberment and our rebirth.

Introduction

The Hero

The hero is a visionary. He must do battle with external adversaries and also, at times, with himself. This battle is generally characterized as a transition of some kind. These are recurring themes: the first has to do with myth and god; the second has to do with trickster, divine and profane. The third has to do with the tale character and with rites of passage, with liminality. Epic is the consummation of all aspects of the society and the oral tradition. The hero can be identified by all three of these ideas. J. R. R. Tolkien wrote of the old English epic poem, *Beowulf* (c. 700 AD): "He is a man, and that for him and many is sufficient tragedy."[1] Tolkien wrote of the transitoriness of life in *Beowulf*.[2] The transitoriness of life is also a theme in the Sumerian epic, *Gilgamesh* (c. 3000 BC). In this poem, the hero is two-thirds god and one-third human. During the course of the epic, he learns the fact of his mortality. The theme is communicated through dualism: Gilgamesh and the trickster Enkidu, the one part god and part man, the other part man and part animal. There is a movement of the one from god to human, of the other from animal to human. They meet in the center, their humanity is affirmed, and their mortality is assured.

Epic deals with the hero confronting his own limitations. To be sure, fantasy swirls on all sides of him. He is frequently aided by fabulous and miraculous agents, donors, and helpers, but that is the point: these exist outside of him. They are not a part of his character: he is not invulnerable. Godlike though he may be, there is an Enkidu side to the character. In *Gilgamesh*, it is the Enkidu side of the hero with which he is attempting to come to terms. Epic, then, occurs within the framework of fantasy, but its focus is the humanity of the hero. In all oral narrative, fantasy and realism exist side by side. Those are the two basic reservoirs of imagery. In oral narrative, there is a vision, a model, a pattern, and that guides the characters in the narrative: their world can only be based on already established models. They are therefore caught up in a prede- termined pattern, and can pattern their own affairs and actions only on it. It is vulnerability that is at the center of epic, and it is for that reason that epic often seems brooding, fatalistic, tragic. In the epic, the oral narrative character has lost his fabulous qualities; the move is toward humanity.

The Trickster

The profane or earth-bound trickster is, like the divine trickster, obscene, aggressive, selfish, amoral. In this, he is closest to the basest of humans. He lacks the sublime connection with the gods, and this is what distinguishes the profane from the divine trickster. Yet, in a way, the profane trickster does retain an echo of the divine connection, if tenuously: he also creates in the sense that he creates a world of illusion; he imposes his own corrupt sense of order on the real world. An agent of chaos, he disrupts harmony; when he establishes harmony, it is according to his own whim, his own sense of order. Trickster combines horror and glee: his is the comedy of the grotesque. With his enor- mous penis, his diminutive size, his love of dance, his amorality, his clownish- ness, he is a grotesque, a rootless, unattached individual who must secure his own survival and psychological wellbeing in a society that espouses traditional values while actually sanctioning dehumanizing modes of behavior. Trickster inherits no place he can call home; he is an outsider. He has no job, he is fre- quently prematurely made responsible for his own welfare; he undergoes a rude awakening, or initiation, that shocks him into an awareness of what he must do to survive. Because he lacks the strength and integrity to impose his will on a hostile world, he adapts himself to diverse situations by serving different mas- ters, inventing clever ruses, or wearing a variety of masks during a peripatetic life of alternating good and evil fortune.

The trickster is outrageous. Humans move from one state to another, but the trickster's is the liminal state, the state of betwixt and between. Trickster is undifferentiated energy, ungovernable. He may appear tame, but in the next instant he shows that he is not. In the trickster and hero, all is change, trans- formation. Enormous untamed energy is in the process of being controlled, funneled. He is always reinventing the world, testing boundaries, relearning the possibilities. This does not justify his acts: in fact, it is difficult to see Trickster in a moral framework. And as we curse and revile him, we understand that he is the representative of us, of our emotions and urges, of our inner world. He is our id, unvarnished, untempered. He is stupid at times, he is brilliant at others. He is small and he is large, but most of the time small, and therefore dependent on his wiles rather than his brawn. We never give him up, because he represents something within us. We can laugh at him because he is, we insist, so inane, so unlike us, at the same time that we understand his likeness to us.

It is not enough to say that he is a safety valve for us, though he is that, doing things to leaders that we dare not do, saying things that we dare not say. Trickster is amiable at times, brutal at others. He is unpredictable. The friendly spider and the cuddly hare may also be deadly. That is the seemingly quirky power of the trickster. He is the clown, who makes one laugh . . . but nervously, because, in his stupidity and witless humor, we see ourselves.

The Trickster and Origins

Origins, etiological events, occur in oral narrative tradition within this framework. Once again, one may argue about whether or not these etiological elements are taken literally by the members of audiences in oral societies. However these arguments regarding the assessment of origins within audiences are resolved, several observations may be made. It may well be that we have been interpreting etiological narratives from the wrong angle. Instead of seeing the end as resulting from the narrative actions that preceded it, perhaps it would be more productive to see the etiological comment as deepening, universalizing, the narrative actions that have just been evoked. Etiological narratives are attempts within the oral narrative traditions to raise human actions to the level of the cosmological. Human affairs influence the way of the world; what humans do has effects on the external world. In fact, the transformation of the world from disorganization, from chaos, into the recognizable and meaningful shapes that it assumes today occurs because of human actions, and human actions can have a disastrous opposite effect on the movement of the world as well. Etiological narratives are no different from other narratives, in this respect, and they are just as significant as devices for the communication of meaning and regulation of human behavior as non-etiological narratives.

Etiological trickster narratives take a variety of forms. In one narrative, the trickster is responsible for the presence of water all over the world because he overcomes the deadly machinations of an old woman. In another, a parrot's act of rescue is commemorated by the change of color of its tail to red. In yet another, a love affair is celebrated by the transformation of the loving couple into oil, the complete mingling of their bodies into oil, which confers a handsome appearance on all who anoint themselves with it. In a fourth narrative, a Winnebago story, a tall man with a big cane abuses other people, striking them with the cane. Hare's bettering of the tall man results in the transformation of the villain into an ant: "You will henceforth remain down there close to the earth and the people will tramp upon you." And finally, Trickster's urgent desire to have the good fortune of someone else results in his efforts to duplicate the actions of the other, but in his haste he makes some errors, and the results are the opposite of what was desired. The narrator informs the audience that people recall this narrative whenever someone leaps at a new thing without first thinking it through. Presumably, Trickster's actions in this narrative are the basis for this think-before-you-leap caution. Each of these etiological events results from the narrative actions that preceded them, and the etiological commentary is little different from that commentary that we experience in the variety of Mantis narratives, where Mantis's family comments regularly and fairly constantly on the activities of this trickster/transformer. The etiological result of the actions in the narrative is also a comment, but the comment is taking different form now, a kind of image. More significant is the fact that the performer seeks to find a broader, more cosmological result of human/trickster activities. Etiological elements are not found only in trickster narratives. From the point of view of structure alone, these etiological endings are not much different from the endings of scores of non-etiological narratives. Because of his triumph over the old woman with the yams, Trickster Ture[3] causes water to be available for all mankind. Because the parrot rescues the queen mother's child from the python, its tail is painted red for all time. Because the couple are so in love, they are melted into oil and become a fount of beauty for all mankind. Because the tall man abuses humans, he is transformed into an ant. Because Trickster Ture is so greedy, he makes blunders that result in his own failure and in the deaths of many people. The etiological endings buttress these narrative activities, they clinch them, they tighten them in the aesthetic experience of the audience, they give these human activities a cosmological significance by making their effects eternal, in one way or another. Other narratives have similar structures: because the cannibalistic Zim abuse humans, they are destroyed. Because children are greedy, they make blunders that result in the flight of the magical bird and in their own punishment. Because she triumphs over the swallowing monster, a woman releases the many people and creatures in its belly. Because the hero rescues the chief's daughter, he is given that daughter in marriage. The essential difference is, of course, that the results in the case of the so-called etiological narratives are much more astronomical, they touch all humans for all times; they are eternal testaments to man's achievements and

How Ture Released the Water[4]

There was an old woman who planted many yams. They yielded (swelled) abundantly. People used to come and work for her and she used to cook them for them. But she never gave water to the people. She alone possessed water, which she dammed from other people. So whenever a man ate the yams they stuck in his throat, and when he writhed with them this old woman attacked him with her big knife and cut his throat with it. This woman killed many people in this way. However, Ture heard about this woman and arose and went to her home to work for her for yams. Ture already knew that she was hiding water from people. So Ture went and searched all around until he found the water she had been keeping from people. Ture drew some of this water in his bottle-gourd and put it in his bag. Then he went also and cut a hollow grass, and put it (one end of it) into his water. After Ture had worked for this woman she took a very large pot and filled it with yams and boiled them. She put them before Ture and went and sat down with her big knife and watched Ture closely, so that when he choked with the yams she might cut his throat. Ture then ate the yams and when they stuck in his throat he sucked up his water with that hollow grass he had put into his bottle-gourd in the bag. So Ture ate up all the yams without their sticking in his throat. This old woman went again and cooked more yams for Ture, nice mealy ones, and sat down again to watch Ture closely for the yams to choke him. Ture ate up all these yams of hers, for whenever they stuck in his throat he drank some of his water. The old woman went again and cooked yams even more mealy than the previous ones. Ture ate only a little and put all the rest in his bag. Ture then took one yam to eat it. After that he began to open wide his mouth and eyes as when something chokes a person. So this old woman jumped up from her place with her big knife and attacked Ture to cut his throat. When she was close to Ture he sprang up and landed a distance from her, and he started off at full speed and fled by the path to her water. She cried out, saying, "Ture, there is no way there. Ture, that is the way to excrement. Ture, there is no way there. Ture, that is the way to excrement." Ture continued to run straight ahead and she shouted after him in vain. Ture then broke her dam and the water flowed everywhere. Ture stood on the far side (of the water) and said, "It is I here, I am Ture, it is I who have dealt with you." That is why water is found all over the world.

man's failures, his goodness and his evil. Other narratives are content with less far-reaching consequences of human actions and human frailties and glories. This is not so in the cases of trickster stories and other etiological narratives.

There are also many trickster narratives that in developmental and percep-tual processes differ not at all from non-trickster narratives. Indeed, the char-acter of the trickster as it is developed in such narratives emerges as fool at times, as hero at others, as villain at others. In fact, Trickster becomes little more than a character who moves about easily and readily through a variety of experiences, and it is the experiences that define the character of Trickster, it is not the trickster who defines the experiences. Such narratives, with or with-out etiological endings, are in no way different from those narrative-images that become the raw materials for the ritualistic artistic experience.

The basic structures of the narratives from a variety of sources and locales are much the same. In fact, those storytellers who tell narratives with etiologi-cal endings and which nevertheless contain structures similar to those in non-etiological narratives are seeking to communicate effects of actions experienced in the earlier part of the narrative. Trickster moves easily in the roles of god, man, animal, and insect, and there are times when his action is motivated, times when his action is unmotivated. But there is seldom any time when his actions lack meaning. And sometimes those actions are linked to cosmological events, other times they are tied to social events, but the fact is that whether the trick-ster is flaunting the most sacred customs of the people or upholding them hero-ically, whether he is transforming the grand scale of the earth or indulging in petty and harmful activities, his actions are not without meaning, not with-out ritualistic significance, not without socially redeeming value. Hlakanyana's actions in the Zulu narratives seem outlandish, without motivation. But his unmotivated actions nevertheless have perceptual significance within the nar-rative itself. It is on actions that we should focus, not on character. Trickster conveniently fits into any role at any time; in a narrative by a Xhosa storyteller, Trickster-Hlakanyana uses his cunning to get the marauding villain, who has been released from captivity because of the compassion of some man, to return to his state of captivity, and there to remain. If Trickster is a problem, his activ-ities are not, and his activities, whether antisocial or socially acceptable, are within the mainstream of the narrative tradition. Ture's self-serving activities in a narrative in which he sings the wrong words and thereby causes the destruc-tion of many people, in which he falls asleep and thereby invites the depreda-tions of the terrible bird, these are typical trickster actions. And these actions would have meaning, social meaning, even without the addition of the first set of images, those that deal with the more heroic actions of the orphan in the same circumstances. Trickster's actions would have social value simply because they would be placed against social values as they exist outside the narrative. In a Xhosa storyteller's version of a baboon's circumcision, for example, the humor of the narrative is augmented by the knowledge of the members of the audience of how sacred the rite of circumcision really is. Add to Ture's activities an image set in which his actions can immediately be contrasted with the opposite actions of another character, and the meaning is intensified.

Trickster narratives seem to fall into two broad categories, perceptually speaking: in the first, trickster narratives are no different in structure and in theme than hero-type narratives; in the second, trickster narratives seem identified with Trickster, they do not seem to carry over into the heroic narratives, and Trickster moves without apparent regard for social niceties. This latter, of course, occurs in both categories, though in the first he is from time to time heroic. The first category is really a category of hero, if these categories mean anything at all, and many if not most of the trickster narratives fit into this first category. The etiological endings occur in both categories, and in fact occur in non-trickster narratives as well. Etiological endings that occur in the first category are generally closely tied to the actions of the narrative, and give cosmological significance to those actions, lending universality to man's behavior. But even with the etiological elements, the narratives of this first category can be analyzed and explained pretty much the way the usual heroic-type narratives are analyzed and explained.

The Hero and the Trickster

When considering the hero, we move into a wonderful and bizarre world, a world peopled by heroes of undeniable stature and of uncertain humanity, a nether realm of cunning and unrepentant tricksters and gods. The measure for these two seemingly extreme characters has been the tale character, the everyperson of the oral tradition. The trickster and the hero seem to stand on either side of the tale character, the one his shameful origins, the other his glimmering vision. Or the one his negative option, the other his positive option. That set of polarities is a viable one. But there are other options. The trickster might be seen as the obverse of the hero, the primordial trickster moving to the sublime order of the hero, in a splendid fairy-tale domestication of the trickster movement. But the most tantalizing option is neither of these. The seemingly antithetical characters are not at all contraries. It makes sense: the hero and the trickster are the most durable of storytelling figures, ancient, unchanging, adapting to contemporary realities but ever the same. A seemingly simple brace of characters becomes a rather complex insight into humanity. It is the combination of the two that is the significant thing: not the movement from the one to the other, not the two as the extremes of the human condition.

The trickster and the hero are trying the limits of their societies and their own natures. Hero pushes back the frontiers of his culture, Trickster pushes back the frontiers of human nature. He is the raw human, newly born, filled with the excitement of his own strength and wit. He moves into the world like a child newly born, trying out his considerable powers on everyone and everything he meets. He is a human walking the earth on the morning of creation, naming things, creating things, fine-tuning the creation, at the same time that he is becoming aware of his own limitations. He is the eternally youthful, and we like that in him. He is forever trying things out, eternally on the cusp of creation. When he sees someone doing something, he must do it too. He wants to be everything. He is a renaissance man gone wild, gone awry. He is the force that occurs when change is taking place. He is the divine trickster present at the greatest change of all, the creation. Trickster is a clown, a master of disguise, of deception. He is often menacing. And he is present at the beginning of things.

What makes the hero of interest is the fact that trickster energy is at the heart of the heroic epic. The trickster clearly embodies, as we have seen, chaos and order. He is amoral, and therefore chaos and order are not of special significance to him, as they are, of course, to us. The hero also embodies chaos and order, but the difference is that the hero has a vision that funnels and focuses those energies, so that society is redefined in a fairly permanent way. Whatever the vision or outcome, the movement in the central part of the epic is no different from that in the central part of either the divine or profane trickster tale. All, tricksters and hero, are in the process of creating. To that extent, they are all mythic. We have defined the limits of their creative activities, but the fact remains that all are creative. The trickster embodies the essential traits of the hero: everything except vision. And the trickster often moves on the grand scale of the hero.

Tricksters are the timeless energy, the eternally liminal, the ordering and the chaotic. They are the alpha and omega, the yin and the yang, the contradictory, the ambiguous, the unending. They are primordial, now sublime and now debased, neither the one nor the other, but a combination that emerges in strange, quirky, and unpredictable ways. We see ourselves in the trickster. It is that trickster who is the heart of the epic, the core of the tale, the soul of the creative myth. Whenever there is chaos and order, the trickster is there. And, for a time, the hero is a trickster, the tale character is a trickster, God plays the role of trickster.

It is at the point that hero and trickster meet in the oral tradition, and in the lives of humans, that the interest of the hero and trickster stories rests. It is at that point that our cosmological, cultural, and personal histories come to a focus, when creation and the gods, society and its heroes, and our own transformations are experienced as identical. That is where the interest of the hero and trickster stories rests. It is precisely at that point at which past, present, and future are sharply focused by means of storytelling that the emotions of the audience are most fully enlisted. It is at the point of tension between chaos and order that we place our emphases: we are present at a birth and a death, at a death and a birth.

There is a compelling reason that the tale is at the heart of the epic. It is not a mistake that the myth is integral to the epic. These are built one inside the other, because in the end they are not distinguishable. Myth, tale, epic, history: they move into and out of each other. We thought that we knew our heroes, but the trickster element in the hero-trickster combination gives us pause. The hero has always given us cause to wonder, has always had his Achilles heel, his vulnerability. Moses errs, Odysseus stumbles, Sunjata falters. In the movement to quintessence, the hero must navigate treacherous shoals and perilous reefs: in such an adventure is his heroism forged. That shaping, paradoxically, is at the hands of the trickster. To move to morality, one moves to one's origins, to amorality. To move to greatness, one descends to hell. To move to the embodiment of a culture, one rends the culture's foundations. To move to wholeness, to psychological fullness, one is fragmented. The storytelling performance is therapeutic to the extent that it provides a safe laboratory for this dismantling and re-creation activity. This betwixt-and-between period, the time of the trickster shuffle, is a season of uncertainty and confusion, of disorientation, of psychological and cultural miasma. Heroic epics are not about heroes, any more than trickster tales are stories about scandalous con-men. Nor, in fact, are the stories about the gods meant to be histories of the heavens. Trickster, hero, God: these characters and their stories are significant only to the extent that they illuminate the lives of you and me, everyperson. Heroic stories are not a category set aside from the common person. God is not a lofty personage with no connection to humanity. Trickster is not a character so low that it is impossible to find an identification with him. The trickster tale, the godly myth, the heroic epic are reworkings of the seemingly inconsequential tale. This explains the presence of the tale in myth, in the trickster story, in the heroic epic. Nor is it simply that the godly myth reveals the god in us, the heroic epic the hero in us, the trickster story the trickster in us. . . . that is so. But it is much more.

In storytelling, all is doppelganger, palimpsest. The modern story is similar to some ancient San rock paintings in southern Africa: clearly evident are the foreground paintings, of San hunters, weapons at the ready, stalking their prey, eland. This image has been painted over another image, now rendered obscure and blurred because of the fresher painting, that background imagery dominated by hooded and masked figures, the mythic images of the gods. The painting is at once a story and a prayer, achieved through what appears to be conscious palimpsest.

The essential tasks of the performer of an oral narrative are to evoke and to channel, to evoke images from a common pool of experience, to organize those images and in the process of organization to have some kind of emotional and perhaps behavioral impact upon the members of the audience, upon the reader, to evoke: usually by means of concrete language to form the evocative image; to channel: by means of metaphor, for metaphor is the active process brought to life in performance whereby the images come into contact and shape experience. Neither evocative image nor the process of metaphor works alone; neither can work in isolation from each other, nor in isolation from an audience, for it is the audience that mentally creates the image influenced by the evocative power of the artist and his crucial guidance as the images are placed into an enclosed space and given form. As the artist calls upon the audience's common experiences and organizes these experiences in a series of evoked images, he shapes our experience and our knowledge of ourselves and the world we inhabit. A musician brings order to a world of sounds, a painter organizes a diversity of colors, a poet arranges a lexicon, but that is to understate the functions of each of the artists, for each brings a kind of order to human experience, each shapes that experience according to his own experience and his own artistic vision, and by shaping experience the artist gives it meaning.

Myth is more than story, it is the shaping process itself. More accurately, myth is the result of the shaping process; a story becomes myth by means of this shaping process. Myth is not myth unless it includes both the developmental and the perceptual processes. This shaping process exists in no vacuum. Myth is not myth until the meaningfulness necessary to the shaping of human experience is achieved. The mere organization of human experience in symbols and images that embody that experience, that in performance fragment human experience, then reorder it and in the reordering provide it with fresh meaning— this organization does not take place without something emerging from the very act of arranging. Images are brought together, and in the bringing together of those images experience is altered. Myth and the metaphorical process that takes narrative and converts it to experience involves both the organization of images—a developmental process—and the meaningfulness that results from the organization—a perceptual process. It is in this organizing that a process of metaphor takes place; that is, the extension of human experience occurs when images are externalized. These images are symbolic in the sense that they stand for human experience; they stand for human experience, however, at the same time that they *are* human experience.

This is the aesthetic paradox of the performance. The complex of images composing a performance does not reflect human experience in any concrete and literal way. If these images reflect human experience at all, they do so in a way peculiar to the art form itself. And the only way to comprehend the meaningful relations that exist between the experience of the work of art and the actual human experience it is reflecting and perhaps even extending is to understand the laws that animate the system. The images that are expressed stand for human experience, accepting the premise that they indeed have something to do with human experience. But the images are themselves experience, not, it is true, the same thing as a routine experience outside the art form. It is an experience that occurs within the work of art, and as such it has its own special quality as experience. But experience it is, a psychological and emotional experience. And most of the nonverbal and many of the verbal elements of the production seem geared to make this aesthetic experience as successful as possible.

The images represent human experience in two ways, both standing for human experience in the wider world, and providing the stuff of experience, "such stuff / As dreams are made on,"[5] within the world of art. These two worlds are bridged during a performance, they are brought into conjunction. And as the images stand for human experience, they impose upon that proxy experience a different kind of experience, one of art, an experience that, by superimposing itself on the larger real-life experience, brings those fragments and those unconnected activities into meaningful organization and arrangement. The one experience achieves organization and therefore meaning by bringing it into contact with an artistic experience. This conjunction and the meaning that it generates is myth. In this process, the various obvious surface attributes of the oral narrative, the functions of these characteristics of oral performance, become quite clear; the magical actions, the supernatural creatures, the recognizable human activities and artifacts, these mix together and provide the raw materials for the artistic experience, which at the same time that it is its own unique kind of experience, snares human experience in the real world, takes those meaningful fragments of experience and arranges them. The arrangement occurs by means of the narrative images; nothing else is operating here, there are no materials save these core-images, all of them quite old, it would seem, all of them having served in this capacity for generations for a variety of artists. The possible arrangement of the fragments of the human experience is finite, and because it is finite and controlled by the relatively small number of images that can be worked into the performance, it is possible to speak of a comprehensive world view that is revealed by this process of metaphor, endowing the former engulfing human experience in the artistic experience, and thereby giving the former its meaning.

In this organizing process, which results in myth, a process that seeks to orchestrate the audience's relationship with its society and the wider world, a number of artistic devices are used, and these devices are used to assist in the establishment of a relationship of meanings between audience and experience. The artist attempts through his or her craft and by means of a pool of common images to restrict that experience first of all, and then slowly to give it meaningful shape. But that meaningful shape does not occur without a lot of prior training, training that the members of the audience have been undergoing since childhood. The common pool of images is one necessary set of materials, and the common experiences in the real world another. Myth is the result of the process whereby the one pool is brought into contact with the other, whereby the daily activities and experiences of the members of the audience are brought into contact with the image pool. and by mediating these two worlds, that of experience and that of image, the artist shapes the former. This process is one of metaphor, a process in which the fragments of human experience are related to an unfragmented artistic experience, and thereby made whole, thereby is fragmented human experience made whole, complete. But it is important, if this process is to take place, that elements of human experience have counterparts in artistic experience, and it is for this reason that the pool of images is significant. These images, developed through the years, respond to central activities of human experience, not the least important of which are the rites of passage. These images become on the one hand extensions of that human experience, and because they are extensions of human experience, and because they (unlike human experience) can be manipulated and organized in a finite setting (the setting of the artistic performance) it is possible to make comments about that human experience. More important, it is possible by means of the artistic experience to duplicate human experience. That is the first thing that must occur during this process of myth. In order for fragmented human experience to have shape and meaning, it must be translated into workable forms, into shapes that are capable of manipulation.

Before human experience can be made meaningful within an artistic framework, it must then be converted into shapes and forms that have artistic value. The repertory of core-images answers to this problem. Once this conversion of the fragments of human experience has taken place, it becomes possible by means of an experience that is not at all like normal human experience to give that human experience shape and meaning. Human experience is so vast, so fragmented, so meaningless in itself. To shape it, organize it, to arrange its parts, it must be worked into elements that are capable of manipulation. Before the artistic experience can take place this movement from the real to the artistic must take place. The threshold into art must be lowered, the audience must be willing to suspend disbelief, all of the approaches to art with which we are familiar must occur. Once this takes place, we are now in another realm. The artist has removed us from the real world, and taken us into a world that stands for the real world, which is symbolic of the real world, so that that real world can begin to come into focus, to make sense. But to make sense, there must be a value system that guides the arrangement of the images in the artistic experience. And the artist has such a system; it is inherent in the very system of images themselves, of artistic images, that is. Whatever arrangement and organization these images may take in actual performance, in one way or another they affirm the society's values, so that the meaningful organization of human experience takes place within a framework of values, so that those fragments are given a meaning that depends not on the whims of the performer but on the values of the society. These values seem to be caught up in the very images themselves. This process of bringing elements of human experience into the world of art is a process of metaphor whereby the images and symbols of the oral narrative tradition are brought to bear on fragmented human experience. The result is to give meaning to that experience, and also to have an impact on human behavior when reentry is made into the world of experience.

The experience of the members of the audience within this process might be termed *ritual*, an aesthetic psychological and emotional experience that has the effect of giving meaning to the nonartistic experience of that audience, an aesthetic experience that is carefully constructed and sustained by the artist, a tradition geared to this aesthetic experience, developed for and constantly adjusting to this critical process. Myth and narrative are not, then, the same thing. But myth is more than a mere category placed alongside "tale" and "legend," as the three separate but equal elements of oral tradition. So-called myths are always having to face the incursion of the narrative, of the tale. And so is legend. The tale finds itself in the myth, in the legend. It is more accurate to see tale as the basis for myth, as the material necessary to the development of a myth. Narrative by itself, as noted, is the stuff of myth, but a narrative in itself as a story, a plotting of images, even when accompanied by nonverbal elements (gesture, etc), is not necessarily myth. In certain performances, narrative becomes myth; in other performances, the narrative remains narrative but not myth. Myth and narrative differ, but myth cannot exist without narrative; this is the basis of the analyses of developmental and perceptual processes in oral performance.

Myth is in fact metaphorized narrative. It is a combination of the developmental and perceptual processes, and it is not one without the other. Myth requires image for meaning; it is both image and meaning. The metaphorizing process means that the developmental elements of the performance are manipulated, and used to move the images into forms and structures that enable the images to achieve meaning. This is occurring within the work of art itself, and it occurs only when the elements of human experience have been transposed into artistic terms. A system of fixed symbols and the presiding thematic image-cluster of the tradition insure that even the most superficial narrative conflict-resolution has some kind of meaning that affirms the society. The performer depends on this system of fixed symbols when he or she constructs a more complex narrative, when he or she moves the narrative into myth. The storyteller establishes a new system of symbols, non-fixed symbols, to complement the fixed system, so that there is now an unstable or temporary symbol system that relates to the fixed system. The broad epic matrix of a society contains the raw materials for myth, then, and the traditional system of fixed symbols makes it possible for human experience to be translated into artistic experience. This educational system of the oral tradition moves, in this respect, on two levels: first a literal level, bedtime stories for children, conflicts and resolutions and little more than that, but at their most literal the narratives continue to educate, to affirm the society, if in no other way than to provide the child with experiences of structure. And so the children become familiar with the imaged language of the system, it becomes second nature to them; they themselves learn to use it, to communicate by means of it, to link narrative to narrative to compose larger narratives, to give the combination of diverse narratives the illusion of union. The combination of diverse narratives becomes a combination and juxtaposition of narrative images, evoking something that goes beyond the image, transforming narrative into myth.

This process is metaphorical in its nature, and as far as the experience of the audience is concerned the process is also ritual. Ritual involves more than the ordering of symbols and images to inject meaning into human experience. Ritual does this, ritual in this definition being the artistic experience itself. But ritual also seeks to influence human behavior, not merely to reflect it and to give it meaning. Ritual seeks to alter reality by altering human relationships with it. Ritual, then, is composed of this dual purpose: first, to give meaning to human experiences by shaping the images that have traditionally symbolized, artistically stood for, crucial and significant fragments of those experiences; and, second, to influence human behavior by aesthetically ordering human beings' relations with the real, constructing a paradigm, a model in which the real and the artistic come into conjunction, in which members of the audience through their rich participation in the performance (verbally and nonverbally) are involved in a ritualistic affirmation of the society, a ritualistic entrance into the world of symbol which breaks down the traditional barriers between art and reality, and the ritual thereby influences the behavior of those involved in the art experience. There are two experiences. The first is an experience in the real world, the world of routine day-to-day life, a world cut into segments, each of which is approached and entered by means of a rite of passage, a world that requires some kind of symbolic system so that human beings' movements within that world have sense, and the human being in that world has meaning. The other experience at once runs parallel to the world of the day to day at the same time that it interprets that world and conditions the behavior of human beings for a more satisfying and productive reentry into the ordinary realm. This is the world of art, presided over by the performer, in which the members of the audience are not passive, but significant participants. This world of art is not to be considered removed from the world of daily experience; there are vital connections between the two. The world of art has many correspondences to the real world: in fact, the elements of the world of art experience relate to the fragments of the world of live experience. This is ritual, the artistic experiencing of life, the artistic organizing of life's experiences, the fragments of life in the real world; in artistic ways, we reenact human experience, and in the reenactment, humans experience meaning. And as humans experience meaning, their own behavior is shaped according to paradigms established by the tradition and, immediately, in the work of art.

Ritual explains and conditions. But it is not the external world that ritual seeks to alter; it is human behavior that it alters, and it is the society's view, society's comprehension of reality, that ritual orders. Ritual depends heavily on symbol and image to accomplish this task, and it requires the full participation of the audience. It is not a vicarious experience then, it is experience itself, an experience that stands for real life experience, a critical social process that regulates human behavior and gives human beings' movements meaning.

Metaphor is the process whereby symbols come into conjunction with reality, and achieve meaning. Narratives are composed of the cultural environment: understandable, recognizable, mingled with the fantastic, the magical, the unreal, the symbol. The symbol makes the connection, the real is embodied in it, and the relationship of the symbols comments upon the real. The connections between the symbols, between the images, and between symbols and images—these relationships and the meaning engendered by these perceived connections and relationships: this is myth. The experience itself is ritual. Ritual and myth cannot be separated. The artistic experience is ritualized real life experience, and the flow of meaning between the two that results from the ritualized experience is myth. The raw materials include the cultural activities and the narratives, or more accurately, the core-images from which the narratives or the developmental processes are developed. More precisely yet, the ritual, that is, the artistic experience, enables the audience to perceive the arrangement, the organization, the structure of the images, their relationships. The entire artistic performance—that is to say, the ritual—is developed to bring the audience to perceive these relationships, for it is in the perception of these relationships that the meaningful harmony of real life and artistic experience is achieved. This act of perception by means of ritual, by means of the artistic experience, is the perceptual process. These narratives are composed of images, with no openly didactic elements. The aesthetic experience, ritual, of the narratives that compose the developmental aspects of the performance is geared to the revelation of the relationships that exist among the various images, among the various symbols, between symbols and images.

A great amount of meaning-potential movement is constantly taking place between these symbols and these images, among the symbols, among the images. Organization and arrangement are essential to the definition of this movement; if meaningful relationships are to be perceived, then obviously meaningful relationships must be constructed. The artistic experience, the ritual, reveals these movements, these interrelationships, to the members of the audience. And the revelation of those movements is a perceptual process that develops from the transposition of narrative into myth. The overall movement then is very complex; human beings are brought into a performance, into an artistic experience, and because certain aspects of their fragmented human experience have been translated into artistic terms, the real life experiences are given meaning. It is then possible for the human being to be released from the artistic experience, and that too is a part of myth, for it means the movement of the human back into the real world. It is not enough merely to bring the human's real life experiences into harmony with the fixed symbols of the tradition; that is not enough because it is not sufficiently precise; it does not adequately respond to the current needs of the members of the audience. Moreover, in order for the two worlds to move into conjunction, certain adjustments must be made. The real must fit snugly into the artistic and the non-fixed symbols are developed to assist in this process. They are a part of the metaphorizing process, which is both image and meaning. They cannot be separated. The non-fixed symbols have an artistic function to perform both as artistic devices and as vials of meaning.

To conclude: the movement into the world of art is no easy task. The leap into art is an essential element of a human's being in the real world. There is not only an entry into the world of art; there is the reentry into the real world, an altered human being whose experience of the real world has now been given fresh or traditional meaning and who can then function in that perplexing world, renewed and assured that his or her movements have meaning. Metaphor, then, is the process, myth is the product; the basic raw material consists of narrative and symbol. Symbols are images that achieve a meaning within a context of images, which stand for certain experiences. And ritual is the process whereby audiences are moved into a perception of relationships, as the performer generates perceptual processes from the developmental.

There are many tensions in an oral performance, and perhaps the reasons for these tensions now become clear. There are tensions between the performer and the audience, as the performer seeks to bring the members of the audience into his or her work of art. But there are other tensions, too—those, for example, of the unfulfilled work of art; the entire experience is in tension until the completion of the work, when it lingers for a moment, then vanishes. There is also a tension between the worlds of experience and art, essential to the perceptual processes of the work of art. And there are tensions within the work too, on the level of conflict and resolution, the tensions that exist among the various characters and actions of the developing drama. There is tension generated by the process of metaphor, between the surface of the work of art and the perceptual elements generated by bringing various narratives into conjunction. These tensions are built into this kind of art form, and it is important that the artist know how to manipulate these tensions without dissolving them.

But what about the artistic experience itself? What actually occurs during an aesthetic experience? If one is altered in the process, then how is one altered? The organization and arrangement of images are readily understood, but can the experience itself be characterized? The members of the audience are prepared for the oral performance, or they would simply absent themselves from it; there is nothing that says that a person must remain there. The threshold is lowered for the experience that is to follow. In addition, the audience has been conditioned by many performances to understand the role it is to play, to understand that for the narrative experience to have its effect, the members of the audience must allow themselves to be manipulated to a certain extent. The effect of the images themselves, with their concomitant verbal and nonverbal artistic devices, will assist in this transposition of the audience from the real work into the world of art. Once audience members are involved in the images, that is, once they are caught up in the verbal and nonverbal elements of the production—and it must be remembered that the performer is at some pains to involve the members of the audience vocally and physically in the performance as well—then they apparently accept with equanimity the arrangements of their fragments of experience, the ordering of these fragments into new shapes. And since they are experiencing the images—that is, since they are wholly caught up in their externalization— then they are also experiencing the world of the performance, for it is nothing more than the series of images that the artist is manipulating, expressing, juxtaposing. It is an experience and, immersed in the world of art, audience members sense that they are experiencing the real world, cut off from the real world, the fragments of experience in that world selectively arranged, altered, adjusted.

The experience that a member of the audience has with the series of images becomes her or his real experience; it is in fact a real experience psychologically. If this is so, and if the performer and the tradition have been successful in finding artistic correspondences to real-life experiences, then the member of the audience will re-experience reality, but on the terms of the artistic tradition, terms that he or she has accepted by becoming a member of the audience, terms known intimately from long experience. This re-experience of reality gives a shape to the audience member's experience that it did not have before, because before, in the real world, there is no shape, there is only experience, a rain of experiences that one encounters daily. The art experience selects fragments from those encounters, arranges them, shapes them. And it is in the shaping of that experience, in the art work, that a new experience is achieved, an experience that, unlike in the real world, makes sense, has meaning, because of the manipulation done by the performer and, as noted, of the many experiences that the members of the audience have had with those images in other performances. By skillfully arranging these images symbolizing shared experiences, experiences that have been significant for the society for years and therefore have taken the form of fixed symbols, the performer begins to manipulate our human experience, to give it meaning; more than that, to give it a socially approved meaning. And, because the experience is socially approved, it also has the effect of conditioning the members of the audience who will internalize the images thanks to the aesthetic experience, to their emotional and psychological involvement in the unfolding and enveloping images.

The art form, then, seeks to comment upon and to give meaning to the real world, not by open commentary, not by didactic preachments (though those are also ways of analyzing human experience), but by the arrangement of images and, through ritual, by the revelation of the relationships between the images. Myth and ritual are very close, a part of the same process, myth being the outcome of ritual. But neither can be understood except in an experiential framework accomplished within a work of art. The work of art is an eminently neat work; there, everything is perfect; there is harmony there, harmony of form and harmony of conflict, things can be handled in the work of art, unlike in the real world, where the proliferation of experiences among other things makes analysis difficult. In the world of art, there is time for arrangement, there is leisure for organization. The images are familiar to us, they embody certain elements of our experience in the external world. The symbols are familiar to us, they gather up many strands of our personal experience. A process then occurs whereby these images and symbols are brought into contact, and new symbols are developed, symbols that exist only for the life of the performance, because a combination of fixed and non-fixed symbols is necessary to carry us through the aesthetic experience, the non-fixed symbols relating the specifics of our contemporary experience to the ancient tradition-sanctioned images and symbols, for there is always the mixture of the contemporary with the traditional in the performances. We are caught up in this process of metaphor; that process is in fact a part of the aesthetic experience. We are not only caught up in it, as we have seen, we are a part of it. The members of the audience are a part of the raw material necessary to the satisfactory completion of the work of art. When we are finally released, we are altered; the work of art has given meaning to our existence. Image sets are brought into contact one with the other, and the addition of a second image set alters our experience of the first one, which in turn has its own impact on the second.

Myth is the product of these various processes, and myth involves the overall theme of the narrative tradition as well. Myth is therefore the product of artistic processes involving narrative at the same time that it is tied to the broad and profound values of the society that evokes the images. Myth is a part of a process and it is also a part of an idea, ideal, value. The impact of myth is largely achieved through the images that compose it, and this is why structures are so vital to the success of the form. Repetition is the key aesthetic characteristic, for it is in repetition that the experience of the audience is intensified; it is in repetition that relationships between images are revealed. The images, in their own way capsulizing fragments of the experiences of the real world, are channeled into structures, which allow them to be repeated but within rigidly defined shapes, necessary to the revelation of relationships. Three of these structures are the expansible image, the patterned image set, and the parallel image set.

(This is not an exhaustive list of structures, there are others.) It is when the images are seen in these structures that the relationships between the images are most visible. But we have seen, too, that it is an experience that we speak of here, not an intellectual analysis. It is the experience of image set A followed by the experience of image set B that reveals the relationships that exist between these two image sets. There is no aesthetic distance here; the audience is caught up in the images and therefore in the structures of the system.

The Argument: The Trickster Box

The trickster is the fundamental building block of storytelling, from the tale to the epic. The deceptively simple profane trickster tale contains within itself the seed of transformation, which is the essential element in all stories: at the heart of these stories are a trickster and a dupe. Such stories have to do with identity: typically, the trickster pretends to be something that he is not in order to fulfill his appetites. At some point, his trickery is exposed, as he comes out of his disguise. At times, the audience does not know who is the real person: the trickster is a master at masquerade.

His antics constitute the trickster box.

Here is the typical trickster formula: the trickster wants something that seems out of his reach; to get that he disguises himself or in some way convinces his dupe that he is what he is not. In that forged identity, he cheats the dupe, gets what he wants, and seldom leaves without telling his dupe what he has done. The trickster himself may be a victim of a tables-turned motif, so that he who is a master at deception frequently becomes the dupe, but whatever the case he is always a part of a gambit of some sort: he creates the scheme, weaves his dupe in that artifice, and the dupe learns what is happening when it is too late. And the trickster is almost always physically inferior to the dupe: he is a diminutive human, perhaps, or a hare, spider, tortoise.

It is a theatrical box that the trickster creates and within which he works his wiles. He must seduce his victim into the box, and once he has him there, he moves in, and for the dupe it is too late. That trickster box is ironically at the heart of most non-trickster tales and heroic epics: it is the trickster's laboratory.

Transformation is an important aspect of story: a change of some kind is being experienced or described, whether a rite of passage or a move to a new society. In most stories, the trickster is not present as a trickster; he shadows the change that is being described. In the epics, the trickster in complex form will inevitably be present, and will be largely responsible for the meaning of the stories.

Some of the World's Trickshers

AFRICA

Abu Nawwas, a man (Arabic / Egypt)

Abu Nuwasi, a man (Swahili / East Africa)

Ananse/Anansi, a spider (Asante / Ghana)

Antelope (Fjort / DRCongo)

Cat (Limba / Sierra Leone)

Chakijana, a mongoose (Zulu / South Africa)

Cock (Kamba / Kenya)

Crow (Kamba / Kenya)

Eshu, a god (Yoruba / Nigeria)

Fox (Khoi / South Africa)

Frog (Igbo / Nigeria)

Giza, a spider (Hausa / Nigeria)

Goat (Limba / Sierra Leone)

Goha, a man (Arabic / Egypt)

Hare (Hausa / Nigeria)

Hare (Kamba / Kenya)

Hare (Umbundu / Angola)

Hare (Swahili / East Africa)

Hare (Kikuyu / Kenya)

Hare (Ila / Zambia)

Hare (Tiv / Nigeria)

Hlakanyana, a man (Xhosa, Zulu / South Africa)

Hyena (Kamba / Kenya)

Ijapa, tortoise (Yoruba / Nigeria)

Jackal (Sotho / Lesotho)

Jackal (Xhosa / South Africa)

Jackal (Kabyl / North Africa)

Jackal (Khoi / South Africa)

Jackal (Hausa / Nigeria)

Juha, a man (Morocco)

Kabulu (Mbundu / Angola)

Kalulu, Little Hare (Lamba / Zambia)

Kamwathi, a man (Kamba / Kenya)

Legba, divine trickster (Fon / Benin)

Maguje, a non-Moslem (Hausa / Nigeria)

Mantis (San / South Africa, Botswana, Namibia)

Monkey (Limba / Sierra Leone)

Mwathi, a man (Kikuyu / Kenya)

Oso-Yurunsu, divine trickster
  (Dogon / Mali, Burkina Faso)
Orphan (Zande / Sudan)
Pakanyanai, a spider (Liberia)
Rabbit (Fon / Benin)
Rabbit (Nyanja / Congo)
Rabbit (Bini / Nigeria)
Spider (Limba / Sierra Leone)
Spider (Ewe / Ghana, Togo,
  Benin)
Spider (Fiort / Congo)
Squirrel (Kikuyu / Kenya)
Tortoise (Umbundu / Angola)
Tortoise (Bini / Nigeria)
Tortoise (Kamba / Kenya)
Tortoise (Nyanja / DRCongo)
Tortoise (Limba / Sierra Leone)
Tortoise (Tiv / Nigeria)
Ture, a spider (Zande / Sudan)
Turtle (Fiort / Zaire)
Usulwe (Ila / Zambia)
Umvundla (Xhosa / South Africa)
Umvundla, Unogwaja, Isibhudu
  (Zulu / South Africa)
Yo (Fon / Benin)

The Americas

Beaver (Nez Perce)
Bluejay (North Pacific)
Coyote (Southwest Great Basin,
  Plateau, Western Plains, etc.)
Coyote (White Mountain Apache)
Coyote (Omaha)
Coyote (Pima)
Coyote (Tewa)
Coyote (Kalapuya)
Coyote (Nez Perce)
Coyote, Old Man Coyote (Crow)

Coyote (Pawnee)
Coyote (Rumsien Costancan)
Gloskap (Algonquian)
Great Rabbit (Algonquian)
Ictinike (Omaha)
Iktome (Lakota Sioux, Dakota
  Sioux)
Inkatomi (Sioux)
Kasiagsak (Eskimo)
Mink (North Pacific)
Nanabozko / Nanabushui, Hare
  (East Woodlands; Ojibwa)
Nihansan (Arapaka)
Nixat (Gros Ventre)
Old Man (Blackfoot)
Orphan (Omaha)
Rabbit (Southeast)
Rabbit (Omaha)
Raven (North Pacific)
Raven (Athapascan)
Sendek (Old Man of the Kiowa)
Sitkonski (Assiniboine)
traveling salesman (United States)
Trickster (Winnebago)
Wihic (Cheyenne)
Wisakedjak (Whiskeyjack) (East
  Woodlands)

Anansi (Suriname)
Chief Ariki (Easter Island)
Coniraya, forest spirit (Peru)
Coyote (Mexico)
Deer (Brazil)
Dan Cacahuate (Mexico)
Fox (Mexico)
Fox (Toba)
Jabuti, Turtle (Brazil)
Monkey (Brazil)
Pedro (Guatemala)

Pedro de Urdemales (Mexico, Chile, etc.)
Rabbit (Brazil)
Rabbit (Suriname)
Stag (Brazil)
Tawkxwax (Mataco)
Toad (Brazil)
Tortoise (Suriname)
Twins, mythical (Amazon)
Uncle Coyote (Nicaragua)

CARIBBEAN

Orula, God (Cuba)
Uncle Bouqui; Uncle Bauki (Haiti)
Andre (Canadian)
Brer Rabbit (Afro-American)

PACIFIC

Maui (Maori)
Naui-tikitiki-a-Taranea (Polynesian)
Rat (Tonsan)
Snake (Australia)
Stupid One (Hawaii)

ASIA

Abunuwasi, the wit (Saudi Arabia)
Andare, court jester (Sri Lanka)
Baba Yaga (Russia)
Badger (Japan)
Bara Mia (India)
Bhar Bitna, a dwarf (India)
Bullfrog (Japan)
Clever Boy (India)
Countryman; Farmer (Nepal)
Farmer (Bengal)
Fox (Caucasus)

Fox (Georgian/Russia)
Fox (India)
Fox (Kazakh)
Fox (Japan)
Fox (Russia)
Hare (Georgian/Russia)
Jackal (Bengali)
Jackal (Hindu / India)
Jackal (Khasi/India)
Jackal (Punjabi)
Kantchil, a mouse-deer (Indonesia)
Kappa, a fabulous being (Japan)
Kichiso (Japan)
Kitchamu (Japan)
Lam-ang, a human (Philippines)
Matalange Laku-Appu (Sri Lanka)
Monkey (Assam / India)
Monkey (Bihar / India)
Muzhik (Russia)
Muzhik (Ukraine)
Niemonen (Japan)
Oaka (Japan)
Oullah (Iran)
Parakeet (Indonesia)
Priest (China)
Shaikh Chulia (India)
Si Kebayan (Indonesia / Sudanese)
Sus (Thai)
Traveler (Burma)
Turtle (Philippines)
Turtle (Tinguian / Philippines)
Uncle Tompa (Tibet)
Vasili (Byelorussia)
Woodcutter (Pakistan)

EUROPE

Cat (Aesop / Greece)
Cat, King Cat (Hungary)

Dwarf (England)
Fox (Celt / Scotland)
Fox (France)
Fox (Germany)
Fox (Ireland)
Fox (Hungary)
Fox (Norway)
Goat (Germany)
Hermes, a god (Greece)
Kayseri innkeeper, merchant, etc.
 (Turkey)

Kose (Turkey)
Loki (Scandinavia)
Musician (Germany)
Old Bob (England)
Peasant (Germany)
Peasant (Armenia)
Prometheus, a god (Greece)
Saemundur (Iceland)
Shifty Lad (Scotland)
Tomas, an innkeeper (Spain)

Part One

The Trickster,
Preparation for the Hero

For the Trickster, Everything Is Identity

The creation myths have to do with origins, the world of the myth, the Age of Beginnings.

Tales also treat transitions, not on a mythic scale but an earthly individual scale. All is physical and concrete movement, all is spatial movement. These movements are accomplished by means of performance, and one of the things performance does is to link its various discrete elements into an aesthetic and social unity. That unity may be fictitious, but not during performance. On the cosmological level, there is change in myth; on the individual level, there is change in tale; on the cultural and national level, there is change in epic. All is change, crisis, transition, a move toward regained equilibrium. But that is not really true. It is not a "regained equilibrium"; that can never occur. It is a new equilibrium. That is why rites of passage are integral parts of the oral tradition. We move from one state of being to another, whether cosmologically, individually, or culturally. We stop being one kind of person or world or society, and we begin life as another person or world or society. This means a regular casting off of one form and a taking on of another. This change occurs ritually and aesthetically in a performance.

What was the norm becomes the past. While we were insiders in the old dispensation, we are outsiders in the new. We are constantly in this state of flux, moving from the old to the new, so that we are simultaneously insider and outsider. And that is one of the challenges of life, that is what makes our various life crises so difficult to endure. The child is an insider to his home, an outsider to his new responsibilities as an adult. During the period of the rite of passage,

29

therefore, he is both insider and outsider, a difficult thing to be. It creates confusion and psychological torment. How can one be both simultaneously? The old is henceforth antisocial; before, it was perfectly acceptable. Now the new, which was asocial to a person in his or her old role, becomes properly social. The trickster through performance binds present and past. The tale is the moment in which past and present are blended in a performance. We are forever reliving, re-experiencing the perfection of the past at the same time that we experience the realities of the present, through performance. The trickster, like gods and heroes and helpers and all others in this fantasy world of the tale, exists both in our time and in myth-time. In the tale, we are merging the two times through the trickster character.

In myth time, animals are humans, humans are animals . . . there is no distinction. Yes, we see the animal characteristics emerging at the end of the tales, a constant reminder to us that the blending is in force, that the ancient Age of Mythology is giving way to the world that we know, when animals have animal characteristics, when humans have human characteristics, when we move into the differentiated world that we know.

The tales are simultaneously depictions of the immediate present, of real difficulties and genuine human emotions, at the same time that they point to the infinite; the human emotions and the problems of the hearth become generalized into cosmological infinitude. This is the power of the performance; it is the potency of the tale. Trickster would have no existence, would have no meaning, would make no sense whatsoever if we did not understand the frame in which he operates. He is forever theatrical. He creates theater in the world that we know, the real world. Without that frame, Trickster's antics are merely obscene and silly. But within that frame, he becomes significant and eternal.

Trickster makes the flawed moment eternal. He ties us to our ancestral past. But within the tradition of the people, he is destroying one part of us and creating another part; he is recreating us, reshaping us, but always within the tradition of the people. We have to differentiate between our own history and the tradition within which that history unfolds. So it is that Trickster recreates our world, but he must first destroy it. He is constantly in the process of taking us back to our origins, destroying what we have, then rebuilding it. We are ever involved in the ritualistic process, the creative moment, because of Trickster.

This is the key: tale is reality, tale is performance; the image is real, the image is fantastic; the tale is the present, the tale is the past. Trickster works within the world that we know: he creates a world of illusion within that frame of reference. But his world would be meaningless without that frame of reference. To comprehend Legba, we must be appalled at his sexual grandstanding with dead

women, his mother-in-law, the king's daughter. Trickster is the theatrical figure: he is the mime, the merrymaker in disguise, the court jester, working his
craft within a setting, then manipulating that setting to his own ends. And that
setting is vital.

There are mighty forces, represented by God, Leopard, Lion. The weak
cannot prevail over them, they have all the power. They create, they establish
boundaries. But in the trickster tale, those boundaries are loosened, violated; the
power of the gods, of the great animals, is called into question, and chaos results.
The great traditions laid down by the mighty are transgressed, and there is a
reversal. Now the traditional world is called into question, authority is under-
mined. Traditional sources of power are confounded. During the moment of
chaos, the world is reconstructed, reversed, and what was up is down, what was
down is up. What was inside is outside, what was outside is inside; the powerful are the weak, the weak are the powerful; what was bad is good, what was
good is bad. But then, the powerful reassert themselves, they take back their
control; it was inevitable, but for a moment, there was something else, before
recreation occurred, and that something else is often embodied in some minor
animal characteristic, an etiological echo.

And if the tale does not show the reassertion of the might of the mighty,
reality, the real frame, does. We always return to the real world. But for the
moment of performance, of fantasy, we return to the time of the beginnings,
to the age of mythology, and with the assistance of the chaos-causer and the
culture hero, the same person necessarily, we reduce reality to a void, and create
an alternative world in its stead. For that moment, concepts of life and death
are reversed, and the death-dealer Legba, for example, is in the ascendancy.
Roles are reversed, the hare is the lion, the lion is the hare. But this is the way
it was before differentiation occurred. Lion as Lion is unimportant. It simply
represents a force that, the trickster tale shows, is ultimately undifferentiated.
And the lowly hare as lowly hare is unimportant. Each exercises its power as it
can, and the struggle is everlasting, for the trickster constantly threatens to
reduce all, then to reshape it so that the roles are forever reversed. This reversal
of roles is at the heart of trickster tales, and of all tales dealing with transitions.
We are constantly destroying, being destroyed, and creating, being recreated,
reborn. We are constantly in a state of transition. Since the end of the Age of
Beginnings, we have been in this state of flux, impermanence, evanescence. Our
lives and our societies are regularly in motion, being transformed, dying and
being reborn. We die at puberty and are reborn, we die at death and are reborn. Trickster takes us on this movement in a fast-forward way. Trickster's
world has as constants destruction and re-creation; hence, the emphasis on the

phallus, the emphasis on deception, disguise, and illusion. And hence, too, the trickster's ability to move between the genders. Everyone attempts to come to terms with the contradictory in the trickster character. But in narrative terms, he is not contradictory at all, nor even ambiguous. He does represent both a creative and a destructive force. But we must not stop there. Consider also his theatrical nature, and the nature of the performance that frames his antics ultimately.

1

African Profane Trickster Tales

Profane trickster tales occur separately or in cycles, often without frames. But sometimes they have frames such as birth and death, with the cycle in between. That is the set-up, the prototype, for a more complex tale, in which the separate tales are now linked by the development and growth of a real-life character, and also through patterns that reflect each other. The trickster is betwixt and between: he stands between worlds; he is the primal self before we put social masks over it, he is the energy within us without any kind of containment, any kind of socializing; he is our deepest wishes, untamed, naked, asocial. When we move from one social being to another, for instance from child to adult, or from the state of being unmarried to a married state, the trickster in us, the real us, is unleashed: unstable, unpredictable, dangerous, even disgusting at times. No social rules are operating during this betwixt-and-between stage.

For the trickster, everything is identity. And identity is the main contribution that the trickster makes to the hero. Trickster and hero, two apparently separate characters in the world's oral traditions, are in fact the same character. The trickster is, as we have seen, an indifferent, amoral, undifferentiated force, as if God the creator had never got around to ordering this part of the universe. He is always on the boundaries, the periphery: Trickster is a liminal being. In the heavens, he is called a divine trickster; on the earth, a profane trickster.

There are many trickster stories in which nothing is accomplished but a trick. This is the energy-potential that the trickster represents: the energy released during the betwixt-and-between stage when no laws are operating, when destructive and creative forces contend with each other, and when, out of these forces, a change frequently occurs. That change does not affect the amorality of the divine and profane tricksters: they can be just as infuriating the next

moment. But when their energies are joined to rites of passage, to transformations, then that force is muted, tamed, redirected. In the end, the trickster continues unaffected, but something has happened, something has been left behind
of a positive and moral nature. The divine trickster leaves a permanent residue,
and so, at times, does the profane trickster. In some of the tales having to do
with the puberty ritual, the trickster actually appears, revealing that betwixt-
and-between amoral energy. In most puberty-rite tales, however, the trickster
is not himself present; only the energy is. The trickster stories embody that
energy in a character.

Disguise, deception, illusion are trickster's tools and weapons. He is an
ambiguous character: usually a male, he is often androgynous. Trickster moves
through the universe trying to satisfy his basic appetites. This is largely the case
with both profane and divine tricksters. If the divine trickster also creates
something permanent along the way, so much the better, but that is not always
his aim. The trickster is outrageous, obscene, death-dealing, uncaring, ignoble.
But this does not mean that he is incapable of socially acceptable practices and
activities. These are usually by-products of his acts, however, rather than conscious efforts on his part. He remains forever an undifferentiated force: he is
never tamed, never domesticated, although he may appear to be so at times,
usually as a part of a sly plan to gain something for himself.

The profane or earth-bound trickster is, like the divine trickster, ribald,
aggressive, selfish, without moral compass. In this, he is the closest to the basest
of humans. He lacks the sublime connection with the gods; this is what distinguishes the profane from the divine trickster. Yet, in a way, the profane trickster does retain an echo of the divine connection, if tenuously: he also creates
in the sense that he establishes a world of illusion; he imposes his own corrupt sense of order on the real world. An agent of chaos, he disrupts harmony; in those instances when he produces harmony, it is according to his own
whim, his own capricious and self-serving sense of order. Trickster combines
horror and glee: his is the comedy of the absurd. With his enormous penis,
his diminutive size, his love of dance, his amorality, his clownishness, he is a
grotesque. He is a rootless, unattached being who seeks to secure his own survival and psychological well-being in a society that espouses traditional values
while actually sanctioning dehumanizing modes of behavior. Trickster inherits
no place he can call home; he is forever an outsider. To impose his will on a
hostile world, he uses trickery, invents ruses, wears masks. The profane trickster stories reveal the undifferentiated energy, represent the period of betwixt
and between: they unmask the enormous energy that is released during the
period of transition . . . sometimes good, sometimes bad, but amoral, actually,

and self-serving. The trickster, profane and divine, always represents the combination of chaos and order.

The trickster is an eternal force that may or may not be molded for socially acceptable ends, but whatever the current ordering of that force may be, in the end, it again becomes an undifferentiated force. Trickster may be tamed for a time, but not forever. He remains the undifferentiated part of ourselves, that part that requires social forming and education.

A South African Storyteller:
"Trickster Gets Married"[6] *(Xhosa/Hlubi)*

A story goes like this . . .

There was a girl called Hlakanyana. One day she traveled, and came to a homestead. An old woman was there, alone.

She said, "Old woman, let's cook each other!"

The little old woman said, "All right, child of my child!"

Hlakanyana dipped out some water and filled the pot. When the pot became warm, Hlakanyana got in.

Then she said, "Old woman! Old woman! Take me off the fire, I'm burning!"

The old woman took Hlakanyana off the fire.

Then Hlakanyana put the old woman in. She made a fire.

The old woman said, "Hlakanyana! Hlakanyana! Take me off the fire, child of my child! I'm burning!"

She said, "No, Grandmother, it's not yet time!"

"My child, my child, take me off the fire! I'm burning!"

"No, Grandmother, it's not yet time!"

The little old woman died, the little old woman died.

Hlakanyana took her off the fire then and put her into a dish. Her two sons were not there, they were out hunting. When they came home, Hlakanyana was already wearing the little old woman's clothing. She took some meat out for them, and they ate, they ate.

In the midst of this eating, one of the sons said, "Oh, what's this? It seems to be a hand! It's good, this!"

Hlakanyana went out. She went, she went, and when she had gone a distance, and was standing alone, she said, "Yeeeeeeeere! They're eating their mother."

Then these two ravenous men went out. They took some sticks, and made her run. They went, they went, they went, they went, and look! a river, and it was full! When they got to the river, Hlakanyana turned herself into a black rock. Then, when the sons arrived, they were unable to find her.

One of them picked up the black rock and said, "If I could find her, I'd do this!" And he hurled the rock to the other side of the river. Then the rock changed, and it became Hlakanyana!

She said, "Yeeeeeeere! You ate your mother!"

She went. She went, she went, she came to a homestead. When she arrived, some men were stitching the thatch on the roof of a house, one was inside, one outside. Hlakanyana got rid of the man who was on top, and then she climbed up. She stitched, she stitched, she stitched, then Hlakanyana went inside. The man who had been inside went to the outside. She stitched, she stitched and stitched, but Hlakanyana was actually stitching the foot of the big man to the roof!

When she had finished doing this, a huge hailstorm came up. Hlakanyana went out.

She said, "Hee! Come down from there!"

There were only the two of them at the house! The hailstorm arrived and pulverized the man.

Hlakanyana started, and she ran and ran. She came to a homestead. When she got to this homestead, Hlakanyana got married. Hlakanyana got married, even though she had a tail! She was dressed in clothes, so that she was beautiful to look at.

Then one day, someone said, "What's this? Since the bride came here to our home, the milk has been disappearing! There's no milk here at home! Let a contest be held!"

He dug a deep hole outside, and put some milk into it. The hole became full. Then it was said that all the people of this homestead should jump. All jumped over this hole, all jumped over this hole. Hlakanyana tarried, not jumping.

Someone said, "Jump!"

She said, "No, I'm afraid."

Again, someone said, "Jump!"

She said, "No, I'm afraid!"

When she did jump, her tail dipped down into the milk. They beat her, they threw her to the dogs! And the dogs fought her, and killed her.

The story is ended, it is ended.

A South African Storyteller: "Pursued by His Own Feces"[7] *(Xhosa/Hlubi)*

Now for a story. . . .

There was Hlakanyana, and he once went to his father-in-law's place. When he was leaving home, his mother said, "Hlakanyana, don't eat any berries along the way! When you see them, you can eat the green ones, but don't eat the red and black ones!"

Hlakanyana agreed. He journeyed. Along the way, he came to some green berries. Since he did not like them, he moved on. Then, along the way, he came to some red berries. Since he did not like them, he again moved on. When he was far off, he came to some black berries, oozing and thoroughly ripe! Hlakanyana wanted them very much. He said, "Well, I'll just pluck one of them!" He plucked them. Oh! He tasted those berries, and they were nice! Hlakanyana ate many of them. Then he went on his way. He journeyed, Hlakanyana walked and walked. Along the way, he had to defecate. And so he traveled and went and defecated. He defecated a lot! Then he put on his trousers again, and walked on.

When he was far off, he heard something singing behind him, saying,

> "Hlakanyana, wait for me!
> I'm going to your father-in-law's place!
> Hlakanyana, wait for me!
> I'm going to your father-in-law's place!"

He was startled, he looked behind. "Oh! It's that shit I defecated!"
He stopped, he went to it. He took it and crushed it into the ground. Then he threw it in the grass.

He traveled on, and when he was far off, he heard that thing again, saying,

> "Hlakanyana! wait for me!
> I'm going to your father-in-law's place!"

He stopped. He saw the feces coming again!
He said, "What'll I do?"
He took it, he gathered it together, he gathered it together. He went to a river, and when he arrived, he crushed it, and the water carried it away. He went on.

When he was about to arrive at his father-in-law's place, he heard something saying,

> "Hlakanyana! Wait for me!
> I'm going to your father-in-law's place."

Oh! He stopped. The feces came along.

"Hey! Hlakanyana!
Why did you leave me behind?
I'm going to your father-in-law's place, too!"

Hlakanyana took it and put it into his pocket.

He went on, and arrived at his father-in-law's place. He had been expected, and he was given some beer.

As he was swallowing it, the feces said,

"Give me some to drink, Hlakanyana!
Give me some beer to drink!"

Hlakanyana pressed the feces down with his hand, pressed it into his pocket. It was quiet then, and it again went down into the pocket.

When Hlakanyana took some beer and again drank it, the feces said,

"Hlakanyana, give me some to drink!"

He pushed it down into his pocket. Again the feces came out of his pocket and disappeared in a pot.

Hlakanyana ran, even leaving his hat behind! He went home, he arrived at his home.

Over there at his father-in-law's place, this feces drank there in the pot, it drank and drank. Then it got up and took the hat that Hlakanyana had left behind, it took a stick and went home. It arrived at Hlakanyana's home, and said,

"Hlakanyana!
After I accompanied you to your father-in-law's place,
You left me behind!"

The story has ended.

A Storyteller from Botswana: "The Hare and the Lion"[8] (*Tswana*)

The hare once said to the lion, "Come, let us make a fold for the beasts."

The lion agreed.

The hare cried, "Fold, make yourself!"

And the fold made itself.

Then the hare said to the lion, "You lie down and pretend to be dead, and I will call all the beasts together. Then rise up and kill them."

The lion lay down as if he were dead, and the hare climbed the poles at the opening into the fold, and cried, "Beeee! Come and see Malacwi dead!"

Malacwi is the name by which the lion was known to the hare and the other beasts of the field.

All the beasts of the field came and entered the fold.

But the tortoise took a stalk of grass and poked it into the lion from behind, and the lion thereupon drew itself away from the stalk.

Then the tortoise said to its young one, "Little tortoise, my child, let us get away from here, for there is no dead thing that can draw itself in on being touched."

And they went away.

Then Malacwi arose and killed the beasts.

The hare said, "Let us say, 'House, build yourself.'"

The lion replied, "Just speak. You're the one who knows everything."

Then the rain came, and the lion said, "Let the house be roofed."

To this, the hare answered, "I know how to call the grass."

And the lion asked that the grass be called.

The hare then said, "Grass, mow yourself."

And the grass was not only mown, it brought itself to the place where they were.

Then the lion said, "Let the roof be thatched."

But the hare answered, "Ah, that is far beyond me."

The lion was astonished, and said, "What do you mean? Is it possible that one who knows how to make things make themselves does not know how to make a thatch put itself on?"

Then the lion climbed on the roof while the hare remained below twisting sinews together.

While he was doing this, he said to the lion, "Let sparks come through the rafters lest you perish with cold."

To this, the lion agreed.

So the hare made a fire, and on the coals he grilled some fat meat. When the meat was cooked, he tied the sinew to the lion. Then he placed a piece of the fat meat on the end of a stick, and said to the lion, "May I swallow this, my elder brother?"

But the lion, in a fierce voice, cried out, "Put it down!"

The hare pulled the sinew with which he had tied the lion, and the lion, feeling the pain, cried out, "Oshe! Oshe!" whereupon the hare broke off the branch from a piece of wood, and said to it, "May this piece of wood kill my elder brother."

He went on doing this until the lion was dead.

When he had killed the lion, the hare ate all the food, and after the lion's skin had become dried up and all the flesh and bones had fallen out of it, he entered the skin in the evening, and went to the house of the hyena.

Speaking in a gruff voice, he said, "Push out your food, push out your food!"

The hyena pushed it out, and the little hyenas spent the night hungry. This went on for some time, until the little ones became quite thin.

Now one day, when the sun was well up and the mother hyena was away, the little ones saw the hare come out of the shriveled-up skin, and dance and sing, "I am a great hare. I have conquered the hyena and the lion. I conquer the hyena."

When evening came, the little hyenas told their mother what they had seen and heard, and she said, "Well, we shall see."

Later, the hare in the lion's skin came speaking as formerly, but the hyena took no notice, just remained at ease. But she took the stone on which her pot stood on the fire, and threw it at the skin, whereupon came a hollow sound from the skin. And the hare burst out and fled, leaving the skin behind.

The hare fled in earnest, and went to visit another hyena. He found the hyena's wife weeding in the garden patch, and said to her, "Mother, seeing you are alone, please let me nurse your children for you. Afterwards, I'll cook for you."

The hyena agreed.

The next day, the hyena went to her garden as usual, and left the hare with the children. The hare looked well after them that day.

On the next day, she again left the children in the charge of the hare. The young hyenas were all of one color, all being very dark skinned.

And on this day, the hare killed one of them.

When, towards evening, the mother returned home, the hare set flesh before her. She asked where the meat had come from, to which the hare replied that while the children were playing he had gone out and hunted young duiker.

"Well! well!" said the hyena.

When the hyena had eaten, she called for her children that she might suckle them. The hare went to bring the children.

Now, as there were ten children, he brought one twice.

The next day, he remained with them again, and killed a second one. This he also cooked and gave to the mother, and once more she ate.

When she called for her young ones to be brought, he brought the eighth one three times, thus making up the number ten.

Day after day, he killed one of the cubs and acted as formerly.

At last, when none was left, the hare was told to bring his younger brothers, that they might suck his mother.

The hare appeared as if he did not understand, and asked who were his younger brothers.

The hyena replied, "Your younger brothers, whom you know."

"I don't know them, mother," was the hare's reply.

"Oh, Hare," said the hyena, "they are those little black younger brothers of yours."

To which the hare answered, "Don't you know that you have eaten them all, and the last of them is the one now in your mouth."

The hyena snatched up something, saying she would kill him, but the hare ran away with the hyena on his heels.

The hare found a hollow tree and hid himself in it.

Then the hyena came to the tree. She asked if anyone was inside, saying to the hollow of the tree, "Mmamorotoroto of the hollow, have you seen a hare pass this way?"

She asked this because she saw protruding eyes though not the body of the hare.

Then an answer came from the hollow of the tree: "Where see we the hare, we of the protruding eyes?"

The hyena drew near, and said, "May this not be it?"

Whereupon the hare leaped out and ran for his life. The hyena followed hard behind him and drove him in the direction of the river.

When he got to the river, the hare changed himself into a large round stone on the bank of the river. Along came the hyena, and she saw the stone.

She cried out, "Oh, one might possibly see the hare on the other side of the river."

So she took the stone and threw it across the river, saying as she did so, "Freeeeee! Tee!"

The hare stood up on the other side, stood upright, and said, "I knew that it would be you, my mother, who would help me to cross the river. Has not my elder sister helped me across the swollen stream?"

And the hyena's heart almost broke.

A Storyteller from Ghana: "How Kwaku Ananse,
the Spider, Got Aso in Marriage"[9] *(Asante / Akan)*

There once lived a certain man called Akwasi-the-jealous-one and his wife was Aso, and he did not want anyone to see Aso or anyone to talk to her. So he went and built a small settlement for Aso to live in. No one ever went into the village.

Now he, Akwasi-the-jealous-one, could not beget children. Because of that, if he and his wife lived in town, someone would take her away.

Now, the sky-god told young men, saying, "Akwasi-the-jealous-one has been married to Aso for a very very long time; she has not conceived by him and borne a child, therefore he who is able, let him go and take Aso, and should she conceive by him, let him take her [as his wife]."

All the young men tried their best to lay hands on her, but not one was able.

Now Kwaku Ananse was there watching these events, and he said, "I can go to Akwasi-the-jealous-one's village."

The sky-god said, "Can you really do so?"

Ananse said, "If you will give me what I require."

The sky-god said, "What kind of thing?"

He said, "Medicine for gun and bullets."

And the sky-god gave him.

And Ananse took the powder and bullets to various small villages, saying, "The sky-god has bade me bring powder and bullets to you, and you are to go and kill meat, and on the day I shall return here, I shall take it and depart."

He distributed the powder and the bullets among very many small villages, until all were finished. All the villagers got him some meat.

On a certain day, Ananse wove a palm-leaf basket. Its length, as it were, was from here to over yonder. Ananse took it to the small villages, where he had distributed the powder and bullets, to receive all the meat they had killed.

Father Ananse took the meat and palm-leaf basket and set it on his head, and set out on the path leading to the Akwasi-the-jealous-one's settlement. When he reached the stream from which Akwasi and his wife drank, he picked out some meat and put it in. Ananse strove hard and brought the palm-leaf basket full of meat and passed through the main entrance leading into Akwasi-the-jealous-one's compound.

And Aso saw him. She said, "Akwasi ee! come and look at something which is coming to the house here, for what can it be?"

Ananse said, "It's the sky-god who is sending me, and I am weary, and I am coming to sleep here."

Akwasi-the-jealous-one said, "I have heard my Lord's servant."

Aso said to Ananse, "Father man, some of your meat has fallen down at the main entrance to the compound."

The spider said, "Oh, if you happen to have a dog, let him go and take it and chew it."

So Aso went and got it and gave it to her husband.

Then Ananse said, "Mother, set some food on the fire for me."

Aso put some on, and Ananse said, "Mother, is it *fufuo* that you are cooking or *eto*?"

Aso replied, "*Fufuo*."

Ananse said, "Then it is too little; go and fetch a big pot." Aso went and fetched a big one, and Ananse said, "Come and get meat."

There were forty hindquarters of great beasts.

He said, "Take these only and put them in, and if you had a pot big enough, I would give you enough meat to chew to make your teeth fall out."

Aso finished preparing the food, turned it out of the pot, and placed it on a table, splashed water, and put it beside the rest of the food. Then Aso took her portion and went and set it down near the fire, and the men went and sat down beside the table. They touched the backs of each other's hands [i.e., eat out of the same dish].

All the time they were eating, Kwaku Ananse said, "There is no salt in this *fufuo*."

Akwasi said to Aso, "Bring some."

But Ananse said, "Not at all, when the woman is eating, you tell her to get up to bring salt, do you yourself go and bring it."

Akwasi rose up, and Ananse looked into his bag, and took out a pinch of purgative medicine and put it in the *fufuo*.

Then he called Akwasi, saying, "Come, for I had brought some with me."

When Akwasi came, Ananse said, "Oh, I shall eat no more, I am full."

Akwasi, who suspected nothing, continued eating.

When they had finished eating, Akwasi said, "Friend, we and you are sitting here and yet we do not know your name."

Ananse replied, "I am called Rise-up-and-make-love-to-Aso."

Akwasi said, "I have heard. And you, Aso, have you heard this man's name?"

Aso replied, "Yes, I have heard."

Akwasi rose up to go and prepare one of the spare bedrooms, and to make all comfortable. He said, "Rise-up-and-make-love-to-Aso, this is your room, go and sleep there."

The Spider said, "I am the soul-washer to the sky-god, and I sleep in an open veranda room; since Mother bore me and Father begat me, I have never slept in a closed bedroom."

Akwasi said, "Then where, then, will you sleep?"

He replied, "Were I to sleep in this open veranda room here, to do so would be to make you equal to the sky-god, for it would mean that I was sleeping in the sky-god's open veranda room, since I am never to sleep in anyone's open room except that of a sky-god, and since that is so, I shall just lie down in front of this closed sleeping-room where you repose."

The man took out a sleeping-mat and laid it there for him.

Akwasi and his wife went to rest, and Ananse, too, lay down there.

Ananse lay there and he slipped in the cross-bar of the bedroom door. Ananse lay there, and took his musical bow [and sang]:

> "Akuamoa Ananse, today we shall achieve something today.
> Ananse, the child of Nsia, the mother of Nyame, the sky-god,
> Today we shall achieve something, today.
> Ananse, the soul-washer to the Nyame, the sky-god,
> Today I shall see something."

Now, he ceased playing his *sepirewa*, and he laid it aside, and lay down.

He slept for some time, when he heard Akwasi-the-jealous-one calling, "Father man"—not a sound in reply except the chirping of the cicada, *dinn!* "Father man"—not a sound in reply except the chirping of the cicada, *dinn!*

Akwasi-the-jealous-one is dying; the medicine has taken effect on him, but he calls, "Father man"—not a sound in reply except the chirping of the cicada, *dinn!*

At last he said, "Rise-up-and-make-love-to-Aso."

The spider said, "M! M! M!"

He, Akwasi, said, "Open the door for me."

Ananse opened the door, and Akwasi went somewhere.

And the spider rose up and went into the room there. He said, "Aso, did you not hear what your husband said?"

She replied, "What did he say?"

Ananse replied, "He said I must rise up and make love to you."

Aso said, "You don't lie."

And he did it for her, and he went and lay down.

That night, Akwasi rose up nine times; the spider also went nine times to where Aso was.

When things became visible, next morning, Ananse set off. It would be about two moons later when Aso's belly became large.

Akwasi questioned her, saying, "Why has your belly got like this, perhaps you are ill, for you know that I who live with you here am unable to beget children?"

Aso replied, "You forget that man who came here and whom you told to rise up and make love to Aso, well, he took me! I have conceived by him."

Akwasi-the-jealous-one said, "Rise up and let me take you to go and give you to him."

They went to the sky-god's town. On the way, Aso gave birth. They reached the sky-god's town, and went and told the sky-god what had happened, saying, "A subject of yours, whom you sent, slept at my house, and took Aso, and she conceived by him."

The sky-god said, "All my subjects are roofing the houses, go and point out the one you mean."

They went off, and the spider was sitting on a ridgepole.

Aso said, "There he is."

And Ananse ran and sat on the middle.

And again Aso said, "There he is."

Then Ananse fell down from up there where he was sitting.

Now that day was Friday.

Ananse said, "I, who wash the sky-god's soul, you have taken your hand and pointed it at me, so that I have fallen down and got red earth upon me."

Immediately, the attendants seized hold of Akwasi-the-jealous-one and made him sacrifice a sheep. When Akwasi-the-jealous-one had finished sacrificing the sheep, he said to the sky-god, "Here is the woman, let Ananse take her."

So Ananse took Aso, but as for the infant, they killed it, cut it into pieces, and scattered them about. That is how jealousy came among the people.

This, my story, which I have related, if it be sweet, or if it be not sweet, some you may take as true, and the rest you may praise me for telling of it.

A Storyteller from Liberia: "Spider"[10] *(Vai)*

There was a spider.

And a great famine came into the country so that there was no rice, no cassavas, no plantains, no palm-cabbage, no meat, no victuals: a great famine had come into the country.

The spider and his wife had been begetting children for a long time: a hundred children. There was no food in the country for them to give to the children.

The spider became sick, it was a feigned sickness.[11]

He said to his wife, "I shall die."

And his wife said, "Do not die. We will work."

The spider said, "No, I shall die." And he said to his wife, "When I have died, do not place me in a reclining position. Instead, set me upright in the hole, and lay boards on me, then put earth on the boards."

His wife consented.

The spider died.

The woman said to her children, "Dig a hole."

And they dug a hole, and they set the spider in the hole: they did not place him in a reclining position, they *set* him in the hole. With boards, they covered the hole.

Then, when evening came, the spider came out of the hole and went to a marsh far away.

He was still alive: he had not died.

He went and met a great woman, a chief. The woman possessed very much rice, very much rice was in her farm, and very much was in the store, and there were very many cassavas in the farm.

But the woman was barren, she had no children.

The spider asked, "My mother, where are your children?"

She said, "I have no children."

He said, "I have a medicine. I will give it to you. Drink it, and you will become with child and give birth."

The woman said, "Give me the medicine. When I give birth, if I give birth to a child, I will give you a whole shed full of rice, two farms of cassava, and a great many plantains."

The spider, because of the famine, agreed. He went away to take out the medicine by the way, and then he returned to the woman.

She killed a goat and cooked rice for the spider, and said, "Spider, here is rice for you."

The spider ate the rice, he was satisfied.

Then he put the medicine into a bowl, put water into the bowl, mashed the medicine into a bowl, put water into that bowl, then mashed the medicine.

He said to the woman, "Bring a strip of cloth."

He tied it around the woman's eyes, and said, "Drink the medicine. And when you have drunk the medicine, you will see me no more. I am going far away. In six months, you will give birth to a male child. Then I shall return, so that you can give me my rice and all my victuals."

The woman agreed. She took the bowl and drank the medicine.

The spider jumped into the bowl, and the woman swallowed the spider.

The spider was inside the woman.

And the woman brought forth a child: it was the spider himself.

The woman gives it water to drink; she cooks excellent rice, and gives it to the spider to eat.

The spider had been within her: her baby was the spider.

The woman did not know that her baby was the spider.

There is an animal in the forest, his name is Deer. He is cunning.

The deer said, "I shall go and see the woman's child, it has been eating the woman's rice for six months."

The deer arrived and said, "My mother, I have come to see your child."

The woman handed her child to the deer.

The deer looked at the child, and he saw that it was a spider. He handed the child to the woman. The woman took the child and laid it within cloths.

The deer went far away to a town, took a switch, returned, then took the cloth from on the baby and flogged it well.

The baby ran, and went far away.

The deer said to the woman, "It was a spider, it was no child. The spider was an impostor."

The spider went to his wife, hear!

All his wife's rice had become ripe, she had very many fowls, she beat rice, and her children killed animals for meat. The woman cooked the rice, she cooked the meat, she put the rice into a bowl, and put the meat into the rice.

The spider came in one evening, and met his wife while she was eating rice.

He pushed his wife's hand, passed on, and stood there. The wife put her hand into the rice. The spider struck his wife's hand again, and said to his wife, "I died long ago, and have now returned."

The wife did not reply.

The wife's child said, "My mother, it is my father."

The wife said, "No, your father died long ago."

The spider came, and said to his wife, "I am the spider."

The wife said, "The spider died long ago."

The spider is an impostor, hear!

Finished.

The Trickster Box

In the first trickster narratives, the profane trickster is in action, two stories having to do with the irrepressible character in the act of tricking someone. In "Trickster Gets Married," Hlakanyana is a trickster in the first part of the tale, as she destroys an old woman, then takes her identity. But in the second section, the tables are turned, and she herself is duped. Identity is a significant theme in each of the two parts: in part one, Trickster disguises herself and becomes the grandmother, and the climax of this section occurs when the woman's sons learn of the true identity of Hlakanyana. In part two of the story, Trickster disguises herself, but when the dupes seek to learn who has been stealing the milk, her identity is revealed when all must leap over the hole.

In the second of the two Hlakanyana stories, the trickster breaks an interdiction, typical of this character, and eats the forbidden berries. Then a pattern develops: Hlakanyana "defecated a lot!" The pattern is emphasized when
the feces sings a song associating it with Hlakanyana. As much as the trickster
may attempt to dissociate himself from his feces, it is impossible: they are
inseparable. Then Hlakanyana, pressing the feces into his pocket, drinks beer
and flees, leaving his hat behind. The feces, his shadow, then emerges from the
pocket, drinks beer, takes the trickster's hat and puts it on, and it takes a stick
and goes home, telling Hlakanyana, "You left me behind!" That final scene, the
feces imitating Hlakanyana, reveals the essential theme here. Identity cannot
be gainsaid.

In the Tswana story, the hare is the trickster, although a tortoise, frequently
himself a trickster, learns of the hare's trickery and departs. And there is an
echo from one of the Hlakanyana tricks when the hare ties the sinews to the
lion and kills it. And then the new identity of the hare is revealed: he moves into
the lion's skin, and initiates a pattern in which he takes the food of the hyena's
children. The hare reveals his true identity when he sings, "I am a great hare."
The hyena throws a hot stone at the hare, and the hare flees, leaving the lion's
skin behind. The hare then becomes a babysitter for another hyena, and he
serially kills the children and feeds their flesh to their mother. And the trickster, as in the Hlakanyana tale, cannot forbear letting the mother know what
he has done: "You have eaten them all. . . ." The hare escapes the anger of the
hyena, the story ending poignantly, "And the hyena's heart almost broke."

Identity is also at the heart of the Asante trickster tale, a profane trickster
story within a mythic frame, since the sky-god plays a role in it. Ananse changes
his name, and thence his identity, and under this new identity he gets Akwasi's
wife, Aso, pregnant. Because Ananse works for the sky-god, Akwasi takes his
wife to the god's town, and the sky-god tells Akwasi to identify Ananse. When
he is identified, Ananse falls from the ridgepole, and because Ananse is the sky-
god's soul-washer, Akwasi must sacrifice a sheep, and then he gives his wife
to Ananse. The mythic element enters the tale when the infant is killed and
cut into pieces that are then scattered, which is "how jealousy came among the
people." Profane trickster stories often have an etiological ending, as this one
does, and these endings are often meant to be ironic or humorous.

Identity becomes a theme in the Vai tale when the trickster spider pretends
to be dead and tricks his wife into supporting his trickery. Spider then meets
a chief, a woman, who is barren. He dupes the woman into thinking that he
has a medicine to cure her barrenness, but then he himself jumps into the medicine and is swallowed by the woman. She then gives birth to the spider. A deer

reveals the spider's trickery: "It was a spider, it was no child. The spider was an impostor." Now the spider returns to his wife, saying, "I died long ago, and have now returned." But his trickery does not work, and his wife now turns the tables on him: when the spider again reveals his identity, "I am the spider," she responds, "The spider died long ago." She is pushing the spider's nose into his own perfidy. And the storyteller ends the tale with the words, "The spider is an impostor, hear!"

2

Mantis and Legba,
Divine Tricksters

Analysis of oral narratives, as with analysis of all works of art, seeks to solve the problem, "How does the poem mean?" not "What does the poem mean?"[12] Frequently, it is not at all difficult to determine the theme of the work of art, but the statement of theme answers few of the aesthetic problems raised by the work being analyzed. Indeed, when analysis is properly carried out, it becomes impossible for the analyst to consider theme apart from the shape of the plot and the form of the total work. Analysis is a means of comprehending the total work of art, and as far as theme is concerned, analysis demonstrates the manner in which thematic experience is revealed in images of sound and sight. If a work of art is an experience, and if we seek to understand that experience beyond its obvious superficial representations, then it becomes necessary for us to grasp the aesthetic dynamics of the form being adapted before commenting on the particular work. Moreover, since every artist depends profoundly on the common experience of the members of the audience, it becomes imperative that those diverse experiences be appreciated also. The particular work is but a representation of the total art tradition.

Analysis concentrates on the particular work, but it is not blind to its wider context and its broader ramifications. This is not to say that the work of art cannot stand on its own. The work of art, or if a larger context is desired the art tradition from which the particular work has its being, has its own integrity. It has its roots in an art tradition, and that art tradition is a product of a culture and a history, and in that sense reflects that culture and affirms it, reveals that history. But it has its reality on a level quite apart from that of historical reality and cultural reality. It is for the historian to discover the structural precepts of history, and it is for the student of culture to determine those of human societies. And so too must art critics develop the tools and reveal the methods whereby we can comprehend the possibilities and limits of oral narrative, for example; their relationships to history and culture will become apparent in the process. Art traditions have their own aesthetic rules that govern the development and externalization of individual works. One cannot comprehend a single narrative, for example, without grasping fully those laws that control the evocation of the work of art. The limits of the tradition and its possibilities must be understood or analysis is crippled.

At its most effective, analysis lays bare the structural elements of the work of art, reveals the affinities among those elements, and seeks to discover the dynamics of those correspondences by comprehending and applying the aesthetic laws that govern the entire system. In the strictest sense, then, no work of art stands on its own, if that means that it is divorced from an aesthetic tradition and artistic system. But it is significant too that the art tradition moves on a level that is not the same as that of history and culture. It parallels history and culture, and in its own special way reflects, even reveals, elements of history and culture. But it does so on its own terms. And because it does so on its own terms, these artistic works become very dangerous and susceptible to the most radiant misinterpretations. Nor can one move blindly from level to level when analyzing a work of art—move, that is, from the metaphorical level of the work of art to the metaphorical level of history, for example. The myths that generate history and the myths that generate art traditions have their separate existence, and while they may grow from a similar set of human needs and experiences, they nevertheless adapt themselves to the structural necessities of the form that they serve. This is why it is necessary to approach works of art as works of art, and not until then will they yield information, experience, that is useful and accurate within the rules and laws and contexts of the art tradition.

If analysis lays bare the structural elements of the work of art, then obviously certain demands are made of the analyst. The art analyst cannot afford to ignore any aspect of the work of art. He must consider all details, he must be able to understand the parameters of the image sets, and to define relationships between the various sets. He must slowly become aware in narratives of those details that are significant and those that, while not insignificant, nevertheless have a lesser function in the works. This is possibly one of the greatest problems for the analyst of works of art: the ability to discriminate, to grasp major structural features of the work of art, and to discover their interrelationships. Once that is accomplished—and it is no simple task—then all questions of theme and content become merely academic. Oral narrative traditions have a life and a structure and a system of laws of their own, and it is up to the analyst to know and to respond to these structures and systems, which are as regular and perhaps even as predictable as those in other forms of human experience, and most certainly should be approached in that manner.

One of the most interesting trickster figures in world narrative fiction is Mantis, the splendidly mercurial trickster of the San of southern Africa. The activities of Mantis, the images evoking his diverse actions, flow most commonly in patterned image sets.

Story One: "The Mantis and the Korotwiten"[13]

The korotwiten is a little bird; it is black, it has white feathers on its shoulders. It was once a man, it was one of the Early Race. It flew, it walked, because it felt it was a man.

Once, the mantis, when he was out hunting, caught sight of the korotwiten hovering over one place. And the korotwiten dropped down, he dived into a little ant-hole, while the mantis stood looking at him. Then he carried out the kaross from another little ant-hole, while the mantis kept looking at the place where he had gone in. He carried out the kaross full of ants' larvae at a different place. And the mantis turned his face towards the korotwiten. Then the mantis went up to him, as he sat tying up the kaross nicely, the kaross of ants' larvae.

The mantis said, "You must please anoint[14] me with your perspiration, for you can do this, but I have to dig ants' larvae out with a stick. Therefore, my hands are sore, because I dig out ants' larvae with a stick."

Then the korotwiten spoke, he said, "You should go up to an ant heap, the ant heap which is there, you should watch."

And the mantis said, "You can give me the power to see."

Then the korotwiten rose up, he flew along, he went to hover; he dived into a little ant-hole while the mantis stood looking. He carried out a karossful of ants' larvae at another little ant-hole.

Then the mantis said, "Truly we can do like this. I can cease being one who digs ants' larvae with a stick."

Men dig out ants' larvae when the springbok are not there; women generally dig out ants' larvae.

Then the mantis broke the bow across his foot, he snapped the arrow in two, he tore up the quiver, he also struck with a stone and split the digging stone, he struck and broke the digging stick, around which he had placed the digging stone in order to dig ants' larvae. He felt that he resembled the korotwiten, he would enter a little ant-hole, when he had slung on a kaross into which he meant to scoop up ants' larvae.

Then he hovered and hovered in the air, he dived into a little ant-hole, and he truly carried out a karossful of ants' larvae at another place. He then went to sit down; while he held the karossful of ants' larvae fast, he said, "Tell me, why is it that we seem always to have been digging? Our hands were sore because we dug, while we might have done like this."

And he again rose and went to hover in the air; he again dived into a little ant-hole; he truly carried out the kaross from a different ant-hole, that was where he brought out the kaross. And he tied up the kaross, he turned aside to take the ants' larvae to the water.

And he went down; the korotwiten was feeding there, for the korotwiten had gone down to the water first. So he reached the water while the korotwiten was feeding there, and he went to feed there.

And the korotwiten said, "I want first to see you at yonder ant-heap, and you must afterwards remember that tomorrow you must give me a share of the new ants' larvae, which you will cut tomorrow, that is what you will give me a share of."

Then the mantis said, "Why is it that my brother did not say so before, for I thought I was really scooping up for my sister's son, Kwammang-a, I really was gathering it for him."

Then the korotwiten said, "You ought to give me a share, because it was I who told you nicely about the ants' larvae. For you should remember that time when you complained that the earth did not feel comfortable to you."

Then the korotwiten shut his mouth, and the korotwiten said, "You had better go home, for I am also going to my home."

And the mantis said, "I will do the same as you."

While the mantis took up the bag of ants' larvae, he slung it on.

And the korotwiten said, "You must seek food at this place tomorrow, and we will talk together and will both go down to the water."

And the mantis returned, the mantis reached home.

Then Kauru, his wife, said, "Oh dear! Where has the mantis left the things that he took with him just now? for he had a quiver just now, and a digging stick's stone."

And the mantis said, "There was a man to whom I went up there, he was entering little ant-holes, he truly carried out a karossful of ants' larvae at another place."

Then the young ichneumon said, "Oh Mantis, where did you leave the things?"

Then the mantis spoke, he told the young ichneumon that he had broken all the things to pieces.

Then Kwammang-a spoke, he said to the young ichneumon, "Child, tell Grandfather it is the korotwiten. When we see him, we keep still, we keep hold of the things and do not break them up, for the korotwiten always acts like this when we look at him."

And the mantis said, "Why does my sister's son, Kwammang-a, speak thus, when he should know that this is a particularly nice man; he has asked me to go out to him tomorrow, so that I may keep hovering and dive into a nice place without its equal."

Then Kwammang-a said, "You can let Grandfather be, for Grandfather does not seem to have placed food for the korotwiten, and we always do so, for we are accustomed, when he speaks nicely to us, to place food for him."

Then the mantis said, "He did speak to me about it; I however thought that he had plenty of ants' larvae."

And Kwammang-a said, "Child, tell Grandfather that we always place food for the korotwiten, then the ground is soft for us. But the ground will always be hard if we do not share with the korotwiten, then the korotwiten is angry and the ground becomes hard for us."

Then the mantis again went out early to meet the korotwiten as he went along, that they might get ants' larvae. He walked along.

The korotwiten was up early, hovering there. He dropped down, he dived into a little ant-hole, he truly carried out the kaross at a little ant-hole there.

Then the mantis went up to an ant-heap that he had seen. He kept hovering there, he dived into a little ant-hole. He truly carried out the kaross at another little ant-hole, he carried the kaross to a bush, he put the kaross down. He sat and tied the kaross up nicely, he went away. He walked up to another ant-heap, he again kept hovering there. He dived into a little ant-hole, he truly carried out the kaross at another ant-hole. He went and put down the kaross. He sat down, he sat and tied up the kaross nicely. Then he poured the ants' larvae into a bag.

Then he descended to the water, and the korotwiten saw that he descended to the water, the korotwiten descended to the water. And the korotwiten walked up to the place at which the korotwiten had laid down the bag. The korotwiten said, "Now, I think you should do this, you should place food before me."

Then the mantis said, "Oh, listen to my brother! Why does my brother speak so? Although he is full of ants' larvae, he speaks so."

Then the korotwiten said, "Oh man, you ought to share with me, for it was you who asked me to speak nicely to you when you did not feel happy. For you were saying, why was it that the ground did not feel pleasant to you."

Then the mantis said, "This person sounds as if he were tipsy with poison, for this is the ants' larvae of which I spoke, that I must go and put it to dry."

And the korotwiten said, "Do so, and you will see tomorrow that the place will hurt you again, for you ought to act as if we had given to you."

Then the mantis did this, he went back, he returned to the people's home.

Then the young ichneumon said, "Oh! Oh! My grandfather the mantis's bag is full!"

Then Kwammang-a spoke, he said, "Just leave off, you shall ask Grandfather whether he did what I told him to do, whether Grandfather shared with the korotwiten?"

And the mantis said that he had not done so, for he had thought that the korotwiten's bag was full.

And Kwammang-a said, "Child, speak to Grandfather and tell him that we are wont to share with the korotwiten. Even if the korotwiten's bag is full, we share. Otherwise, he always gets angry, and the ground will not open."

Then the mantis said, "The place is not one into which we could vanish," for he had been diving into an ant-hole.

Then Kwammang-a was quite silent, for Kwammang-a felt that he meant to do so.

And the mantis woke up early, he went out early to seek an ant-heap that he had located. And he went along, he reached the ant-heap, he went to hover above it. And he kept hovering there, he dropped down, he tried to dive in, he plunged on to his brow. And he cried with the pain in his brow.

He got up again, for he thought that he did not seem to have entered the hole properly.

He got up again, he again hovered above, he dropped down, he again crashed on to the front of his head, while blood flowed.

And he got up, he went home.

And the young ichneumon said, "Oh! Oh! Who can have done this to my grandfather, the mantis?"

And the mantis told him how he had himself plunged onto his face when he meant to enter the ant-hole.

Then Kwammang-a spoke, he said to the young ichneumon, "Child, tell Grandfather that I wanted him to share with the korotwiten, for he seems to have thought that the earth would not be hard for us if the korotwiten were angry because we had not divided with him."

Then the young ichneumon spoke to the mantis, he said, "Father wishes me to say that he told you to share with the korotwiten, for the earth would be hard for us if the korotwiten were angry."

So Kwammang-a felt that he had thus spoken to the young ichneumon, and the young ichneumon had told the mantis while he was quite silent. Because he would not speak in haste, he had spoken to the young ichneumon.

He was silent, quite silent.

Commentary: "The Mantis and the Korotwiten"
A little black bird with white wings, the korotwiten, dives into an ant-hole and emerges with ants' larvae. Mantis sees him and asks the bird to anoint him with its perspiration, so that Mantis too would be able to accomplish this marvelous task. That is the full image set, and the central act of the image set is the movement of diving into the ant-hole and the emergence with the ant larvae. Now an entire narrative performance is created about this single rather straightforward action. But Korotwiten goes on its way, and continues to dive, continues to come up with the tasty food. Mantis continues to watch, as the image set is repeated. And then Mantis, blind to what his actions mean, breaks his bow, his arrow, tears up his quiver, breaks his digging stick, because, he insists, he can do the same thing, he can duplicate the action of the korotwiten bird. And so he "felt that he resembled" the bird, and he too hovers in the air, he too dives into the little ant-hole, and he too comes back with his cape filled with ant larvae. He has successfully navigated the magical pattern established by that little bird with white-tipped wings. Why, Mantis wonders, have we been digging for larvae all this time? This is a much easier way! And he dives into another ant-hole, and another, and so the actions are being repeated, the model is being repeated precisely in terms of image. That is the basic element of the artistic tradition. And before Mantis goes home, the one detail necessary to bring the narrative to its conclusion is added, the detail that will make it possible for the model to be altered and the narrative to make its point. The mere continued repeating of the image set will result in no meaningful experience. The detail: Korotwiten insists that, on the next day, Mantis must share the ant larvae that he gets with the bird; after all, the bird showed him how to get that food. But Mantis is arrogant. We always used to get our ant larvae in this way, he sneers. Mantis had always known it, he didn't require the assistance of Korotwiten. So he owed the bird nothing. At his home, Mantis's various relatives are concerned that he has broken up his weapons and digging implement, and his son realizes that it is Korotwiten who has caused this: "For the korotwiten always acts like this when we look at him." And he warns Mantis to place food for Korotwiten, for "the ground will always be hard if we do not share with the korotwiten." The point has been doubly made, and the narrative proceeds now with the repetition of the basic image set of this performance, the diving into

the ant-hole. The next day, Mantis goes back to the ant-holes, and continues to dive in, returning from the hole with ant larvae. When the bird arrives and asks that Mantis share his food, "Oh man," the bird says, "you ought to share with me, for it was you who asked me to speak nicely to you when you did not feel happy. For you were saying, why was it that the ground did not feel pleasant to you." But Mantis refuses, and the bird warns Mantis that the ground "will hurt you again" on the next day. And so the repeating of the basic model continues, and Mantis returns home with much food. Again, he is warned by those at home that he must share with the bird. And on the next day, the pattern is repeated, the pattern being the diving into the ant-hole and the returning with ant larvae, but now the pattern is altered: "And the mantis woke up early, he went out early to seek an ant-heap that he had located. And he went alone, he reached the ant-heap, he went to hover above it. And he kept hovering there, he dropped down, he tried to dive in, he plunged on to his brow. And he cried with the pain in his brow. He got up again," he will seek to duplicate the model yet again, "for he thought he did not seem to have entered the hole properly. He got up again, he again hovered above, he dropped down, he again crashed on to the front of his head, while blood flowed. And he got up, he crept home." And so with another scolding by his relatives, Mantis's antics bring the narrative to a close.

In analyzing a straightforward narrative such as this one, the isolating of the image sets is not difficult. The image set basic to the performance—basic in the sense that all actions and the theme flow from it—is, as I have said, the repeated movements into the ant-hill, then back again with food. Korotwiten does it, and establishes the pattern, and then Mantis follows, and continues to repeat the model. There are several reasons for the repetition of the pattern. First of all, the pattern is repeated to move the narrative forward toward its resolution, a resolution that would not have been attained had the problem of sharing not been introduced between the repeated image sets, when the bird asks that Mantis share the next day. But it might be noted that, in this narrative, the plea for sharing in itself becomes a repeated element: first, Korotwiten requests it, then Mantis's family requests it, then Korotwiten again, and then the family again and finally, as the narrative ends, the family repeats its plea for sharing. The second reason for repeating the basic image set is to establish Mantis's success at the diving, returning sequence. And the more successful he becomes, the more arrogant he becomes, so that the repetition develops a kind of intensity on the level of the character of Mantis, Mantis who insists, as he often does, that he has nothing to learn, that he has had this wisdom for a very long time. Side by side, then, the repeated elements develop, the image of diving, the image that contains the warnings about sharing. And then, because he does not heed the advice, the final image set occurs, when Mantis crashes into the earth and hits hard ground rather than an ant hole. The point of the narrative has been made, the theme revealed. And it is quite obviously a theme that revolves around sharing. It is not a difficult matter to reveal the image sets in this narrative then, the job of the analyst. One can see the repeated sets, all of them quite the same, and then the final one, with its alterations. The relationship between that last set of images and the earlier ones provides the dramatic experience of the rather didactic image sets that weave into those that primarily depict action.

Story Two: "The Mantis and the Cat"[15]

The mantis rose up on the morrow. He walked out, because he was angry. He went wrathfully along. He met the cat going along singing. The cat sang that the lynx mocked at him, because he could not run as fast as the lynx did. Thus the cat sang as he went. The mantis ran to meet the cat, as he came along. The mantis asked him: "What are you singing about?" The cat answered: "I am not singing about anything."

The mantis said: "Your little head is trembling, you were singing about something."

The cat said: "Your eyes have warts on them. I will hit your head, I will break it."

The mantis said: "O Cat, hit my head, I will hit your head!"

The cat struck at the mantis's head; the mantis drew back. The mantis struck at the cat's head; the cat drew back and hid his head in the ground. The mantis hit the cat' s tail. The cat got up and struck at the mantis's head. The mantis drew back and struck at the cat's head. The cat drew back and hid his head in the ground. The mantis hit the cat' s tail, because it was above the ground, and the cat's head was in the ground. The cat hit the mantis's head and broke it.

The mantis quickly got feathers, he flew away. He called to the hartebeestskin bag: "O Hartebeest's children, leave here, we must fly."

The hartebeestskin bag said: "Let us follow!"

The shoes said: "We will really follow, for the mantis has said so."

The quiver said: "We will do so!"

The cap said: "O Kaross, let us follow!"

The bow said: "O Stick, we ought to follow, for the mantis says so."

They ran off.

The mantis flew along the sky; he flew into the water, he splashed in the water, he jumped out, he rejoiced: "The mantis has done this." His things ran past him at the water. The mantis quickly called to them, he said: "Lie down there quickly, for yonder is our home and the ichneumon would laugh at you; you must lie down there quickly and I will carry·you."

The·quiver said: "The mantis left us, we had to come home."

The shoes said: "We really must lie down to wait for the mantis." The shoes did so, they waited for the mantis. The mantis boasted: "What man is our equal? Our name is the mantis!" He walked forward. He walked slowly up to the hut, for he was limping; he sat down.

The ichneumon said: "Who has hit the mantis's head with a stick?"

The mantis said: "It was the cat who hit my head with a stick!"

The ichneumon said: "O Mantis, we always feint at the cat's head, the cat hides his head in the ground, we look to see where his head is, we strike, break- ing it."

The mantis said: "O Ichneumon, you must go on telling me about it, you must not go to sleep. For day will soon break for me, and I want to go early and look about for another cat, that I may quickly break its head."

The day soon broke; the ichneumon said: "O Mantis, do let me sleep! You must find the spoor."

The mantis ran out of the house, he ran to seek a cat. Again he saw the cat come singing, and ran to meet him. The cat stood still. He feinted at the cat's head. The cat quickly put his head into the ground, thinking that the mantis would strike his tail again. The mantis saw his head just above the ground; he struck at it and hit it. The mantis asked whether he had meant to offer him his head.

The cat rose up, the cat said: "The ichneumon told you about it, that is how you found my head."

The mantis said: "You are lying, I had forgotten."

The cat said: "You had not forgotten, the ichneumon told you."

The mantis said: "That is not true; you stand there telling lies. It slipped my memory, I had not really forgotten, but I did not think of it. I really am cunning."

The mantis feinted at his head once more. He again put his head into the ground. The mantis saw his head standing there and struck, hitting it. The mantis sprang away, he boasted: "See, our name is the mantis! What man is equal to us?"

The cat rose up and said: "The ichneumon told you."

The mantis said: "A lie has misled you. I am the cunning one. The ichneu- mon did not tell me. I had merely forgotten about you." He went forward, he picked up the quiver, he slung it on. He picked up the kaross, he wrapped it

round him. He picked up the bag, he slung it over his shoulder. He picked up
the bow, he put it under his arm. He picked up the shoes, he put them on. He
picked up the stick, he carried it. He returned home; he laid down the quiver,
he laid down the bow, he laid down the stick.

The ichneumon asked him: "Did you see the cat?"

The mantis said: "I did see him."

The ichneumon asked: "What happened to you?"

The mantis said: "Nothing happened to me," for he was boasting. He said:
"I feinted at the old man, he hid his head in the ground, I saw it."

The ichneumon said: "Did you get him?"

The mantis said: "I truly struck it, I hit it. The old man rose up and said you
had told me, that was how I knew about him. I told the old man that I had
merely forgotten. The old man said that you had certainly taught me. I told
him, he was standing telling lies."

The ichneumon said: "O Mantis, you are foolish, you are deceitful. I taught
you; I, a child, taught you, a grown-up man. You are foolish, you are cunning, you are deceitful." Thus they talked there. The womenfolk laughed at
them. The ichneumon said: "You agree with me. Is not the mantis foolish and
deceitful?"

Commentary: "The Mantis and the Cat"

The foolishness of this trickster becomes the theme in a narrative that has precisely the same structural pattern. And again, Mantis finds it impossible to
admit that he has received assistance from members of his family. He meets the
cat, and they start fighting. The cat strikes at Mantis, then buries its head in
the ground. Mantis strikes at the cat's tail, because that is the only thing above
the ground. The pattern is established, the image set involves the fighting of the
creatures, the cat strikes Mantis, then buries its head, Mantis strikes but only
hits the cat's tail. This pattern is repeated until the cat breaks Mantis's head.
Mantis escapes by developing feathers and flying away, and his bag and shoes
and quiver and cap fly along with him. Mantis flies into the water and boasts
that he is Mantis. Then he goes limping home. His grandson tells him how to
fight with the cat, and, with this new knowledge, Mantis/Trickster is prepared
to alter the pattern, which was established, and to break the cat's head. When
they meet on the next day, Mantis strikes the cat's head rather than its tail. The
cat insists that the grandson must have told Mantis what to do, but Mantis
argues that he had only forgotten how to fight the cat. Again they fight, and
again Mantis hurts the cat. And again they argue. Finally, Mantis picks up his
belongings and triumphantly returns home. He tells his grandchild what has

occurred. And, says Mantis, when the cat "told me that you had certainly taught me, I told him he was telling lies." And his grandson taunts Mantis, "Oh Mantis, you are foolish, you are deceitful. I taught you; I, a child, taught you, a grown-up man." And the women laugh at Mantis as the narrative ends. Here, too, as in the previous Mantis narrative, theme and image set are bound together. The image set centers on the fight between the cat and Mantis, the first set of images has the cat victorious, the second has Mantis as the victor. Between the two sets of repeated and patterned image sets is the advice given to Mantis by his grandchild. Mantis boasts throughout this narrative that he is an incredibly wise and cunning creature, but in fact, of course, he is not, and the narrative images bear this out. In the first narrative, the detail that provides the reason for the alteration in the patterned image sets is the demand of the bird that Mantis share the ant larvae. In this narrative, the detail that alters the pattern is the advice given to Mantis by his grandson. But the point of the narrative is not simply the fact that Mantis is now victorious over the cat. We realize that the mantis did not himself alter the image sets. It took a small child to do that, to provide Mantis with the information needed to make the necessary changes in the image set to bring the narrative to a satisfying close. And, as with the previous narrative, that of the korotwiten, the material that accompanies the basic image set is also repeated: the advice given, and the insistence on the cat's part that the grandchild had told Mantis, and finally the grandchild's repeating of that point. The foolishness of this puffed-up trickster then is a part of the theme, but the theme requires the boastfulness of Mantis as well, and that is the reason for the inclusion in this narrative of Mantis flying to the water, then boasting of his capabilities even as he limps home. The structure of the narrative is quite simple; the pattern is established of the fighting, and the pattern is altered. It is in the alteration of the pattern that the point of this narrative is made.

It is obvious in these brief analyses of the two Mantis narratives that there are really two kinds of structural relationship here. There are the basic patterned image sets themselves. In the first of the narratives, these involved the hovering, the movement into the ant-hill, the movement out with the ant larvae. In the second Mantis narrative, the basic patterned image set had to do with the fight between the cat and Mantis. But simultaneously, in each of the two narratives, there were other repeated images, which were of a more didactic nature than the basic image sets, though these were indeed image sets. In the first narrative, these images centered on the warnings, the repeated warnings, to Mantis to share with the korotwiten, and these warnings were repeated at the very end of the narrative. In the second narrative, these secondary images centered on the fact that Mantis received advice from a child, these images including the act itself, the cat's insistence, twice, that this is in fact what happened, and Mantis's insistence that it did not happen that way, and finally the grandchild's own insistence that he, a mere child, had to tell Mantis how to handle the cat. There are two kinds of narrative images, the primary image sets, those depicting the basic repeated actions of the narrative, a developmental repetition; and those images that are more didactic, perceptual repetition. Those image sets that are purely action sets, which move the plot toward its resolution and which are devoid of didacticism, lesson, theme in any overt way, are developmental repetition, in the sense that the repeated images develop the conflict and move it toward resolution. Those images and image sets that comment on the action images are perceptual repetition, in the sense that these images are included in the narrative to provide a thematic perspective for the more basic repeated image sets. The Mantis narratives obviously contain in separate repeated channels action images and thematic images, something that is not so obvious in many oral traditions, but something that is vital to an appreciation of the structures of these traditions.

Story Three: "The Mantis and Kutegaua"[16]

Kutegaua used once to set fire to the lairs of wild cats. Then he got into the fire and brought out the wild cats, and those cats had no equal in beauty.

Kutegaua would pick up a firebrand, he would walk up to a lair, he would set fire to the lair; he would get into the fire when the fire was burning, yet the fire would feel cool and not feel hot, because it felt that he was the one who owned the fire. Therefore, the fire did not burn him, the fire also did not scorch his apron, for he was clad in a cat-skin that was scorched like the west wind's clouds, a black cat-skin it was.

He was wont, when he had set fire to a lair, to say,

> "Kutegaua, n bagen, bagen, gaua!
> Kutegaua, n bagen, bagen, gaua!"

Then he would spring through the fire and he would bring out the cats. He laid them down, he took out a knife, he skinned them, he cleaned them, he put earth on the skins.

Then he picked up a firebrand, he walked on to another lair; he went and set fire to it, he sang again,

> "Kutegaua, n bagen, bagen, gaua!
> Kutegaua, n bagen, bagen, gaua!"

He kept passing through the fire, he kept coming out of the fire while he was singing, and he brought out cats, and there were no cats as fine as these which he took out of the fire. And he laid them down, he skinned them, he cleaned them, he put earth on their skins, he took a firebrand, he walked up to another lair. He again set fire to it, again he sang, again he sprang into the fire; again he brought out cats, again he skinned them.

He collected them, collected the cat-skins; he rolled them up, he put them on his shoulder because he was going home. And he really went home because the sun was setting, because he was going to sleep.

And early next morning, he took a firebrand in order to seek lairs that he had remarked. These he sought.

Then the mantis came by, the mantis caught sight of him making a fire there, and the mantis went right up to him. And just as the mantis was looking, he jumped into the fire, and the mantis said, "Blisters, oh blister him! What ho! What person can be doing this? He is getting into the fire!"

And just as the mantis came up exclaiming, he dragged out cats unequaled in beauty.

And the mantis said, "I should like to know what these things can be."

And the mantis said, "You really must give me the next cat, for you are rich in cat-skins. You should give me the next cat."

Then Kutegaua said, "If you go to the lair that stands yonder and set fire to it, you will see."

Then the mantis said, "You might give me the next cat, for this fire is scorching me."

And Kutegaua said, "Ho there! Go back! Go and light a fire, and you shall feel whether the fire will scorch you."

Then the mantis took a firebrand, he went up to a lair. He set fire to the lair, he said,

> "Kutegaua, n bagen, bagen, gaua!
> Kutegaua, n bagen, bagen, gaua!"

for he imitated Kutegaua, because Kutegaua had always said,

> "Kutegaua, n bagen, bagen, gaua!"

And he jumped into the fire, he dragged out cats, he laid them down. He took a firebrand, he walked to another lair, again he set it on fire, again he sang like Kutegaua; he jumped into the fire. Again he dragged out cats, he laid them down.

Again he took a firebrand, because he was glad that the fire did not burn him; therefore, he would not start skinning. He dragged out cats, he laid them down, he took a firebrand, he walked to another lair, because he was glad, that was why he would not start skinning. Then he dragged out cats, he laid them down; he took a firebrand, because he was glad that the fire did not burn him, and that the fire felt cool. Then he gathered up the cats, because he meant to skin them.

Then Kutegaua came to him, Kutegaua came to see what cats he had got. Then Kutegaua asked him for the cats which he himself saw. Kutegaua asked for some of them, he said, "You must give me these two cats."

Then the mantis said, "I cannot do so, these are the cats that I had planned to take to Kwammang-a."

Then next day he came again and set fire to lairs and jumped into the fire. He dragged out cats, he took them along, he laid them down. He took a firebrand, he went to another lair, he set it on fire. Again he sprang into the fire, again he dragged out cats, he laid them down; again he went to another lair.

Then, when he felt that he had plenty of cats, he gathered them together because he meant to skin them.

Then Kutegaua came to him, Kutegaua saw that he was going to start skinning.

So Kutegaua came up to him and said, "You must give me of the cat-skins lying here, a share of them, for I let you off about yesterday's cats. These cats are the ones of which you must give me part."

Then the mantis replied, "These cats are the ones of which I meant to make a kaross, for you can see that my kaross is like this."

Then Kutegaua said, "You must give me a share of these cats. Then I shall merely look at the new cats, whose lairs you will presently set on fire. At them, I shall merely look." For he would not beg from him again, because the mantis would have just given him some cats.

The mantis said that he would not do so, for he had not yet made the kaross, for he had intended to make a kaross and he had not made it.

Then Kutegaua said, "You shall give me these cats, a share of them, for you acted like this about the cats for which I asked you before, you went on like this." And he exclaimed, "You must give me these cats, a share of them."

Then the mantis said, "You really sound as if you mean to insist, although I tell you that I have not got a kaross."

Then Kutegaua exclaimed, "Oh man! You shall give me a share of these cats or else you will find out what the fire feels like, because you act like this while we are wont to give to one another."

Then the mantis told him he had always known how to go into a fire.

Then Kutegaua spoke and said, "Wait, you shall feel the fire tomorrow. You seem to think fire cannot scorch you."

And the mantis said, "That is false, you know the fire feels cool."

Then Kutegaua said, "Wait, you will see. When you have taken these cats away and gone to lie down, you will wake up early tomorrow, you will start early and come to make fires, thinking you will enter the fire unharmed. But those cats shall be burnt up, the fire shall burn you badly when you try to enter the fire."

Then the mantis said, "That one seems to want to deceive us."

Then he went away, he went to sleep.

Early in the morning, he took a firebrand, he went early to pairs that he had remarked, he went to them early, while Kutegaua stayed at home because he was angry with the mantis, that was why he stayed at home.

Then the mantis set out, he reached a lair, he set fire to the lair, he sang again, as Kutegaua had done, he sang of him. Then he sprang into the fire, and he was scorched in the fire.

He exclaimed, "Hartebeest's children, you must go!" and he flew down, he popped into the water. And he exclaimed, "Our mate! lie down in the old place. The person has done this!" When he had said this, he cried out, "Oh blisters! Oh dear! Oh dear! Oh dear!" for he was howling about the fire's blisters, for the fire hurt him. He said he would not set lairs on fire again, for the fire was burning him as the fire had not done yesterday.

So he took up his things, he returned home.

Then the young ichneumon exclaimed, "Who has done this, has burnt my grandfather the mantis?"

Then the mantis told the young ichneumon that he had burnt himself by jumping into the fire because the fire had felt cool the day before, therefore he had jumped into the fire.

Then Kwammang-a spoke, he said to the young ichneumon, "Child! Tell Grandfather that Grandfather does not seem to have given Kutegaua every other cat. For we are wont to do so when we want the fire to be quiet and feel cool for us, that we may get quietly into the fire. For the fire always burns off our skin unless we give Kutegaua every other cat, for Kutegaua gets angry. Therefore we are wont to give him every other cat."

Then the mantis replied that he thought Kutegaua was rich in cat-skins.

Then Kwammang-a replied, "We are wont to give to him, even if he is rich in cat-skins. For then the fire is always quiet and feels cool to us, we get quietly into the fire. But the fire always burns us if we do not give him every other cat."

Commentary: "The Mantis and Kutegaua"

Mantis encounters Kutegaua, who habitually sets fire to the lairs of wild cats, and then it goes into the fire and brings out the wild cats. The fire feels cool to this creature, not hot; he kills the cats, skins them, and cleans them. This is the model for this performance, and Kutegaua goes from lair to lair with this fiery business. One day, Mantis sees this activity, and Mantis begs for one of the splendid-looking cats. Kutegaua invites Mantis to do the same thing that it is doing, and he imitates Kutegaua, doing and saying what it does and says, and Mantis too is not burned. He too gets the wild cats. And so it goes, the model being repeated by Mantis and Kutegaua. Then Kutegaua introduces into the narrative the demand that results in an alteration in the pattern. "You must give me these two cats," it insists at one point, but Mantis refuses. The next day, the patterning continues, Mantis getting more and more fine-looking wild cats. And again, Kutegaua asks for some of the cat skins, and again Mantis refuses; he plans to make a cape of the skins. The argument goes on, and finally Kutegaua warns Mantis, "You shall give me a share of these cats or else you will find out what the fire feels like, because you act like this while we are wont to give to one another." Mantis then insists that he does not need Kutegaua anyway, "he had always known how to go into a fire." Kutegaua says, "Wait, you shall feel the fire tomorrow. You seem to think that fire cannot scorch you." And so, on the following day, Mantis begins the pattern again. But this time, when he reaches a lair and sets fire to it, "he was scorched in the fire." He has been badly burnt, and when he gets home, Kwammang-a repeats what Kutegaua had warned, "Grandfather does not seem to have given Kutegaua every other cat. For we are wont to do so when we want the fire to be quiet and feel cool for us, that we may get quietly into the fire. For the fire always burns off our skin unless we give Kutegaua every other cat. . . ." Once again, the basic developmental repetition is that of the primary image set, that dealing with the movement into and out of the fire with no ill effects. And the parallel image set is again the didactic one, the continued warnings of Kutegaua that occur alongside and complementary with the primary image set, that Mantis must share the cats with Kutegaua. This presents the material for alteration, and Mantis's character does the rest; Mantis of course refuses to share, insists that he does not need Kutegaua anyway, and so when he seeks to repeat the pattern, he is scorched by the fire, and the narrative can come to an end. But again, it does not end until the secondary thematic image set is completed, and again Mantis is taught by members of his family how he can go through life without finding himself in trouble constantly.

These sets of images, developing simultaneously, the one commenting on the actions of the other, the perceptual providing a context of cultural accept-ability for the developmental repetition, are still rather uncomplicated in the San narratives, the sets of images on the one hand developing the plot, the other barely a set of images in any visual sense, with characters speaking and commenting on the actions in the other narratives and thereby pronouncing the theme. But this dual structure is important for oral narrative traditions, and seems to suggest a development of thought in oral narratives so far as struc-ture is concerned that might be stated as follows: the most ancient structural form that still operates within the oral system seems to be the purely repeated image set, a repetition with little alteration in the images themselves. From the expansible image develops patterned image sets that allow more complex nar-ratives and therefore more complex themes to develop. But in the patterned sets, theme is not readily revealed. The emphasis, as with the expansible image, remains on the surface linearity of the narrative, and that linearity exerts an influence on the entirety of the performance, so much so that plot dominates all and the manipulation of plot is a difficult aesthetic problem.

It becomes necessary to develop an artistic counterpart to the plot, the mere movement from conflict to resolution. A kind of running commentary is devel-oped, some kind of extra-image element that complements and supplements the repeated image sets, endowing those sets with meaning. What is happening with the developmental repetition, with the repeated image sets, the pattern-ing, is that the expansible image is now becoming even more complex. This occurs in Greek drama, when ancient dance and song evolve into dramatic representation, a chorus simultaneously developed that provides an intellectual and perceptual context for the action unfolding on the stage. But the chorus is not merely an adjunct to the dramatic action, it is artistically woven into the action of the narrative, so that the chorus helps to develop the conflict and res-olution even as it comments upon that conflict and resolution. The chorus remains aloof from the action, thereby enabling it to comment freely on it, but the chorus is sufficiently a part of the action to ensure that its pronouncements of meaning flow cohesively from the drama itself. This blending of didacticism with action is a common characteristic of African art forms, and art forms of oral societies generally. In oral narrative traditions, as the repeated image sets are being externalized in a more perceptual context, the running commentary is de-veloping into a more complex form. Like the Greek chorus, it does not become non-dramatic exegesis; it is closely associated with the main action of the nar-rative. And so a kind of parallelism develops, in which the narrative action becomes related to a narrative commentary, which is itself a part of the action.

The expansible image set, then, is the simple repetition of an image set. From the beginning of the narrative to its end, with no structural alteration in this basic imaged movement, one image set is repeated, nothing more. Patterning, on the other hand, involves the channeling of the expansible image set into new molds; now the expanded image set becomes a model, and this model, a complex of images, is repeated in typical traditional expansible image manner, but at the end there is an alteration in the image set, or the injection of something into the narrative between the image sets that nevertheless results in the alteration of the image set when next objectified, and that has a dramatic effect on the movement of the narrative and perhaps reveals a theme as well. This is the form that the expansible image set takes, then, when it develops into patterned sets. The expansible image set is repeated a number of times to insure the establishment of the model, and then the model is altered, the simple alteration of the model sufficient to communicate to the audience the meaning of the narrative. But the movement is again toward more complex themes and therefore more complex narratives, and so this patterned parallelism is further developed. And there are two kinds of parallelism in the oral narrative traditions, one in which patterned image sets are combined with image sets of a didactic nature, the other in which two parallel sets of expansible images are simultaneously developed, or developed serially, but the one set is not a duplication of the other as occurs with patterned image sets. The paralleling set is not precisely like the model; it reflects the model, but with an entirely different image set.

It is a metaphorical movement. The second set of images is acting upon the first, so that an entirely new perception is generated by the relationship, by bringing the sets of images into parallel relationship. Patterned image sets deal with similar image sets; parallel image sets deal with unlike image sets. But at the same time, parallel image sets are parallel in the sense that each image set, though different on the face of it, reveals the same theme. The second and/or third sets, which parallel the first and/or second sets, extend the meaning of the first, comment upon the first, or in reflecting the theme of the first thereby reveal it. This can be seen in a theme's incipient form in the patterned image sets of Mantis. The basic patterning is of the pure patterned image set variety, as in most of the trickster narratives. What is changed in the overall structure of these Mantis narratives is the addition of the commentary, those images that show members of Mantis's family commenting on his actions in a decidedly didactic way; these two are images, but the emphasis is on theme rather than action, and in the patterned sets of the developmental variety, the emphasis is quite the reverse. The artists are obviously seeking to give the patterned developmental repetition a context of meaning, and hence the addition of the paralleling set of images, those dealing with the family's constant warnings and exhortations. The one complements the other; that is, the one set of images acts as a commentary on the other. This is the foundation for the complex parallel image set structure.

One of the most complex narratives illustrating this use of paralleling imaged commentary is a Mantis narrative that Bleek entitles "The Mantis Takes Away the Ticks' Sheep" and "The Mantis and the All-devourer," two narratives that, as Bleek notes, are really parts of the same story.

Story Four: "The Mantis Takes Away the Ticks' Sheep" and
"The Mantis and the All-devourer," by ‖Kábbo[17]

|kággen, the mantis, went to the ticks' house. They saw him, and said to each other, "What man is coming here?"

Another said, "|kággen is coming. We'll creep into the sheep's wool, and let him come into the house. Let the little child remain here, he can look after the pots on the fire. Then the old man will come into the house as the child sits here alone. Now, you must all carry knobkerries. We'll listen to |kággen, when he approaches the child. He'll question the child, because he'll see that we're not in the house."

The ticks then went into the sheep's wool.

|kággen went up to the child. "Am I like a fighting man, that the people have fled in fear of me? But I'm just a quiet man. There's no one here but this black child. The others have gone, leaving him sitting alone in the house tasting the contents of this pot. The houses have no people!"

But the people were listening in the sheep's wool.

|kággen said, "Let me just put my quiver down and take out this fat and eat it—because the people have fled in fear. As for this child, I'll first eat until I am satisfied, then I'll knock him down because he has no sense."

A tick fell down from the sheep's wool.

|kággen saw him, and asked, "Where did you come from?"

But the young man tick was silent. He lifted the pot and placed it carefully on the fire.

Then his sister fell down, his older brother fell down and snatched the pot. Other ticks fell down at other fires.

The other ticks that were still in the sheep's wool whispered to each other, "You must fall down one by one!"

A big young man tick slipped down beside |kággen, and he sat there holding |kággen by his cape.

THE MANTIS

This is a Xhosa view of the origin of the mantis: One day, there was a big thunderstorm in a certain village. A big house in one homestead was struck by lightning. People were asked to come and extinguish the blaze. They tried and tried, but gave up. Suddenly, there appeared a thin, weak, green insect. It perched on the burning house, and the fire immediately subsided. The people at once called that insect the Child of Heaven.[18]

And this is Dorothea Bleek's view: "The mantis is the favorite hero of [San] folklore. He is gifted with supernatural powers, yet shows great foolishness. He is sometimes mischievous, sometimes kind, at all times very human. His wife is the dasse [rock-badger], also called Kauru, as the mantis too has several other names. . . . Besides his own children the mantis has an adopted daughter, the porcupine, who is really a child of the All-devourer; but fear of her own father has led her to leave him and live with her adopted father. The porcupine is married to Kwammang-a, a mythical person not identified with any animal, but seen in the rainbow. . . . This strange couple have two children, young Kwammang-a, who is brave and quiet like his father, and the young ichneumon, who is a great talker, always lecturing his grandfather the mantis on his foolish doings. . . . Although the mantis has creative powers and can bring people to life again, [San] did not worship him, yet they prayed to his creation, the moon, and to other heavenly bodies. He seems to me to be just a sort of dream [San]. . . ."[19]

His older brother slipped down on the other side of |kággen, and he held him by the other side of the cape.

Another tick made a rustling sound as he dropped down, *vvvv*.

Their father, an old tick, was still up in the sheep's wool. He said to another, "You must wait! Hold the stick, ready to strike. Many people are down there, sitting about on the ground. They'll beat him while we knock him down, as he sits among the people."

|kággen drew back. He said to himself, "Let me move a little further away." He pulled at the cape that was fast to the ground.

Then the old tick fell upon him, and knocked him down. Another tick fell on the mantis, he beat |kággen's shoulders, he struck with the knobkerrie. Another tick sprang out here, on one side, and he beat |kággen's side. Another tick leapt down on him, he beat his other side until |kággen screamed.

Then |kággen slipped out of the cape. The ticks rushed together and struck at him. He called out as the ticks beat him.

|kággen was going. He called to his hartebeestskin bag, and the bag came to him. The quiver arose by itself, and came to him. The stick came, the bag came. |kággen went away first, his things followed him. He went flying into the water, he swam across, he walked up the water's bank.

He said to the hartebeest's children, "Wait for me over there, so that I can come to you slowly to carry you. The people have beaten me badly, and I must go home slowly."

The ichneumon saw him, and said, "|kággen comes, he's coming over there. He's coming slowly. The ticks seem to have beaten him, as they're accustomed to do because they're angry people. |kággen remembered that he has wings, that's why we see him returning. He'll not sleep well tonight."

|kággen sat down, and said, "The people to whom I went must have been hidden. I didn't see them. They kept coming out from above, they kept sliding down. They beat me while the sheep were in the kraal."

The ichneumon said to |kággen, "You went to the house to which people do not go, at which they merely look in passing when the sheep are in the kraal, and go to their own homes. For those people are black, they are accustomed to beating a man to death because of those sheep. They go into the sheep's wool, and we cannot see them. They keep a lookout, they see a man first, while he's still far off. They hide their bodies in the sheep's capes hanging up there. Then they keep falling down, and they beat a man from all sides."

|kággen agreed with him: "That's just what they did. One man knocked me down, others dropped down and struck me. I didn't pick up my stick and strike back, I got up and left my stick. My things were still lying on a bush. The quiver came after me to the water where I went to wash off the blood, the other things followed me."

The ichneumon said, "You're sitting there shivering because you went into cold water to cleanse your wounds. You might have died without our knowing. You had to go into the water because of your tricks, because you went to play tricks on the people you did not know! Nobody goes to them, because they drink blood! They are black people, they are bloody-handed. Their houses are always black, because they are angry folk."

|kággen said to him, "Ichneumon, don't teach me, I'm an old man! I feel as if I would like to sit listening to stories, that's what I would like to hear. You always scold me. But I think that I'm the one who should be angry. Now I'm not going to talk any more, I'm going to lie down. My head aches. And don't say that you don't sleep well, because I really ache! I shall writhe in pain!"

|kággen lay down to sleep, he covered his head.

The ichneumon said, "You always act like this."

|kággen lies there, he moans, he dreams that all the ticks' houses arise and come. "The sheep rise up, the sheep come and stand in front of his house, and the ticks' houses are at the side of his houses, while the ichneumon is still asleep. The ichneumon will see when he awakens—the capes of the ticks are here, all their things are here, their knobkerries with which they beat him are here. Those ticks will soon feel the cold, even though they are asleep. They shall sleep very heavily, they'll feel as if they were wrapped up even though they are not, as they lie in the cold. They'll feel as if they are lying inside houses, but they'll wake up and miss them. And they shall not see the spoor of their sheep, for the spoor will have gone into the air, the kraal will have mounted upwards with the sheep in it.

"Then they'll first miss their fire early, for their fire will have gone with the house, the pots will have entirely disappeared. Those people will not cook for their knives will have gone. I shall be cutting up sheep with them, while the ticks are walking about in their bare flesh, no longer possessing the things they once possessed. Now they will have to drink blood, because they will no longer have a fire as they used to have. Real people will henceforth cook, while the ticks walk entirely in the dark. They will have to continue biting the bodies of things, they will have to drink the blood of things and no longer eat cooked meat."

The ichneumon awoke.

|kággen said, "Icheumon, are you sufficiently awake to look out at the thing that's bleating like a sheep outside? It seems to have come to us early while we were asleep here." The mantis lay there, he questioned the ichneumon while he still had his head covered.

The ichneumon got up and came out. He saw the sheep, and said, "People, get up! Get up, and see the sheep standing in this kraal that my grandfather |kággen has brought! Sheep are here, and the houses have come with them! And look at these pots that he has brought! Look at the ticks' capes, in which we shall lie wrapped up! Now I can keep warm from this cold in which I have always lain uncomfortably. The knobkerries with which they beat my grandfather are here—I shall possess them, so that I can beat the people! My grandfather |kággen will take the old fellow's knobkerries, and I'll take my fellow-children's knobkerries, because they helped their parents to strike my grandfather |kággen when he was alone."

The rock-badger got up. She said to |kággen, "|kággen, why did you take away the people's sheep?"

|kággen answered her as he lay there, "It seemed right to me, because those people attacked me, they wanted to kill me in their anger. Then, because they fought me at their fire, I felt that I wished those angry folk over there should no longer warm themselves at a fire. They shall now drink raw blood because they lack a fire, they cannot make a fire. They cannot cook, they also cannot roast meat to feed themselves. Now they shall walk about in their flesh. In these pots here the San shall some day cook, because they shall have a fire. We who are here will then also be as the ticks now are. We'll eat different things, because we too shall lack fire. You, the ichneumon, will then go to dwell in the hills with your mother. She will truly become a porcupine, she will live in a hole, while Grandmother Rock-badger will live in a mountain den, for her name is really 'Rock-badger.' I shall have wings, I shall fly when I am green, I'll be a little green thing. You, the ichneumon, will eat honey because you will be living on the hill. Then you will marry a she-ichneumon."

The porcupine called to Kwammang-a: "Oh Kwa! Look at the sheep standing here, |kággen has brought them! We don't have to eat them, because the tick-people did not see them go, they'll not know where the sheep have gone. The sheep went straight up into the air as they stood in the kraal. The other things went up with the sheep. The sheep came out of the sky, they stood here. The things also came out of the sky and sat down here, while the people were asleep over there."

The ichneumon said, "|kággen! Now leave these people's things alone, let them keep their houses."

|kággen replied, "Do you not see why I thought it right? These people did bad things to me, they wished me to tremble with the pain of my skin. I want those people to see what I can do and recognize it. They would not give me food, so that I could eat and then return to my home. Had I been able to return comfortably, I would not have done this to them. Now they must truly suck blood, for they lack a fire altogether. They must walk about in their flesh that is black, because they cannot find capes. They'll walk about at night with their naked bodies. They must sit in the cold, because they have no houses. They'll continue to bite the hare's ears to drink its blood. The old tick will always bite men's skins, he'll suck out blood because he lacks a knife altogether. They'll suck blood with their mouths, when they have bitten through the skin. They'll fill themselves with blood, they shall truly be blood-bellies. And they will continue to bite the sheep. Men will search through the sheep's wool, dividing the wool, throwing the ticks down on the ground and crushing them, because they are sheep's ticks." |kággen said, "Now I want you, the ichneumon, to catch some fat sheep for Father to cut up for us and hang up to dry near the house. For I don't feel

like cutting up, because I'm still writhing in pain. The swelling must first be over, then I can cut up, then I shall hang meat to dry at my house—because I want the sheep's fat to be dry, so that the women can render it, so that we can moisten the dry meat that we've been crunching, the quagga's meat that was white with age and not tender. So now, I want you to cut up the old sheep— let the young ones wait a little, because we'll not finish these sheep, there are so many. I want the porcupine to go out tomorrow, when she has cooked and put aside the meat that she has dried, and invite the man over there to come and eat these sheep with me, because I've counted them and see that they are plentiful."

The porcupine said, "Do you really want me to go to the man who eats bushes? He'll come and swallow all the sheep as they stand in the kraal! And don't think that these bushes will be left, because we'll all be swallowed with the sheep. He is a man who devours things! He walks along eating up the bushes as he passes, the bushes among which he walks."

|kággen said to her, "You must go to your older father, the All-devourer, so that he can help me to eat up these sheep and drink this soup—because I've poured some of the soup away because I feel that my heart is upset. Fat has taken hold of my heart, I don't want to drink more soup. So I want the old man over there to come, he'll drink up the soup and then I can talk, for I don't talk now. So fill the sack there with cooked meat and take it, then he'll come. Otherwise he might refuse."

The porcupine said, "People do not live with that man, he is alone. People cannot hand him food, for his tongue is like fire. He burns people's hands with it. Don't think that we can hand food to him, because we'll have to dodge away to the sheep over there! The pots will be swallowed with the soup in them! Those sheep will be swallowed up in the same way, for the man over there always does so. He doesn't often travel, because he feels the weight of his stomach which is heavy. I, the porcupine, live with you, even though *he* is my real father, because I fear that he may devour me and I know that you will not devour me. Nevertheless, I'll bring him tomorrow. Then you'll see him with your own eyes."

The next day the porcupine went, she carried cooked meat. She arrived at her father's place, the place of the All-devourer. She stood there, and took off the sack of meat.

She said to her father, "Go! Cousin there invites you to come and eat the sheep over there, for his heart is troubling him. He wants you to come. I have told you, now I'll go on in front because I don't walk fast."

She shook out the meat from the bag onto the bushes. The All-devourer licked up the meat and the bushes with it, he gulped down the bushes too. The porcupine slung on the bag. She went forward quickly, she walked on giving directions: "You must climb up to that place from which I came, you'll see the sheep standing there." She felt that she was going in fear of the All-devourer. She was the first to reach the house.

|kággen asked her, "Where is Father?"

The porcupine answered him, "He's still coming. Look at the bush standing up there, watch for a shadow that will come gliding from above. Watch for the bush to break off. Then look for the shadow when you see that the bushes up there have disappeared. For his tongue will take away the bushes beforehand, while he is still approaching behind the hill. Then his body will come up and the bushes will be finished off right up to where we are, when he arrives. We'll no longer sit hidden here. Now I want the ichneumon to eat plenty, for of that meat he will never eat. For the man who comes yonder, the bushes are finished, the sheep will likewise be swallowed up."

The All-devourer followed the spoor of the porcupine. As he went, he ate up the bushes. He climbed up the hill, finishing off the bushes, while his shadow glided up to |kággen's house. It fell upon |kággen. He looked at the sun, he asked where the clouds were, for the sun seemed to be in the clouds.

The porcupine said to him, "There are no clouds there! But I want the ichneumon to go and hide this pot away for me, for he truly feels the shadow of the man coming over there, it altogether shuts us in, the sun will seem to have set when he reaches us. His mouth sits black along there—it is not a shadow, it is what the trees go into."

|kággen saw the All-devourer's tongue. He asked the porcupine, "Is Father holding fire in his hand? for a fire is waxing red over there!"

The porcupine answered him, "It is the man coming there, his tongue is red. He is near, that's why you see his tongue. We'll get out of the way here. We'll not hand him anything ourselves, just put down something for him, because his tongue would singe our hands if we held anything out to him. I want the rock-badger to hide the other pot so that she can still have soup. Now she herself can see the stomach, it truly extends to either side of us! We do not hear the wind, because he is coming. The wind does not blow, because he always makes a shelter when he stands. He does not sit down, he stands. He'll first eat the things up, for they are still plentiful. He has put in a layer of bushes at the bottom of his stomach, he has partly filled it, but he has not filled it up yet. That's why he is still seeking food. For he is a man who fills himself to his trunk. If he looks around and finds no food, he'll swallow these folk, because they invited him to come to eat food that was not enough."

The All-devourer arrived, |kággen placed food for him. The All-devourer gulped it down quickly. |kággen took soup and poured it into a bucket. The

All-devourer swallowed the bucket. A pot was still keeping warm. |kággen took meat that had been put away in a bag, he put it into a bucket; he pushed the bucket towards the All-devourer. The All-devourer put out his tongue, he licked and scorched the mantis's hands. |kággen pulled his arms quickly away, he sprang aside, knocking against the rock-badger.

The rock-badger said, "Why does |kággen spring aside from the man whom he invited to come? The porcupine told him not to give anything to the All-devourer with his hands, but to put meat on the bushes."

|kággen took meat and put it in the pot.

He said to the young mantis, "Child, make a good fire for the pot. My hands are burning, keeping me sitting where Grandfather scorched me. For you can feel his hot breath! His tongue feels like that too!"

The rock-badger said to him, "You ought to ladle out sheep's meat and put it on the bushes."

|kággen did not hear, he sat spitting on his hands to cool them. He ladled out another bucketful. He again pushed the bucket to the All-devourer. The All-devourer licked |kággen's hands. |kággen sprang aside, losing his balance, and tumbled into the house. He got up, he sat licking, cooling his hands.

He said to the ichneumon, "Ichneumon, give me meat to cook, for you see it is as Mother told us—the buckets seem to have vanished."

The ichneumon said to |kággen, "Mother told you that it would be like this. You would not listen, you invited the big cousin whom people know, whom no one invites, because his tongue is like fire."

|kággen called to the young mantis, "Go and fetch me the meat that the porcupine hid, for you see this bucket of meat has been devoured. You must look at the stomach."

|kággen brought two buckets, he ladled out meat. The rock-badger nudged him, he winked at her. He slung a bucket forward with meat in it, then he slung another bucket forward alongside of it. The All-devourer's tongue licked his ear, he tumbled into the house. The rock-badger spoke to him, he winked at her.

She said, "|kággen, leave off winking at me! You must feed Cousin, whom you invited here. You must give him plenty to eat, for the porcupine told you that she did not want to fetch him because his tongue is always like this!"

The All-devourer gobbled up both buckets, he licked up the meat that was on the bushes of the house, he devoured it together with the bushes.

|kággen said to the ichneumon, "Ichneumon, you must cook at that place, and bring the meat that is on the bushes, because the buckets are all finished.

I'll give the old man a pot that is hot to swallow, for you see that the bushes are swallowed up. I shall no longer sit and cook in the bushes when the wind blows."

The All-devourer stepped backwards, he licked up Kwammang-a's home-bushes, he devoured them quickly with the meat on them.

|kággen said to the ichneumon, "Ichneumon, quickly bring a sheep, you must cut up a sheep quickly, for you see that the bushes have been swallowed with the meat!"

The All-devourer asked for water. |kággen lifted a whole water-bag, and placed it before him. The All-devourer's tongue took up the water-bag, he swallowed it with the water in it. He licked up a thorn bush.

|kággen said to the young mantis, "You see, we shall not eat, for that thorn bush has been devoured, although it has thorns." |kággen said to the ichneumon, "Ichneumon, fetch that water there that is in the water-bag, for you see that this water-bag has been swallowed. Grandfather turns his head seeking more water. He himself has devoured everything else, he still seems likely to gobble up our beds! I'll truly sit upon the ground if Grandfather eats up all the things in my house!"

The All-devourer licked up the porcupine's things, he swallowed them quickly. |kággen said to his son, the young mantis, "See, Sister's things there have been devoured, Sister sits there on a bare place. The sheep will soon be devoured."

The All-devourer looked towards the sheep, his tongue took up all the sheep, he swallowed them quickly while they were still alive.

|kággen said, "Haven't the sheep been quickly swallowed? before I had cut them up as I had meant to do! And the bushes have vanished, swallowed up! We're sitting on a bare place. Now I no longer have those things that I brought here so that I might possess them!"

The porcupine winked at the ichneumon. "Ichneumon, I tell you, your younger brother must spring away. Father will be swallowed if he goes on act-ing bravely like this, and Grandfather |kággen is the one who takes, he'll cer-tainly be swallowed!"

The All-devourer called his name, he who is a devourer of things whom |kággen called to come to him.

He said to |kággen, "|kággen, bring out the things you invited me to eat, the real things that I, a devourer of things, should eat!"

He advanced, he burned the mantis with his tongue.

|kággen said, "I who am |kággen invited you who devour things to my home. You came and finished off my things. You should not now ask for the real food

for which I invited you—those sheep that you've devoured, that was the food that I invited you to eat. There is no other food."

The All-devourer quickly devoured |kággen, and |kággen shut up. The young mantis sprang away, he took up the bow. The All-devourer looked towards Kwammang-a. Young Kwammang-a sprang aside, he ran away. |kággen was quite silent because he was in the stomach. The All-devourer stood opposite Kwammang-a, he said that he was really going to swallow his daughter's husband. Although he was handsome, still he would swallow him for he felt inclined to do so. He advanced, and he quickly swallowed his daughter's husband with the bed on which he was sitting. The stomach of the All-devourer now hung down almost to the earth.

The porcupine wept, she stood sighing. The children came from afar.

The porcupine asked the young mantis, "Are you a fierce man?"

He was silent.

She asked him, "Are you angry?"

The young mantis was silent, because he felt angry.

She also questioned her son, young Kwammang-a. She turned as she sat, she heated a spear, she asked her son, "Are you angry? You must remember that Grandfather's tongue resembles fire. I don't want you to flinch if your heart is like Father's heart."

Young Kwammang-a sat still, they agreed to cut *his* grandfather open. She took the spear out of the fire, she drew it burning along her younger brother's temple. The fire burnt his ear, he sat still. She reheated the spear, it became red hot. She put the spear burning hot into her younger brother's nose. Tears slowly gathered and stood in his eyes.

She said to him, "A mild person is his, whose tears slowly gather."

She heated the spear, she placed it burning hot to her son's ear-root, her son sat still. She heated the spear again, she said to her son, "Grandfather's tongue is like this. I don't want you to flinch from him, if your heart is like your father's heart." She took the spear out when it was red, and put it into her son's nose. She looked at his eyes, they were dry.

She said to herself, "Yes, a fierce man is this. That one is a mild man. This one is fierce, he resembles his father. That one is mild, he resembles his father |kággen, he is a runaway." She said to her son, "Remember, Grandfather's tongue is like this. You must sit firmly when you go to Grandfather."

The children went in wrath to their grandfather, they approached him as he lay the sun. He arose, he stood up, and waited.

Young Kwammang-a said to the other, "Mother wished me to sit on one side of Grandfather, and you to sit on the other side. Because you cut with the left hand like your father, you must sit with your left arm outwards, the arm in which you hold your spear. I will sit opposite on this side, so that I may have my right arm outside, the arm in which I hold the spear."

The All-devourer scorched the young mantis's temple with his tongue. He walked forward, he scorched with his tongue the root of his grandson young Kwammang-a's ear. He said that this little child seemed very angry. He walked forward, he scorched the root of the young mantis's ear with his tongue, the young mantis sat still. He went forward again, he again scorched the young mantis's other ear with his tongue. Young Kwammang-a looked hard at the other, he signed to him to hold his spear fast, and he held his own well. The other held his spear well, because he had said beforehand, "You must cut one side, while I cut the other side. Then we must run away, while the people pour out."

He sprang forward, and cut. And the other cut too. They ran away, while their fathers poured forth. The sheep also poured out, the buckets poured out. His father sat on the bed. The pots poured out, the things poured out. His grandfather doubled up and died.

The children said, "Bushes, we have cut you out! You should truly become bushes, you'll grow at your place, you'll be what you were before. The place will be right again, and these sheep will wander over it, they'll graze over it and again return to the kraal which will be as it was before. For that man who now lies here, who ate up the bushes, he shall utterly die and go away, so that the people may gather dry bushes and be able to warm themselves."

The young mantis spoke, he felt that he truly resembled his father, his speech resembled his father's speech—it came true.

The rock-badger gave |kággen water, she said to him, "|kággen, you must only drink a little."

|kággen said, "I'm dying of thirst, I must drink up the eggshellful!"

He gulped all the water down, and he fell. Kwammang-a still waited.

The porcupine said to the rock-badger, "Take that long stick lying there. You must beat your husband on the shin-bone with it until he gets up, you must hold his face fast and rub it."

The rock-badger took the long stick and hit |kággen on the shin. He started up quickly, he sat there shivering.

The rock-badger reproved him: "I told you to drink only a little, because you would be like this if you gulped down all the water. But you would drink! nearly killing yourself, so that you fell down!"

The porcupine gave Kwammang-a water, she said to him, "Kwammang-a, you must only drink a little, you must soon put the water down—when you have just wet your mouth. You must sit down and wash yourself a little, for you have just come out of the stomach. After a while you can drink plentifully, when you feel that your body is warm."

Kwammang-a drank a little, he put the water down and did not gulp it all. He washed himself, he drank, and then he drank plentifully.

His wife cooked meat for him which she had kept hidden away, for she had told the ichneumon to hide some for her so that they could eat it when the children had dealt with the man who was devouring them and he lay dead.

"We must eat here, for he lies over there where the children have killed him. Then we'll travel away, leaving him lying outside that house. We'll move away, seeking a new home, because the man lies in front of this home. We'll live in a different house, which we'll make our home."

They traveled to a new home, and left the house at which the man who had devoured the people was lying.

At this new home, they always lived in peace.

Commentary: "The Mantis and the All-devourer"

In the first part of the narrative, the repeated image is that of Mantis under attack by the ticks. Mantis has intruded upon the ticks' household, and in those early days ticks, like the mantis and other creatures, were all men. He is attacked by the ticks, the repeated images focusing on the ticks as they fall from their hiding places and strike out at the trickster. Beaten, he returns to his home, and as usual it is up to his grandson to tell him what he did wrong. "You went to the house to which people do not go, at which they merely look in passing, when the sheep are in the kraal, and go on to their own homes." The usual patterned form is being followed here, the mantis having difficulty with some creature, and members of his home sounding the theme. The mantis, in pain, sleeps, and dreams that the ticks are deprived of all of their possessions, sheep, clothing, fire, furnishings. From that time on, ticks will not have fire, they will not cook their food, "They will have to continue biting the bodies of things, they will have to drink the blood of things and no longer eat cooked meat." And when Mantis awakens, that is in fact what has happened. All of the material goods of the ticks have been transported to Mantis's home, and his grandchild calls everyone, "People, get up! Get up, and see sheep standing in this kraal that my grandfather Mantis has brought! Sheep are here and the houses have come with them! And look at these pots that he has brought! Look at the ticks' capes in which we shall lie wrapped up! Now I can keep warm from this cold in which I have always lain uncomfortably. The knobkerries with which they beat my grandfather are here—I shall possess them, so that I can beat people!" Why did

Mantis take these things? "It seemed right to me, because those people attacked me. . . . They shall now drink raw blood because they lack a fire, they cannot make a fire. They cannot cook. . . ." This etiological judgment is developed by Mantis into a vision that involves his family and himself:

> In these pots [of the ticks] the San shall someday cook, because they shall have a fire. We who are here will then also be as the ticks now are. We'll eat different things, because we too shall lack fire. You, the ichneumon [his grandson], will then go to dwell in the hills with your mother. She will truly become a porcupine, she will live in a hole, while Grandmother Rock-badger will live in a mountain den, for her name is really "Rock-badger." I shall have wings, I shall fly when I am green, I'll be a little green thing. You, the ichneumon, will eat honey, because you will be living on the hill. . . .

And so all of this activity of the mantis and his friends is to lay the civilizing groundwork for the coming of the San peoples, when all of these creatures of nature, now man-like, will assume their natural shapes and will take their proper places in the natural order. And the ticks have been cursed and put in their place by Mantis/Trickster/Creator/Transformer, "They must sit in the cold, because they have no houses. They'll continue to bite the hare's ears to drink its blood." In this first part of the narrative, Mantis himself plays the role of commentator, but not only does he comment on the actions of the ticks and their beating of him, he curses them— and in detailed fashion, and repeatedly, notes the effects of the curse.

In the second part of this narrative, Mantis invites All-devourer to come to his home to help Mantis to eat the sheep. The porcupine, his wife, warns him not to invite the All-devourer. "People do not live with that man, he is alone. People cannot hand him food, for his tongue is like fire. He burns people's hands with it. . . ." But she invites him nevertheless, and he becomes like the cannibalistic Zims in Xhosa and Zulu narrative tradition. He is insatiable, he eats everything, "The All-devourer licked up the meat and the bushes with it, he gulped down the bushes too." He eats everything in sight, the sun is shadowed by him. "We do not hear the wind," says Porcupine, "because he is coming." Mantis's hands are scorched by this fantastic creature, which drinks buckets of soup, and continues to lap up every bush in sight. All-devourer then licks up all of Porcupine's possessions, then all of the sheep, everything, his stomach hung almost down to the earth. All is barren, all of the things of the ticks have now been gobbled up by this creature. Even Mantis's son, Kwammang-a, is swallowed. And now, Kwammang-a's wife teaches her child how to attack

All-devourer; she heats a spear, puts it burning hot on her son's ear. The All-devourer's "tongue is like this. I don't want you to flinch from him. . . ." Then she puts the red-hot spear to his nose. Remember, she warns him, the All-devourer's "tongue is like this. You must sit firmly when you go" to him. And so the child is taught. And then he goes to do battle with All-devourer and is able to withstand the heat, and he cuts the All-devourer open. And "their fathers poured forth. The sheep also poured out, the buckets poured out. His father sat on the bed. The pots poured out, the things poured out" from the All-devourer who doubles up and dies. Everything is as it was before.

In the opening set of images, Mantis is attacked by the ticks, and for this he curses the ticks and foresees the time when all creatures of nature take their proper places in the San scheme of things. In the second set of images, All-devourer swallows all of the possessions of Mantis and his friends, including some of the friends. Mantis had invited the All-devourer, and once invited he cannot be got rid of. Mantis's grandchild is then taught by his mother to withstand the heat of All-devourer, and then the child does battle with the beast, cuts it open, and releases all of the things inside.

The basic actions of the two image sets are, as noted, these: in the first, the ticks are made to yield all of their properties and domesticated animals and fire to Mantis and his friends, materials which, Mantis says, the San will someday use, "because they shall have fire." In the second set of images, the son of Mantis causes All-devourer to yield up the same artifacts and materials, the things of San civilization. In the first image set, the ticks are cursed to suck blood forever, never to cook again, to remain the noxious insects that the San know today. In the second, the All-devourer is cut open by the child/hero, then destroyed. The parallelism between the two sets of images becomes obvious. There is a tone about these narratives, even in translation, which is mythic, Mantis in the opening set of images has a vision of the way things will be in the future, when the mantis and the other man-like creatures become insects and animals, and the San take over the earth, an earth prepared for them by these earlier mythic creatures. In the second set of images, a more common narrative as far as oral traditions are concerned, the hero cuts up the swallowing villain and releases the materials and the people who will form the future populace.

Fire is an essential motif in this narrative; fire that Mantis gets from the ticks becomes paralleled with the fire represented by the All-devourer, which the young mantis must learn to control for it to become useful. The first narrative, in this sense, deals with the acquisition by man of fire, the second with the taming and controlling of fire. Fire in itself is destructive, as we see when All-devourer destroys all of the artifacts of civilization. Controlled, it can be made to yield all of these materials. Mantis wrests fire and its secrets from the ticks, but he is stupid, he does not know how to control the fire, and, in this sense, the narrative assumes the bungling-host pattern typical of trickster narratives throughout the world. Trickster learns how to do something by watching others, but when he seeks to do the same, he is excessive in some way, and is overwhelmed rather than aided by the material he seeks to control. That is precisely what occurs in the opening set of images: Mantis cannot control what he has attained. It remains, as always, for his grandchild to show the way to control; it is the grandchild who learns to withstand the heat, it is the grandchild who finally brings All-devourer under control and achieves the materials of San civilization.

The structure of this complex narrative, then, is little different in development and perception from the earlier ones. In those more straightforward narratives, Mantis is in the process of losing the battle when he is assisted by a member of his family, an assistance Mantis chooses not to acknowledge. In the more complex narrative we have just considered, Mantis again stands to lose everything. This time, instead of being told in a didactic way how to handle the situation, another image set is added, with action rather than didacticism the essential element, and in that parallel image set is the point of this performance made, its theme revealed. It is a complex theme, which is involved with the earliest mythic history of the San peoples, their origins, the beginnings of San society. In other narratives in the Bleek collections, Mantis goes about creating various things, at the same time that he learns how to conduct himself with other creatures and humans. He is at once creator and student; through his stupidity, he is made to learn; through his creativeness, he endows the earth with its creatures, at the same time revealing such emotions as love. Mantis signals in these narratives his future in San civilization, the god who created and who then was subsumed in nature, along with his fellows, as the earlier civilization (composed of animals and insects) gives way to San society. That is the theme of this set of parallel actions, and the parallelism is no different from the patterning of the earlier narratives. Mantis does things badly in the first part of the narrative, and in the second he sees them done properly by his grandchild. Things threaten to get out of hand because of Mantis's incompetence in the earlier part of the narrative (his inability to deal with All-devourer), and things are brought under control in the second part (the grandchild's destruction of All-devourer).

The movement of the San narratives has definite thematic purpose; there is a movement toward knowledge, a movement from stupidity toward awareness. This is the central thematic movement of the Mantis trickster narratives, a movement toward an understanding—and this movement toward enlightenment takes different forms. We have seen it in those narratives in which Mantis/inept trickster learns, and profits from his knowledge, although he is loathe to credit the knowledge. And we have seen the etiological enlightenment, the advent of fire and the civilization that follows in its wake among the San peoples, but within the same context of the earlier and simpler forms of movement toward awareness. In other etiological narratives, this pattern and thematic movement persists.

This myth occurs at the end of the golden age, the beginning of the age of creation. The enmity that is beginning between |kággen and the ticks suggests the differentiation characteristic of this period. The San are about to be created. |kággen will take the things of civilization from heaven, where they belong to the ticks, and transfer them to the earth, where they will become the materials of San culture. The audience is present at the birth of San civilization. The myth operates on the premise that God dreams, and so things happen: God dreams, and San civilization is born. And now, God orders the world, putting all beings and things into their proper places.

But humans do not yet know how to make use of the things that God has given them, as is suggested when all things are destroyed, when God's creation is swallowed up. Humans must learn how to deal with the great forces that God has given them; those forces are here suggested by the unrestrained fire of the All-devourer. Such energy can be creative, but destructive, too. So it is that young Mantis and young Kwammang-a are taught by Porcupine, and they learn to withstand the fearsome force of All-devourer, untamed fire, and thereby bring about a second creation, demonstrating that humans have learned to deal with God's creations.

The first pattern is introductory: it establishes the conflict, the provocation that will move God, |kággen, into action, motivating succeeding events: ticks fall down from the thatch and beat him. The second pattern is the main pattern; it has to do with creation and re-creation. Creation is the result of |kággen's dream, a dream that grows out of the ticks' behavior. When God awakens, all around is the fulfillment of the dream: differentiation has occurred. But the pattern is broken when the creation is undone by the destructiveness of All-devourer. In a subsidiary pattern, young Mantis and young Kwammang-a, the new generation, are educated, and this results in the re-creation. The primal wresting of fire and the things of civilization from the ticks, the ordering of the creatures of the earth and of the society of humans: these are what the first part of the story is about. For humans to be civilized, nature (the ticks) must be properly ordered, must be put into its place. |kággen prophesies the way all creatures, including himself, will find their proper place in the San scheme of things. For humans to be civilized, fire (All-devourer) must be brought under control. They are the same: the stealing of fire from the ticks, the controlling of fire that is All-devourer; the destruction of the power of the ticks, the destruction of the power of All-devourer.

Story Five: "The Mantis Makes an Eland," by ‖Kábbo[20]

|kággen, the mantis, once did this:

Kwammang-a, his son, had taken off a part of his shoe and thrown it away. |kággen picked it up, and went and soaked it in the water at a place where reeds stand.

He went away, then came back again, came and looked. He returned home again when he saw that the eland was still small.

Again he came to the water, he found the eland's spoor at the place where the eland had come out of the water to graze. |kággen went to the water while the eland was seeking the grass that it eats. |kággen waited, sitting by the water. He was on the water's bank, opposite the eland's spear. The eland came to drink there. He saw the eland as it came to drink.

He said, "Kwammang-a's shoe-piece."

The person walked up while his father trilled to him.

Then |kággen went to get some honey, he went to cut it. He came and put the bag of honey down near the water. He returned home.

Before the sun was up, he came back, came to pick up the bag. He approached while the eland was in the reeds.

He called to it: "Kwammang-a's shoe-piece."

The eland got up from the reeds and walked to his father. His father put down the bag of honey. He took out the honeycomb and laid it down. He kept picking up pieces of it and rubbing it on the eland's ribs, at the same time splashing the ribs, making them very nice.

Then |kággen went away, he took the bag to seek more honey that he cut. Then he came back and laid the bag down near the water. He returned home.

Once more he came and picked up the bag; once more he went up to that place and called the eland out of the water, saying, "Kwammang-a's shoe-piece."

The person stood shyly in the water. Then he walked up to his father. He had grown. His father wept, fondling him.

|kággen again worked, making the eland nice with honeycomb. Then he went away, while the eland walked back into the water, went to bask in the water.

|kággen did not come back for a time, and for three nights the eland grew, becoming like an ox.

Then |kággen went out early. The sun rose as he walked up to the water. He called the eland, and the eland rose up and came forth. The ground resounded as he came.

|kággen sang for joy about the eland. He sang,

> "Ah, here is a person!
> Kwammang-a's shoe-piece!
> My eldest son's shoe-piece!
> Kwammang-a's shoe-piece!
> My eldest son's shoe-piece!"

Meanwhile, he rubbed the person down nicely, rubbed down the male eland. Then he went away, he returned home.

Next morning, he called young Ichneumon, his grandson, saying that young Ichneumon should go with him, they would be only two. He was going to deceive young Ichneumon.

They went out and reached the water while the eland was grazing. They sat down in the shade of the bush by which the eland's spear stood, where he kept coming to take it.

|kággen said, "Young Ichneumon, go to sleep," for he meant to deceive him.

Young Ichneumon lay down as the eland came to drink; the sun stood at noon, and it was getting hot. Young Ichneumon had covered his head because the mantis wished him to cover it. But young Ichneumon did not sleep, he lay awake.

Then the eland walked away, and young Ichneumon said, "Hi, stand! Stand! Stand!"

|kággen said, "What does my brother think he has seen over there?"

Young Ichneumon said, "A person is standing over there, standing there."

|kággen said, "You think it is magic, but it is a very small thing, it is a bit of your father's shoe that he dropped. It is not magic."

They went home.

Then young Ichneumon told his father, Kwammang-a, about it, and Kwammang-a said that young Ichneumon must guide him and show him the eland. He would see whether the eland was so very handsome after |kággen had rubbed him down.

Young Ichneumon guided his father while |kággen was at another place— he meant to go to the water later on. Meantime, they went up to the eland at the water while |kággen was not there. Kwammang-a knocked the eland down and was cutting it up before |kággen came. When |kággen arrived, he saw Kwammang-a and the others standing there, cutting up the eland.

|kággen said, "Why could you not first let me come?" And he wept for the eland, he scolded Kwammang-a's people because Kwammang-a had not let him come first and let him be the one to tell them to kill the eland.

Kwammang-a said, "Tell Grandfather to leave off! He must come and gather wood for us so that we may eat, for this is meat."

Then |kággen came, he said he had wanted Kwammang-a to let him come while the eland was still alive, he should not have killed the eland when |kággen was not watching. They might have waited to kill the eland until he was looking on, then he would have told them to kill the eland, then his heart would have been comfortable, for his heart did not feel satisfied about his eland, whom he alone had made.

As he went to gather wood, |kággen caught sight of a gall there, it was the eland's gall. He said he would pierce the gall open, he would jump on it.

The gall said, "If you do, I shall burst and cover you."

Young Ichneumon said, "What are you looking at there? Why are you not gathering wood?"

|kággen left the gall, he brought wood and put it down.

Then he again looked at the place where the gall had been. He went to the gall, he again said he would pierce the gall open, he would jump on it.

The gall said that it would burst and cover him.

|kággen said he would jump on it, the gall must burst when he stepped on it, when he jumped on it.

Young Ichneumon scolded |kággen again. He said, "What is it over there that you keep going to see? You do not gather wood, you just keep going to that bush. You're going to play tricks instead of gathering wood."

Kwammang-a said, "You must hurry. When you have called Grandfather, let's go. The gall lies over there, and Grandfather has seen it. So you must hurry. When Grandfather behaves like this about anything, he is not acting straightly, he is playing tricks. So, when you have called Grandfather, we should start to leave the place where the gall is."

They packed the meat in a net while |kággen untied his shoe, he put the shoe into his bag. It was an arrow bag that he had slung on, next to the quiver. They carried the things, and headed for home.

On the way, |kággen said, "This shoe string has broken."

Young Ichneumon said, "You must have put the shoe in your bag."

|kággen said, "No, no, the shoe must be lying back there, where we cut up the eland. I must go back and get the shoe."

Young Ichneumon said, "You must have put the shoe in your bag. Feel in the bag, feel in the middle of the bag, to see if the shoe is there."

|kággen felt in his bag, he kept feeling above the shoe. He said, "See, the shoe is not in the bag. I must go back and pick it up, the shoe is truly over there."

Young Ichneumon said, "We must go home! We really must go home!"

|kággen said, "You can go home, but I must go back and get the shoe."

Then Kwammang-a said, "Let Grandfather be! Let him turn back and do as he says."

Young Ichneumon said, "I just wish that |kággen would listen for once when we speak."

|kággen said, "You always go on like this! I really must go and get the shoe."

Then |kággen turned back. He ran up to the gall, he reached it. Then he pierced the gall, he made the gall burst. And the gall broke, covering the head of |kággen. His eyes became big, he could not see. He groped about, feeling his way. As he groped about, he found an ostrich feather. |kággen picked up the feather and sucked it. Then he brushed the gall from his eyes with the feather.

He threw the feather up, and said, "You must now lie up in the sky, you must from now on be the moon. You shall shine at night. By your shining, you shall light the darkness for men, until the sun rises to light up all things for men. It is the sun under which men hunt. You, the moon, glow for men, while the sun shines for men. Under the sun, men walk about, they go hunting, they return home. You are the moon, you give light for men, and then you fall away, you return to life when you have fallen away, and you give light to all people."

That is what the moon does: the moon falls away and returns to life, and he lights up all the flat places.

Commentary: "The Mantis Makes an Eland"

In "The Mantis Makes an Eland," Mantis with great love creates a splendid beast from a piece of his son's shoe. This is the repeated element of the narrative, little more than an expansible image set, in which Mantis slowly gives life to the creature, Mantis the creator. But then, his son destroys the eland, for no good reason, and Mantis is sorrowful. He takes the gall, the least regarded of the parts of the eland, the part that is thrown away, and he pierces it, creating darkness, presumably for the first time. The creation of darkness thus has a very real connection with the repeated image sets in this narrative. The creation of Mantis has wantonly been destroyed, and because of that destruction, night comes. Mantis mitigates his curse somewhat, by providing a moon made from a feather, but darkness remains as a testimony to man's needless destruction of living beings. The thematic movement of this narrative, again, is clear. The etiological aspects of the end of the narrative are definitely related to the repeated image sets and the aftermath, that is, the destruction of the eland, which results, dramatically, in the end of the repeated sets.

In this particular narrative, there is a different kind of structure from the earlier ones we have considered. There is no simultaneous developmental and perceptual repetition. Instead, the first part of the narrative is composed purely of developmental repetition, which is stopped by the destruction of the eland. The perceptual element of the narrative now follows from that interruption, from the destruction of the repeated image set. The repeated sets act as a generator in this narrative, generating the movement of the final part of the narrative, the etiological part. The creation of darkness is not a simultaneous development here; it is rather a resulting development. But there is more to this narrative than merely a resulting development.

That final part also has its repeated elements, the repeated attempts of Mantis to get back to the gall to do with it what he wishes. And he is initially kept from doing so by those who have committed the act of destruction. Both Ichneumon and Kwammang-a know that Mantis is going to play some kind of trick (as they put it) on them, and that this trick results from their destruction of the eland. Finally he is allowed to return to the gall, and when he does, he bursts it and creates the darkness. There is a tension in this second repetition of the narrative that corresponds harmoniously with the first. In that first set, Mantis lovingly creates his eland; in the second, he persists in returning to the gall. The act of creation is matched by an act of destruction, for darkness is the memorial to destructiveness in this narrative. The joy of creation in the opening images is now matched by darkness, groping.

That joy of creation is also matched by the attempts of Mantis, as the narrative comes to its end, to return to the gall, and the attempts of the guilty ones to keep him from doing so, a tension that has its origins in guilt and destructiveness and which is given vividness and meaning by its correspondence with the joy of creation. To speak of theme in this narrative, then, it would not be enough merely to say that Mantis creates the darkness in retaliation for man's destructiveness. That is indeed true. But theme is experience in the oral narratives, and experience in this narrative includes that joy of creation, the wantonness of the destruction, and the stubborn movement toward retribution.

The Mantis narratives have a purposeful movement, then, leading from where we were to what we are, contemplating problems of origins, and sounding central social themes. Mantis at his most destructive is always attached to some significant theme. These are the people of the early race, we are told again and again.

The story raises a major theme in myth, a question that is asked but never really answered: it has to do with the situation that humans find themselves in. They are instructed not to destroy God's creations; to do so is to upset the delicate ecological balance, inviting the wrath of God and nature. But they cannot survive without doing just that. This paradox is built into the final part of this myth.

DEVELOPMENTAL AND PERCEPTUAL PROCESSES

The oral narratives operate in ways similar to those that animate poetry in literate societies. The basic analytical approach to oral narrative traditions must focus on the image, its development into an image set, and the movement from one image set to another. This is the developmental aspect of oral narratives. The analyst should seek to reveal the relationships that exist between the various images and the diverse image sets, for these relationships once understood will reveal the thematic and ideological, and the perceptual elements of the performance. It should be obvious that these two cannot really be separated during an actual performance; the developmental and the perceptual aspects of a performance both depend on the same images and image sets. The basic difference is that the developmental quality of the narrative centers on the surface and linear movement between images, their flow one to the other. Perceptual aspects of the performance are not so involved with this surface movement; indeed, they are a way to escape the tyranny of that surface movement, something that early writers in the western world did not really comprehend until relatively modern times. The perceptual approach to an oral narrative takes larger chunks of the performance and considers their interrelationships; the developmental approach is consumed with detail, with the logical and cohesive movement of characters in action toward some kind of climax. But while it is true that two quite different processes are operating during the performance of an oral narrative, the perceptual and the developmental, it is also true that there is a complex relationship between these two processes. The perceptual cannot exist without the developmental, and that statement in itself is a rather ridiculous statement, because the perceptual process depends entirely on the developmental, its very materials are those that are the linear sequential movements of the developmental repetition of the performance.

The question for the analyst must center on the critical dynamics of these two processes, how it is that one (the developmental process) gives birth to the other (the perceptual process). In the analyses of the San Mantis narratives, it becomes clear that it is possible for the developmental and perceptual processes

to exist side by side, one of them having the focus for a time, then the other taking over. In the Mantis narratives, the developmental process is caught up with
the actions and antics of Mantis, and the perceptual process is developed by the
didactic commentary, of members of Mantis's family, his child and grandchild,
mainly, who continuously act to give meaning to Mantis's actions by criticizing
Mantis when he returns to them, often bloodied by his conquests. That is one
way in which these developmental and perceptual processes may coexist. The
processes can quite readily be identified in the San narratives, and their functions are indisputably those of moving the narrative forward and of commenting on that movement. In these Mantis narratives, the narrative developmental
aspects of the production move alongside the perceptual, and there is never any
doubt as to the thematic elements of the performance, Mantis is constantly
being analyzed and preached at by characters within the narrative. But it is not
the performer who is preaching, it is members of the cast of characters of the
narratives. Even in these more obvious perceptual narratives, the performer is
at some pains to allow the narratives to speak for themselves, in the sense that
performers never step out of their role as performers, although they do rather
obviously put the themes and the morals into the mouths of the characters of
the dramas. That is one way in which the developmental and the perceptual
processes may be combined in performance.

There is another and rather complex mixture of developmental and perceptual aspects of performance, in those trickster narratives that have etiological
endings or which contain within themselves etiological images. These mixtures
have been seen in the Mantis narratives. In these narratives dealing with the
beginnings of things, and specifically those that deal with Trickster as the cre-
ator/transformer, there are several characteristics worthy of note. In some of
these trickster/creator narratives, the etiological parts of the narrative are inter-
woven closely with the actions in the earlier parts of the narrative. That is, the
etiological ending does not seem to have been merely pasted on to the end of
the narrative. That is the case in the San Mantis narratives. But there are also
those narratives in which the etiological endings seem uncomfortable in the
narrative, seem not to be a logical and cohesive part of the action. Here, too, the
etiological aspect of the narrative seems to be the major perceptual element in
the performance, and so the developmental elements occur first, and then the
perceptual are affixed apparently awkwardly to the end. The developmental
part of the narrative acts as a kind of generator for the etiological ending. The
etiological elements are caught up in the perceptual processes, in most cases.

There are also narrative categories in which repeated elements, while present, do not cradle the perceptual elements in large part. Still, there can be no

doubt but that the perceptual flows from the developmental process, but something additional is added, and this too flows from the narratives in the San
Mantis collection. Here, the expansible images and the patterned image sets
continue to move the conflict toward its resolution, but there is a great emphasis on the use of details to communicate the perceptual elements of the performance. Nongenile Masithathu Zenani is a foremost practitioner of this kind
of perceptual-developmental process.[21] Again, the two cannot be divided, but it
is clear that she places great emphasis on detail, and that it is through detail—
connected to the developmental processes, it should be emphasized—that the
perceptual elements of the narrative are revealed.

To categorize the various means whereby the developmental and perceptual
processes in the narrative are organized and revealed: the narrative in which the
developmental and perceptual processes are externalized so that the perceptual
becomes a running commentary on the developmental; the narrative which is
largely composed of a developmental sequence moving from conflict to resolution without concomitant perceptual processes, and the perceptual element
takes the form of a moral, a homily attached to the end of the image sets; the
narrative in which the perceptual elements are etiological, and those elements
may or may not flow logically from the developmental sequence in the performance. Another type has the developmental and perceptual processes organized and revealed not by repetition but by a series of diverse images or image
sets that, in some way, turn in upon themselves and thereby comment on each
other. This can take the place of parallel image sets, in which one set of images
developed by repetition comments upon another developed by repetition, in
which case the former is the perceptual process and the latter the developmental. In other narratives, the repetition may be absent, and an image or series of
images may be reflected in another image or series of images, the images developed not by means of repetition but by arrangement, the arranging of diverse
images in a series, and in that series, a perceptual process is revealed. This
complex mechanism is evident in many narratives in which repetition plays no
obvious part. Repetition is of course involved here, in the sense that the series
of unlike images or image sets repeats itself perceptually, thematically.

Developing awareness is the reason for parallel image sets and the perceptual process in any case. The parallel imagery is a highly developed form of
perceptual process, and here, unlike those categories in which didacticism is
more open (the Mantis narratives, for example, and the etiological), theme is
achieved in a more complex way, by turning one image set against another, by
juxtaposing imagery. Through the juxtaposition alone the perceptual process is

revealed. Juxtaposition here simply means that the second (and third) image set(s) follows the first, nothing more than that, although there is no doubt but that there are many internal correspondences between the image sets, and theme is generated merely by the juxtaposition. But the juxtaposition is of diverse image sets. In these complex narratives, the developmental process is in control from very beginning to very end, there are no didactic elements to interrupt it. The plot is tight, even though the narrative is composed of more than one separate narrative. The illusion of union is very important, and the performer introduces interlocking and transitional images and details to give the overall series of narratives the illusion of being a single narrative. Hence, the developmental aspects of the performance are important to her. Hers must not appear to be merely a picaresque sequence of loosely connected narratives, it must seem to be a tightly constructed single piece of narrative action. And so there is not really much room or sympathy for a perceptual element in such sophisticated narratives that would interfere with or even complement this all-important developmental process. But this is in no way to suggest that the perceptual elements are unimportant. They are as important in these parallel image sets as they are in any others of the categories mentioned in this inventory. In fact, the perceptual elements are of supreme importance in these narratives. The developmental aspects, in fact, are really the means of revealing the perceptual elements. This is the way the system has evolved, and it will be possible one day to trace its roots. In these narratives, it is not so easy to separate the perceptual from the developmental processes, layer by layer, as one can in the etiological and the Greek-chorus-type narratives. But this is not simply to say that the second and third image sets comment upon the first. If that were the case, then one could indeed separate the perceptual from the developmental processes. Simply by removing the second and third sets, we would isolate the perceptual processes. Now it is indeed true that if we were to shave off from the narrative all image sets except the first we would not have much of a perceptual element, though that does not necessarily mean that there would be no ideological element left. In parallel imagery, it really does become very difficult to separate developmental from perceptual elements. But there is an evolution of processes involved here, and by comparing what is occurring in parallel imagery with the other developmental/perceptual categories, it is possible to discover the perceptual elements in the parallel imagery.

What analysts are concerned with is the way a work of art works; they attempt to understand how a poem works at the same time that they appreciate that movement. The aesthetic system that underlies, motivates, and animates oral traditions is important: the system that makes understandable and meaningful the arrangement of images and their unique internal relationships one with the other and with the system as a whole. And there is the relationship of that art system with a wider world. First, however, we seek to comprehend the art system. In heroic poetry, for example, this is the web of special relationships that exist between historical incident and personage on the one hand and image on the other; in oral narrative, for example, the relationships that exist between society and custom on the one hand and image on the other contribute to it. The dynamics of the system that produces the individual works of art must be understood. An oral narrative system is a system, and is therefore not haphazard. It is a highly developed and detailed system, remembered through the generations and communicated. That system involves its transmission and its means of communication. In this communication system, there are two elements that must be considered and analyzed, the developmental and the perceptual. Sometimes these are connected with repetition, with both of these processes, and sometimes they are not.

LEGBA, A FON DIVINE TRICKSTER

Characters in the Legba Stories[22]

Legba, seventh and youngest born of Mawu; divine trickster, linguist of the gods

Mawu, the Creator; the female portion of the androgynous Great God Mawu-Lisa; the moon

Hevioso, another name for So, second born of Mawu; androgynous deity, chief of the thunder pantheon

Agè, fourth born of Mawu; deity of the hunt

Gu, Fifth born of Mawu; deity of iron, war, weapons, and tools

Awè, first human to learn magic, "chief of magic"

Agbanukwè, husband of Kpoli and father of Legba

Kpoli, mother of Legba, Minona, and Aovi; principle of the Fa divination complex

Minona, sister of Legba; goddess of women and of the hearth

Aovi, brother of Legba and Minona; embodiment of the principle of punishment for transgression of moral code

Fa, cult of divination; personified as principle of foretelling destiny; master of Legba

Metonofi, ruler of the dead; first king of the earth

Nundè, wife of Legba

The Story: "How Legba Became Guardian of Men and Gods:
Why the Dog Is Respected"[23]

There were three children of Agbanukwè and Kpoli. The first was a sister whose name was Minona. The second was called Aovi, the third Legba. These three formed a little funeral band. And so, one day, when a great man died in the faraway country of the man Adjaminako, they went to help at the funeral. Each of the three had been married, and each had killed his mate. When Minona killed her husband, she cut open his stomach and ripped out his intestines. When Aovi killed his wife, he cut off her head. And Legba killed his by giving her a blow on the head with a stick.

Now, when these three came to the funeral, they played their drum, and made up funeral songs, and people liked what they did. So they were given many, many, many gifts, many, many cowries.

Now, King Metonofi was also at the funeral. He had married his eldest daughter to the King of Adja. But this king was impotent, and had not been able to lie with her. This gave the king much shame. So he gave the girl to his eldest son.

Now, at the burial they met Fa, Legba's master. Before Fa could speak, it was necessary that Legba be at his side.[24] The son of the king of Adja had come to find Fa, and he told him all that had happened between his father and the daughter of Metonofi. And he told that his father had given him the girl for his wife. He asked Fa for a powder that would make him potent, and would remove the shame from his family.

Fa told him to go home. In three days he would send him a good powder. But Legba, who kept the sack that contained Fa's medicines, said, "Your sack is here. I can take the boy behind the house and give him the powder immediately."

So Fa said, "Yes," and instructed Legba to give the boy some of the white powder. For Fa had two powders, one that was white that gave potency, and one red, that rendered men impotent. But when Legba got the sack, he gave the boy some of the red powder.

The burial over, Legba and his two brothers [the word is used for both male and female siblings] started on their way home. When they came to a crossroads, they sat down to divide the gifts they had received. They divided the cowries into three piles, each of equal size. But one cowry remained over. They tried again and again to divide the cowries equally, but no matter how they divided the pile, one remained.

So Minona said that, since she was the eldest, she would take it. But Aovi disagreed, and said that, since he was the second, it should go to him. Legba also laid claim to it, saying that the others had had much to eat before he was born.

There was a great discussion, but the three could not agree.

While they were talking, along the road came a woman who had been collecting wood to sell in the market-place, and she carried a bottle on her head. They called to her, and asked her to divide the cowries equally. She tried and tried, but every way she tried there was always one over. So finally she asked, "Who of you is the eldest?"

Minona replied, "It is I."

So the old woman said that in her country when three divided something and there was one over, this went to the eldest. So she gave Minona the extra cowry. In an instant, Aovi cut off her head, and Legba struck her with his cane. Then they threw her body into the bush. But Legba went off into the bush where the body was, and lay with the dead woman.

When he returned, they resumed their quarrel, until a woman came down the road on her way to the well to get water. They called to her and asked her if she would divide the cowries for them. She tried and tried, but always one cowry was left over. So finally, she asked, "Who among you is the second?"

Aovi replied, "It is I."

She said, "In my group, when there are three among whom something is to be divided, and one is over, the first doesn't take it, or the last, but the middle one." And she gave the extra cowry to Aovi. Instantly, Legba struck her with his stick, and Minona slit her stomach and ripped out her intestines. And, when they had thrown her body into the bush, Legba again went where the corpse lay and had intercourse with it.

After a time, a third woman came, this time on the way home from the market. They invited her to distribute the cowries. She tried and tried, but always after an equal division had been made, there remained one. So she asked, "Who is the youngest?"

Legba said, "It is I."

So she gave the extra cowry to Legba, saying, "In my group, when three divide something and there is one over, we give it to the youngest, for the older ones have eaten before he was born." At this, Minona ripped open her intestines, and Aovi cut her head off, while Legba took her body into the bush, and he lay with the dead woman.

By now Legba had had enough, and so he told his brothers he was going into the bush to look for something. Legba was a great singer, and he still carried with him the sack of his master, Fa. In this sack he now found a carved figure which he turned into a dog. He whispered to the dog to go past the brothers, who were still trying to divide the gifts from the funeral, and he told him what to do. Then he rejoined them.

Now, no sooner did he come back, than a dog came down the road. So they invited him to divide the cowries. He tried and tried, but always there was one over. So with his paws he scratched a small hole, and said, "In my group, when three divide something and one is left over, it is for the ancestors." And he buried the extra cowry in the hole.

Now, all three of the brothers were satisfied, and they blessed the dog. Na said, "You will lead all the *vodun* that I command. You will always be in the lead."

And Legba said, "You will lead all men. You will never let them lose their way." They blessed the dog again, and he went on his way. But Legba went into the bush, where the dog came to him and was changed once more into the statuette.

When they came home, the son of the king of Adja, to whom Legba had given the red powder, was there with Fa. He said that he, too, had become impotent.

Now, in those days, everyone had to come and consult Fa before he did anything. And so, when Metonofi announced that any man who could have intercourse with his daughter would be given half his kingdom, all the men came to consult Fa. But Legba gave them all the red powder, and made all the men of the kingdom impotent. When the men complained to the king that Legba had rendered them impotent, Metonofi looked for him to punish him. But Legba ran away to the house of Ayo, his mother-in-law.

It happened that his father-in-law was away, and Legba had to sleep in the same room with her. During the night he lay with her, and in the morning he returned to his village.

There they arrested him at once, and brought him before the king, who now summoned all the men of the kingdom to come and make their complaint. When the men of the families of the three women who had been killed by Legba and his brothers at the crossroads saw Legba, they accused him before the king of their deaths. And Legba's father-in-law also made complaint that Legba had slept with his wife. And all the men of the kingdom accused Legba before the king of having given them the red powder.

Now, the first case was up for trial. The king asked Legba if he had killed the three women. Legba replied, "No, it was Aovi." He said he had intervened and had helped to divide the cowries so as to save other deaths. But the brothers denied the guilt of Aovi, and said that a dog had finally settled the matter. At this, Legba said that he was the one who had commanded the dog. He told that he had changed a carved figure into a dog, and to prove his words, he took the carving and, before the eyes of everyone, changed it into a dog.

Now all the people saw that Legba had spoken the truth, and Metonofi ordered that Legba be guardian of men and women, and of all the gods. He told Minona to return to her home, and henceforth live in the houses of women, whom she would command. He told Aovi to live among the gods. But Legba, he told could live anywhere he wished. So Legba came into the houses.

After this, there was the second complaint to be disposed of. The trial took place after two days. Legba was asked, "Did you lie with your mother-in-law [an act hateful to ancestors and gods]?"

And to this he answered, "Yes." But he explained that she had slept in the place where his wife usually slept. And so judgment was given in this case. Metonofi said that since he had already made Legba guardian of all, he could not revoke this. But because Legba always created scandals, he was not to live in houses, but that his place would always be in front of houses.

After two days, the third complaint was brought before the king for judgment. It was the complaint that Legba had given the men of the kingdom the powder that made them impotent. "Did you give the good powder?"

Legba replied, "Yes." So they told him to bring the powder he had given the men that they might see.

While he was gone, Legba mixed the blood of a pigeon with the good powder, making it red. In the red powder he put water in which caolin had been mixed, thus turning it white. When he came back with the two powders, Metonofi asked the men, "What color was the powder given you?"

All cried out, "The red, the red!" So they told Legba to take the red powder himself, and Metonofi told everyone to return in two days, when they would see whether the red powder had made Legba impotent.

When all had reassembled, they found that Metonofi had caused a little house to be made, and in it he had placed his daughter, the wife of the King of Adja. The men were told to enter, one by one, to see if they could lie with his daughter. None of them could accomplish sexual intercourse, and one by one they left her. They were sad, because they were impotent. But there were some who said that it was not good to try it this way. With everyone waiting anxiously, they could not be expected to accomplish what was desired of them.

Legba, however, told the king that these men knew nothing. He, Legba, would have intercourse with the king's daughter in public, if they wished it. And so, it being his turn, Metonofi told him to enter the house, and that if he accomplished intercourse with his daughter, he would reward him well.

Now Legba had made drums, and these he caused to be played as he entered the house where the girl lay. No sooner had he entered, than he deflowered the king's daughter. There was blood all over the house. This done, he came out of the house still naked, with his penis erect, and when he approached anyone, he went through the motions he had made when he was with the girl. And all this time his drums were being played.

Metonofi was very pleased with what had happened. He told Legba to take his daughter as his wife. And he ordered that from that day on, this drum should be played everywhere in remembrance of his daughter. He also said that Legba might sleep with any woman he chose, without any distinction. And as Legba was wise, he named him intermediary between this world and the next. This is why Legba dances in the way he does everywhere.

Legba gave Metonofi's daughter to his master, Fa, and Fa invited all the men of the country to his house to celebrate the marriage. When all were there, Legba gave everyone a drink, putting the good powder in the liquid. And at once each recovered his potency.

On that day, Legba was named Aflakete, meaning, "I have deceived you." And he gave the name Adje to the girl. The name means cowries, since it was for cowries that they had killed the women.

That is why Legba is now found everywhere. To go to a *vodun*, one must first pass Legba. To make Fa, one must pass by Legba. And all men and women must have their Legba as a personal guardian. And this is also why the dog is respected as the animal of Legba.

Commentary: "How Legba Became Guardian of Men and Gods: Why the Dog Is Respected"

The story is in three parts, corresponding to the three court trials. In each of the three parts, Legba is the chief figure: the killing of the three old women, and he has sex with them; sleeping with his mother-in-law; the potency medicine, Fa and sex with the king's daughter. In each of these three parts, Legba is crossing boundaries, violating taboos: murder and sex with corpses, sex with a mother-in-law, manipulating the virility of men. But in the court trials, Legba proves himself innocent, revealing himself a trickster: he argues that he stopped the murdering, that he is not a murderer; and his behavior is therefore deemed proper. He thought he was sleeping with his wife; and again his behavior is deemed proper. He takes the same medicine as the men, and shows himself virile; his behavior is deemed proper. It is trickery, but it satisfies the court. This leads to the etiological elements: trickster as god of the hearth and as mediator between gods and humans.

Legba is pure undifferentiated energy . . . but look at what happens. The court cases, as major social and cultural institutions for the ordering of human behavior and conduct, reveal that what Legba did was correct: he did not kill

the women, he kept others from killing them; he did not sleep with his mother-
in-law, or if he did he was sleeping, he thought, with his wife; he did not make
the men impotent, he will show everyone by taking the medicine himself. Out
of the wild activities, trickery and deception or not, comes socially acceptable activity, keeping men from murdering, sleeping with one's wife rather than
one's mother-in-law, ritualizing sex. In the process of being domesticated and
shaping us, Legba becomes the god of the hearth, of the home, of doorways, of
the liminalities.

What about his trickery? His trickery here becomes the means of the shift,
from the wild one to the domesticated one. Trickster is playing the role of the
pre-cultural human and the role of the cultured human. The court trial and the
trickster's trickery are the transitional devices. The final suggestion of domestication, acculturation, occurs when we find that the unbridled wild sex with
the king's daughter also has a cultural niche; it is ritualized (as we see when
he emerges from the house), and ritual is a crucial cultural activity, having to
do with rituals of puberty, marriage, and other passages, all of which transform
humans from biological beings to cultural beings. This tale deals with this transition, these rites of passage.

Part Two

The Trickster in the Hero

THE BASIS OF EPIC

The heroic epic is a grand blending of tale and myth, heroic poetry and history. Separate epics contain a greater or lesser degree of each. History is dominant in *Sunjata*, heroic poetry and tale in *Ibonia*, tale and myth in *Mwindo*, tale and myth in *Gilgamesh*. In all four epics, poetry plays a crucial if not dominant role. Epic is not history: it combines history and tale, it combines worlds of reality and fantasy.

This is the storyteller's laboratory, in which a tale becomes an epic. We can also discover here how the tale remains an integral part of the epic. This section involves a discussion of the basis of epic, how patterns, tales, history, and the trickster are worked into the character of the hero, resulting in epic.

The epic becomes the grand summation of the culture because it deals with the major turning points in history, always with a towering, complex historical or nonhistorical figure who symbolizes the turning point and links that turning point to tradition. The epic hero is inevitably revolutionary, but his story does not signal a total break with the past. Continuity is stressed in epic; in fact, it is as if the shift in the direction of the society is a return to the paradigm envisioned by ancient cultural wisdom. The effect of the epic is to mythologize history, to bring history to the essence of the culture, to give history the resonance of the ancient roots of the culture as these are expressed in myth, imaginative tale, motif, and metaphor. In heroic poetry, history is fragmented, made discontinuous, a necessary preliminary to epic. In epic, these discontinuous images are given a new form; the tale helps in this regard. And the etiological aspects of history, that is, the historical alteration of the society, are tied to the etiology implicit in mythology; that is, the acts of the mortal hero are tied to the acts of the immortals.

The significant genre involved in the epic, then, is not history but tale/myth. This is what organizes the images of history, giving those images their meaning. History achieves significance when it is juxtaposed to the images of the tale/myth tradition. This suggests the great value the oral societies place on the imaginative traditions: they are entertaining, certainly, but they are also major organizing devices. The tales take our routine, everyday experiences of reality and place them in the fanciful context of conflict and resolution with the emotionally evocative motifs of the past, thus giving them a meaning and a completeness that they do not actually have. So also in epic is history given a form and a meaning that it does not possess. This imaginative environment revises history, takes our historical experiences and places them into the context of the culture, gives them cultural meaning. The epic is a blending, then, of the ancient culture as it is represented through the tale/myth tradition and historical event and personage.

We shall look, in this storyteller's laboratory, at four of the elements involved in the shift from tale to epic: the cycle of tales, patterning in and between the tales, the relationship between tale and history, and the injection of the trickster into the developing heroic epic. Each of the four stories that has been selected includes all four of these characteristics; I shall emphasize one of the four in each of these epics.

3

The Winnebago Hare

THE FOUNDATION OF EPIC:
BRINGING THE TALES INTO AN EPIC CYCLE

The Winnebago hare shapes himself; as he shapes himself he is shaping the world of the people out of Grandmother Earth, and Grandmother Earth regularly chronicles the changes that Hare is himself undergoing. The storyteller records the origins and then the fall of humanity, the final differentiation of animals and the origin of death.[25]

The melancholy hero is born.

The hare has to do with differentiation. The grandmother is the earth in the process of being shaped by Hare. As the hare shapes himself, he is shaping the world of the Winnebago out of Grandmother Earth, as she reflects Hare's changes. Once he is shaped and the earth is shaped, he can be swallowed. The trickery and creation then continue, and result in the origin of menstruation. The fall of the trickster, regarding his power to order things and to pass that power on to humans, results because of the trickster's blunders. There is a final differentiation of animals and the establishment of rituals, followed by the origin of death by Grandmother Earth; Hare weeps for his people; he establishes the medicine rite with the hope of a better life for the people, knowing, however, that they will nevertheless die.

Part 1. Birth: The hare, conceived without sexual intercourse, is born after seven months. [Sometimes, he tears his mother to pieces during childbirth.] His mother dies, and his grandmother raises him. He is mischievous, and he keeps moving further from home.

Parts 2, 3, 4, 5 have to do with the bow and arrow:

Part 2. Trickster Hare sees a man: the man seems weak to him, so he blows at him, but he cannot blow him over (this becomes a pattern). The man shoots Hare with an arrow; his grandmother removes it, calling the man Hare's "uncle."

Part 3. Getting wood for arrows: Trickster Hare is fascinated by the arrow, but he cannot make it go. His grandmother will teach him. First, make a bow. Grandmother sends him for hickory, wood for making arrows. He gets poplar, but that is no good. Then she sends him for turkey feathers for the arrows, then for glue made from a fish. Trickster begins target practice. The grandmother identifies trees, etc., teaching him to make weapons for survival.

Part 4. Getting feathers for arrows: one day, he goes for feathers, is carried off by an eagle to its nest. When the parents are gone, he kills four young eagles, takes their feathers, skins one and wears it, flying like an eagle to the earth. He puts the feathers into the hollow of a tree, sends his grandmother to get them, but a streak of lightning flashes from the feathers. Hare keeps sending her back. He refuses to give her one of the feathers, and from that time makes his own arrows.

Part 5. Getting arrow-points: Hare's grandmother instructs him to get tobacco from his first grandfather, and take that to the second grandfather to get arrow-points. The pattern here is that, as Hare nears the first grandfather, he makes himself very tall and keeps leaping closer to the grandfather, who keeps increasing the amount of tobacco he will give Hare. Finally, Hare scatters the grandfather's tobacco over the ground (an etiological detail), and kills the grandfather, who turns out to be a grasshopper. He tells his grandmother. Following the story's pattern, she curses the hare for killing her brother: "Oh, you ugly big-eyed creature, you must have killed my brother." When Hare threatens her as well, she recants, says she is glad, as "he was withholding from your uncles the tobacco belonging to them . . . ," stating in essence that Hare created tobacco for humans.

Part 6. Getting arrow-points: now Hare goes to the second grandfather, who has the arrow-points at various points on his body. Following the pattern, Hare, again tall, leaps at him as formerly, and the grandfather gives him inferior points from his wrist and ankle. Then Hare clubs him, kills him, forcing him to scatter his flints over the earth (the Winnebago believe that arrowheads are found on the earth: an etiological detail). He takes the arrow-points home, and tells his grandmother. She curses Hare: "Oh, you ugly, big-eyed, big-eared creature, I hope you did not kill my brother." He threatens her, she recants. When he presses an arrow, the lodge is filled with lightning.

Part 7. Hare and Sharp-elbow (evil): Hare shoots an elk, tells it to fall dead on the outskirts of Sharp-elbow's village. Next day, he goes after it; it is gone except for its entrails. An old woman tells him that warriors took the elk, that the chief Sharp-elbow pulled the arrow out. Trickster wants his arrow. The old woman is making soup with some of the elk's blood; she offers some to Hare: he does not understand that he is to drink it (part of the pattern). Then Hare sends the old woman's grandson to Sharp-elbow to get the arrow, but Sharp-elbow kills him. Hare takes a whetstone, goes to Sharp-elbow, breaks his elbows and knees with the whetstone, then takes the arrow and shoots it through Sharp-elbow, kills his children and wives, freeing the people, giving them back to their former chief (though they offer to serve him). He goes home, tells his grandmother. She curses him: "Oh you big-eyed, big-eared, big-footed creature, you have killed my brother." He threatens her, she blesses him. (Note that she is creating him, giving him his features in her descriptions.)

Part 8. Hare and the bear: Hare goes to visit his grandfather, Bear. (Note that at this early time, animals and humans are the same: Hare himself is an example of this.) Hare apparently eats the acorns he brought for Bear, then, in typical trickster fashion, he blames Bear for eating them. Hare sets dung and feathers around Bear's place, instructs the dung to give a war-whoop in the morning. Following the pattern, he shows Bear his arrows, Bear fears none of them, but finally does fear the fourth. Next morning, the war-whoop rings out, Hare shoots Bear in the place Bear dreamed he would. Hare tells his grandmother, who says, "Oh, you big-eyed, big-eared, big-footed creature, you must have killed my brother." He threatens her, she blesses him. (The etiological element is bear meat.)

Part 9. Hare and his grandmother: his grandmother is the earth. Bear is Earth's husband. She gets the hind-end, which contains the penis. They go to get Bear's remains. Grandmother apparently gets lost and dirty, and loses her pack; Trickster by means of a trick name learns that she is lying. They eat Bear, but differentiation is occurring, as Trickster understands her womanhood.

Part 10. Hare gets a slit-nose: he visits his uncles, heads without bodies. On the way, he creates a boat from a crab, and has the wind blow him across the water. His uncles give him a knife with which to eat, he slits his nose, another hare characteristic. Following the pattern, his grandmother comments on this when he gets home. (Note that these uncles are ogres, evil beings, and are consequently a part of his challenge, his growth to manhood.)

Part 11. Hare destroys evil: Hare visits the heads again, and they decide to eat him. A chase follows, patterned: they gnaw the tree down, etc. Finally, he sings them to sleep, or so he thinks, and a chase again ensues. He leaps across a creek, they do too and are drowned. He grinds up the evil heads, they become relatively harmless fast-fish that nibble at people's ankles. This is etiological.

He goes home to his grandmother, who again curses him for killing her brothers, then blesses him.

Part 12. Hare creates ants: he sees a tall "man"; it is an ant, much taller than he. The ant crushes the hare. Grandmother seeks Hare, finds him crushed: "Oh, you big-eyed, big-eared, big-footed, slit-nosed, evil creature, get up and come away from here," and she raises him from the dead. Etiologically, this is his rebirth. Next day, he makes himself very tall, crushes the ant, and thereby creates the ant, an etiological act.

Part 13. Hare's trait: burnt buttocks. He comes on a nice road, decides to snare the one who built it. The pattern dictates that his snares are broken. Grandmother educates him: she makes a snare out of her hair, it is tough. Then he snares the sun. His grandmother, angry at what he has done, strikes him: "So you are up to your tricks again, you big-eyed, big-eared, big-footed, slit-nosed, evil object." He borrows a knife from his grandmother, cuts loose what he has snared. It is a shining object (the sun). As he releases it, he is scorched by the sun, and hence gets a hare's trait of "burnt buttocks."

Part 14. Hare and the swallowing monster: Hare is now complete, therefore, the swallowing monster motif. The pattern is swallowing and disgorging. He is swallowed, then disgorged when his grandmother goes to find him. But he returns to the monster, and is again swallowed: there are many people inside the monster, alive and dead. He is vomited up four times because the swallowing monster does not like his taste. But then he tells the people he will save them if they find something in his head. They look, and find flints there. He cuts the monster's inside, then its heart, killing it, and he releases the people. They kill all the children borne by this monster, along with the monster's pregnant wives, so that it has no progeny. Hare's grandmother first curses Hare, then blesses him.

Part 15. Hare and the wildcat: Hare encounters a wildcat, and boasts that he will fight anyone, but when he sees the cat he changes that to "play with" anyone. In the pattern, the wildcat gives chase and Hare escapes in a hole. The trick follows when the wildcat asks how Hare can be brought out of the hole. Hare sends him to his grandmother to get matting to set on fire to smoke him out. As the wildcat goes on that errand, Hare gets out, substitutes acorns. The cat returns, sets the fire, the acorns answer for Hare, then explode, the cat thinking the explosions are Hare's eyes and testicles. Then Hare moves in, traps the cat with a forked stick, burns it to death, and takes the cat's remains home.

Part 16. Origin of menstruation: using trickery, so that he can have all the food for himself, Hare throws some of the cat's blood at his grandmother, saying that she is having her menses. She must then go and build a menstruation lodge: the pattern dictates that he keeps sending her further away to build the lodge, a safe distance from him and the food. He pretends (by feigning voices) that others have arrived to eat the food, but he actually eats it all. Another trick follows: he tells his grandmother that it is unseemly for them to be living together, that an old man with one eye (he came to the meat-eating festival that never really took place) wants to court her. She agrees. Hare then takes out one of his eyes, and goes to his grandmother and has sex with her. In the meantime, mice have gnawed at the eye.

Part 17. Origin of one of Frog's traits: Hare hears a loud voice threatening him: this is the pattern. Finally, the frightened Hare finds that it is just a small frog. He kills it, and opens its mouth to see how it could have spoken so loudly. It has long teeth, so Hare (playing the role of creator) removes the teeth (an etiological explanation).

Parts 18, 19, 20, 21. Why humans must work for what they want.

Part 18. The pattern here is that people pursue Hare. But this is a ruse by an old man with a bandaged head to get Hare to come to his house. (It was actually a woodtick that the old man had planted in Hare's ear, not people shouting at him.) The pattern: the old man feeds Hare in a magical way, a kettle and a plate do the man's bidding. The problem: the man has been scalped, and he wants the clever hare to get the scalp back. If he does, the man says, "I will give you the power to order things about as I do and you will then be able to pass on that power to your uncles and aunts [that is, to humans]." The next day, Hare sets out.

Part 19. The etiological significance here is the origin of beavers' paws. Hare, on his trip, goes to beavers to ask that one transport him across a lake. They agree, then ask which young beaver will give itself as Hare's food. All agree to do that, because when they are dead they are brought back to life. There is an interdiction: Hare must leave all the sinews attached. But Hare breaks the interdiction, breaks some sinews, so that when the beaver comes back to life, its paws "are drawn together": an etiological consequence.

Part 20. The beaver takes Hare across the lake, tells him she'll wait for him as he gets the scalp. In this pattern, Hare speaks to the chief, learns all his habits, then kills the chief and masquerades as the chief. He goes to the chief's home, doing all the things the chief normally does. But a pattern develops: the chief's wife is suspicious each time Hare-as-chief does something. Finally, he gets the scalp, which is a part of the chief's headdress, and flees, with all in pursuit. The beaver overturns their boats with her tail, and they get safely to the other side of the lake. Hare gives the old man his scalp back, throwing it on his head, and the old man is transformed into a handsome man. Before he leaves, he gives Hare what he had promised, but with an interdiction: Whatever you wish for will be yours, but never ask for the same thing four times in succession, and never harm the woman who lives in the partition of the lodge; she is in charge of all these things. Then the deity goes into the sky as thunder echoes.

Part 21. Following the pattern, Hare breaks the interdictions, asking for a more beautiful woman until he has sexual relations with the woman in the partition. Both interdictions are broken. The etiological result: this is why we have to work at the present time for every thing that we want. Then the lodge disappears, and hare begins to regret his mischievous ways: "When will I be of any use in this world?" He tells his grandmother what he has done, and she curses him: "Oh, you big-eyed, big-eared, burnt buttocks, evil creature, you!" People will, she says, always be sorry for what the hare had done, but Hare says she is just jealous.

Part 22. Cleaning the earth of evil beings, installing hunting rituals, giving animals their traits with regard to humans: Hare "began to think of the work he had been appointed to do." He says that he has not trampled on all the evil beings that have been abusing humans, pushes abusive birds further into the sky, tramples evil spirits under the earth "so that the people might live in peace here." The pattern: preparing animals for the humans to eat. All the animals gather together; he fattens them as food for humans, gives them their animal traits. Differentiation is occurring: elk, bear, horse, mink, skunk. And he establishes rituals, ceremonies to overcome animals like the bear in the hunt.

Part 23. Creation of death by Hare's grandmother/Earth: Hare concludes that "the people will live peacefully and forever." But his grandmother says that all will die, and so will she, because she/the earth is too small to accommodate all. Hare weeps for the humans.

Part 24. Conclusion: Hare creates the medicine rite. He kills all birds of the air that are evil or abusive of humans, and he kills evil spirits. He was sent by Earthmaker to teach the people on earth a better life, and that is why he roamed over its whole extent. He did away with all hindrances to the people. He called the people his "uncles and aunts," because his mother was a human being: he was born of an earthly, human mother.

Conclusions: The hare and the grandmother—Hare: differentiation; Grandmother: the earth, being shaped by the hare. As the hare shapes itself, it is shaping the world of the Winnebago out of Grandmother Earth. And Grandmother Earth regularly chronicles the changes that the hare is itself undergoing. Once he is shaped and the earth is shaped, he can be swallowed. The trickery and creation then continue, to create the origin of menstruation. After this comes the fall of humanity: Hare is given the power to order things and pass that power on to humans, and he messes it up. The final differentiation of animals follows, and the origin of death by Grandmother Earth. Hare weeps for his people, and originates the medicine rite, giving rise to a better life for the people.

THE CENTRAL ROLE OF RHYTHM IN THE CONSTRUCTION OF TALES AND EPICS

Cycle is the key now, as we gather the various parts of the oral tradition together into a single and unified work. But at first it doesn't seem to be single and unified; it seems to be a disparate gathering of trickster stories.

In the Winnebago Hare Cycle, a series of typical trickster stories provides the rhythmical background of the lengthy story. These separate trickster tales are bound together by the patterns of the story: the grandmother's curse, the slow and halting creation of the universe, Hare as a character-in-a-state-of-becoming, moving toward humanity, being shaped along the way. The sun and the frog are created, as Hare shapes Grandmother Earth. Death comes into the world, followed by cultural rituals. The many trickster stories, with their predictable and fairly obvious (and brief) plots, the easy patterns, the clear motifs: these are the rhythmical background, the patterned pull of the story. To what end?

These are the materials: the many trickster stories, each self-contained, each known to the audience; the linear movement, from conflict to resolution, in this case, the creation of the earth; the patterns: the gradual shaping of Hare and Grandmother Earth, the creation of Frog and Sun, of cultural ritual, of death. These create the story. What is the effect of this combination? The emotions of the members of the audience are engaged. It is music and dance, a regular, rhythmic, patterned undercurrent that establishes the context for the story. The audience knows the trickster, knows his stories; it is repelled by his antics, amused by his activities, delighted by his pratfalls. At the same time, something sacred is happening, something earth-shaping: the world is being formed, members of the audience are present at the morning of time, and their emotions are a part of a force that is at work forming this world, a force that is at once familiar and outrageous and sublime. That combination of emotions forms the core of the destructive-creative activities of the trickster, and it is crucial that the audience's emotions be woven into these creative activities.

The trickster stories are the rhythmical drumbeat of the larger story, the pattern of dance-like movements that, wavelike, move with a mesmerizing predictability in the background, coloring that background, evoking and shaping our emotions into a formal frame within which the linear story unfolds, the shaping of the world as we know it. The two parts of the story are obvious in themselves; the many familiar trickster stories, the linear movement (the storyteller alerts us to the pattern: the grandmother's comments to the hare, the hare's shaping of the grandmother). It is the combination that we are concerned with here. There are times when we are simply in the presence of the typical trickster. So we should not look for something weighty every time the trickster tricks. We have to look at the entirety of the cycle, as the storyteller keeps the trickster character firmly in our minds. To grasp the overall meaning of the story, we have to look at the story overall. Like a complex drumbeat, the many trickster stories provide the essential rhythm of the story. Then these emotion-laden, emotionally evocative trickster motifs are worked into the form of the story, so that the linear narrative, the creation of the earth, or whatever the linear narrative happens to be, occurs within the tight and evocative embrace of this web and weave of trickster tales. And this is the way the epic is created, against the background of tale and myth. The trickster moves to a new identity; in the background are motifs having to do with creation: a world, or a hero, is in the process of growth. Built into this world, integrated into the character of the epic hero is the trickster, inevitably, a part of the world for better or for worse, but essential in the creation of that world, that hero. It is a construction formed out of a cycle of tales, the separate tales relatively insignificant but becoming earth-shaking when put together, held together by the trickster character, the template of the epic hero.

The patterning evident in this cycle of tales, the presence of the trickster, and the altering of human history are what give these stories the germ of epic.

4

Ibonia

THE FOUNDATION OF EPIC: PATTERNING THE TALE INTO EPIC

Epic describes the feats of a heroic character, dramatizes the transformation of a society or culture in a major way. A hero is one who, with one foot in the past and one foot in the visionary future, moves the society from one dispensation to another . . . or symbolizes that movement. As the epic progresses, an epic process becomes evident: the hero becomes representative of the essence of the culture. The hero necessarily contains elements of both what the society was and what it is to become. The members of the audience, through their identification with the hero and by means of the emotionally evocative images that provide linkages to the cultural past, become imbued with the essence of the culture. The epic makes a community of the audience, and ties its members to the past through the theatrical experience. Epic is, in this sense, a ritualistic experience. The divine trickster connects heaven and earth, god and human; the epic hero links heaven and earth, god and human, fancy and reality, tale/ myth and history, cultural continuity and historical disjunction. Father Sky welcomes his five sons: the Prince of the East, of the North, of the West, of the South, and the Prince of the Middle. But Father Sky is disappointed with the Prince of the Middle because he has not sired a child. Cannons are fired for all the sons, but that for the Prince of the Middle is fired into the ground. Mythic imagery in this epic includes the five sons visiting Father Sky: they connect the heavens and the earth. Nature responds to the acts of Ibonia and his mother. Ranakombe has supernatural abilities. Rasoabemanana's ordeal takes her to the corners of the universe, to the heavens. And there are etiological elements: various landforms come into being because of the actions of Rasoabemanana

IBONIA[26]

A Movement to a Union with Iampela
Key Characters: Ibonia and Iampela
The Basic Movement: Bringing Ibonia and Iampela together as one
The Mechanics of the Movement:
    Myth: the diviner and the four corners, etc.
    Tale: Raivato: keeps Ibonia and Iampela apart (pattern)
    Commentary: heroic poetry (praises)
Trickster, the Engine of the Movement: Ibonia as youthful transgressor, Ibonia as
    Raivato's retainer.
    Disguise: Ibonia as Raivato's retainer
Hero: Ibonia (move to union with Iampela)
Physical Strength of the Hero: He overcomes Raivato, other impediments
Frailty of the Hero: A trickster nature; a sense of loss
A Diminished Nature: A loss of his other side, his loved wife
New Possibilities: A movement to a new kind of world with built-in safeguards
    (traditions) against evil
Definition of Hero: In his movement to oneness with the woman he loves, he
    establishes the ritual of marriage within the context of God and the struggle
    between good and evil.

and Ibonia. Heroic poetry in the epic includes Ibonia's self-praise, the inventory of villainy, and the ritual of naming.

The Tale: "Ibonia"[27]

Once, there were two sisters who had no children, so they went to work the divination at the house of Ratoboboka.

As soon as they came in, she asked, "Why have you come here?"

The sisters replied, "We are childless, and so have come to inquire by divination here of you."

Then Ratoboboka said, "Look into my hair."

The elder one looked and saw only a bit of grass. She said, "I saw nothing, Mother, but this bit of grass."

Ratoboboka replied, "Give it to me, that is it."

Then the younger woman searched, and saw only a little bit of broken charm, red in color.

She said, "I saw nothing, Mother, but this little bit of a red charm."

Ratoboboka replied, "Give it to me, that is it."

Then Ratoboboka said, "Go alone to yonder forest to the east. When you have arrived there the trees will all speak and say, 'I am the sacred child-charm.' But do not speak for all that. Take the single tree that does not speak there, last of all. Take its root that lies to the east."

So the two sisters went away. They came to the forest, and each of the trees said, "I am the sacred child-charm [i.e., that causes the barren to give birth]."

Nevertheless, the sisters passed them all by.

When they came to the single tree that did not speak, they dug around the tree, and saw one of the roots that struck eastwards, and they took it away.

When they were on the road, the sisters vowed, saying, "If we should bear boy and girl [i.e., if one have a boy and the other a girl], they shall marry each other."

When they came home, they each drank of the charm.

Accordingly, the elder one became pregnant, and after a half year had passed the younger was also with child. When the time came for her to be delivered, the elder sister bore a daughter, and she gave it the name Rampelasoamananoro.

In time came the day for her younger sister to be delivered, so she went to the south of the hearth to bring forth her child. But the child in her womb, they say, spoke, and said, "I am not a slave, to be taken here to the south of the hearth," so his mother went north of the hearth. But the child spoke again, "I am not a prince, to be taken to the north of the hearth." Then his mother took him to the box, but the child said, "I do not like to be smoked." After some time, the child said, "Make me a big fire of wood." So they made it. Then it said again, "Swallow a knife for me, and take me to the west of the hearth." So he was taken there. Then, at that place, with the knife his mother had swallowed he ripped open his mother's womb, then leaped into the fire that burned brightly there—after having patted the wound that he had made by tearing open his mother, so that it was healed. His father and mother endeavored to save him, lest he should be killed when he went into the fire, but when they put out their hands to take him, their hands were broken and they were unable to take him. And so it happened with their feet as well.

After a while, the child spoke: "Give me a name."

His mother said, "Perhaps you should be called Fozanatokondrilahy, for I hear that he was a strong man."

But the child did not like it.

So his mother mentioned another name, and said, "Perhaps Ravatovolovoay then, for he, I understand, was famous for his strength."

But he did not like that either. So the child gave himself a name. He said,

> "I am Iboniamasy, Iboniamanoro:
> Breaking in pieces the earth and the kingdom;
> At the point of its horn, not gored;
> Beneath its hoofs, not trampled on;
> On its molar teeth, not crushed.
> Rising up, I break the heavens;
> And when I bow down the earth yawns open.
> My robe, when folded up, but a span long;
> But when spread out, it covers the heavens,
> And when it is shaken it is like the lightning.
> My loin-cloth, when rolled together,
> Is but the size of a fist,
> But when unfolded, it surrounds the ocean;
> Its tongue, when girded, causes the dew to descend,
> And its tail sweeps away the rocks.
> Ah! I am indeed Iboniamasy, Iboniamanoro."

Having spoken thus, he came out from the fire and went to his mother's lap.

After he had grown up, he had a dog called Rampelamahavatra.

One day, while Ibonia was hunting in the fields, that famous man called Fozanatokondrilahy came seeking him.

He inquired of his parents, "Where is Ibonia?"

They replied, "He has gone for pleasure into the forest."

Then Fozanatokondrilahy took Ibonia's dog, and the parents could not prevent it.

When Ibonia returned from hunting, he asked his parents, "Where has my dog gone?"

They replied, "Fozanatokondrilahy has taken it."

Ibonia said, "I am going to fetch my dog, Father."

But his father would not let him do so. He said, "Why, Child, even the crocodiles in the water are sought by Fozanatokondrilahy, and found. How can you fight with him without coming to harm?" But seeing that he would not be warned, his father made him fetch a great stone. He wanted to test the strength of his son. He said, "Since I cannot persuade you, fetch me yonder big stone to make me a seat." Ibonia went to the stone and brought it. Then his father let him go.

So off he went, and caught up with Fozanatokondrilahy.

When Fozanatokondrilahy saw Ibonia, he said, "What are you seeking here?" Ibonia replied, "I want my dog!"

Fozanatokondrilahy asked him, "Are you strong?"

"Yes," Ibonia replied, "I am strong."

No sooner had he said that than Fozanatokondrilahy seized him and threw him more than the length of a house.

Ibonia, in his turn, seized Fozanatokondrilahy and threw him also as far as the length of a house.

So they went on, first one and then the other, until each had thrown his opponent as far as ten house lengths.

Then Fozanatokondrilahy said, "Let's not throw each other any more. Instead, let us cast each other down."

So he lifted Ibonia up and cast him down. But Ibonia did not descend fully: he stuck in the ground as far as his ankles.

Then Ibonia, in his turn, cast down Fozanatokondrilahy, who descended as far as his knees.

So they went on with each other, until Fozanatokondrilahy was forced completely into the ground, into the rock on which they were contending, and Ibonia then pressed the stones down upon him so that he was fully covered up.

Ibonia then called together Fozanatokondrilahy's subjects and asked them, "Will you obey the living or the dead?"

Fozanatokondrilahy's wife and people replied, "We will obey the living."

They became Ibonia's subjects, and he departed with all his spoil.

On his way back, a number of people met him. They were skilled in various ways: some were swimmers in deep waters, others were able to tie firmly, still others were able to see great distances, others were able to give life. Ibonia showed kindness to all these, and gave them a share of the spoils that he had obtained.

He returned to his village. When he arrived, he could not find Rampelasoa-mananoro, his betrothed wife, because she had been taken by Ravatovolovoay.

He asked his parents, "Where is my wife?"

They replied, "She has been taken by Ravatovolovoay."

So he said, "I am going to fetch my wife."

When they heard that, his parents warned him: "Don't do that, child. Ravatovolovoay is extremely powerful!"

But he would not stay.

At last, his father became angry, and he took gun and spear to kill Ibonia. But he could do nothing to harm him, for the spear bent double when he hurled it.

Then Ibonia planted some arums and plantain trees, and said to his parents, "If these wither, then I am ill. If they die, that is a sign that I also am dead."

That being done, he went away, and came to an old man who took care of Ravatovolovoay's plaintain trees. He asked him, "What is it that you take with you when you go to visit your master?"

The old man replied, "A few plantains and some rice with honey, my lad."

Ibonia slept there that night. In the morning, he plucked off the old man's hair from his head, so that the whole skin from his body came away with it. Then Ibonia covered himself with that skin, and he fetched some plantains and prepared rice and honey to take to Ravatovolovoay.

He came to Ravatovolovoay's village, and when the people there saw him they said, "The old man has come." They did not know it was Ibonia because he was covered with the old man's skin.

He said, "I have come, Children, to visit you."

So they took the plantains and the rice that he had brought to the prince—for Ravatovolovoay was a prince. They cooked rice for the old man, and gave it to him in the servants' plate. But Ibonia would not eat from that. He said, "Fetch me a plantain leaf on which to eat. You know well enough how well my wife and I live, so why do you give me a plate like that?"

On the day following his arrival, it was announced that the prince would engage in a sport, throwing at a mark with a cross-piece of wood. So the old man went with the rest. When they came to the place where the mark was set up, the prince aimed at the mark but not one of the people could hit it.

Then the old man said, "Just give me a cord, let me catch hold of it."

They gave him one, and he was successful with the one the prince had missed.

The prince said, "This is not the old man, but someone altogether different. Give me a spear and gun so that I may attack him."

But the old man said, "Who else is it but I, my son? I am only revealing the strength that I used to possess."

As they went on with the game, the old man pressed in with the rest, but did not obtain what he had aimed at—the cross-piece went into the earth and brought up a hedgehog, then dipped into the water and brought out a crocodile.

Ravatovolovoay said, "Did I not tell you that this is not the old man, but someone else?"

Again, he sought to kill him, but the old man spoke as before, and Ravatovolovoay again refrained.

On the next day, the prince's orders came: "Today, we shall try the tempers of the oxen. Therefore, make ropes to catch the stubborn ones."

When they began the game, many of the stronger oxen could not be caught.

Then the old man said, "Just give me a rope."

They gave him a rope, and he caught the strong oxen and held them.

When the people saw this, they wondered.

When the prince saw it, he said again, "This cannot be the old man! It must be someone else."

But the people replied, "But who else can it be?"

The old man answered again as he had done before, that he was no one else, that he was merely revealing his strength.

So the players dispersed.

The following night, Ravatovolovoay went to his other wife.

Then the old man went to the house where Rampelasoamananoro was, and said, "Let me lie here by the side of your feet."

But she said, "What a wretch you must be, old man, to say such a thing to me! To speak of lying at my side!"

But when the people were fast asleep, Ibonia took off the skin of the old man with which he had covered himself, and there was a blaze of light in the house because of his shining skin.

Then his wife knew him, and said, "Is it you who have come?"

"Yes," he said, "I have come to fetch you."

He told the people to go out of the house. When they had gone out, he bolted and barred the doors, then sat down to wait for the morning, so that he might show some marvelous things to the people of the village.

Then Rampelasoamananoro said to Ibonia, "How shall we free ourselves from this place?"

He replied, "Don't be afraid! We'll get out all right. But listen to what I say: do not speak to me or beckon to me, because if you do either they will kill me."

In the morning, when Ravatovolovoay awoke, he found that the door of the house where Rampelasoamananoro was was locked.

He said to the people, "Isn't it just as I told you? That this is not the old man, but another person?"

When he tried to break open the door, the door became like a rock, and he could not force it. Then he set fire to the thatch of the roof; it would not burn, but also became as rock.

All attempts were unavailing, and at last Ibonia and Rampelasoamananoro prepared to go out. Ibonia caused a profound sleep to fall on all the people outside the house. Everyone slept.

Then he said to her, "Let's go, but remember, do not speak to me or beckon to me."

They went out, and stepped over all the people who slept along the road they traveled. When they came to the gateway, Ibonia beckoned to a lad and told him to awaken the people. So the lad awoke and roused all the people, including Ravatovolovoay.

The prince said, "Quickly, bring guns and spears! And come, let us pursue them!"

Away they went, shooting at them with their guns. But when the smoke rolled away, there was the pair, going along without any harm. They went on without any mischance, until they arrived at a waterside. When they got there, the wife beckoned to him, to ask him where to ford the water. The moment she did that, Ibonia was struck by a bullet. He fell back into the water, he was dead.

Then Ravatovolovoay came up to Rampelasoamananoro and asked what she wished to do, to follow the living or the dead?

She said, "I shall follow the living, sir," at the same time excusing herself to him.

So Ibonia met his death, and his parents looked at the arums and the plantain trees which he had left with them as a token. When they saw that they had dried up, they lamented him, because the things that he had given them as a sign about himself were dead.

But the friends to whom he had given presents when he came from conquering Fozanatokondrilahy had by no means forgotten him. One day, Joiner-together and his companions said to Far-off-seer, "Look out for Ibonia, lest some harm should have befallen him."

He looked, and said, "Ibonia is dead. A stream is carrying away his bones."

Then Far-off-seer and Joiner-together and Life-giver said to Strong-swimmer, "Go and gather those bones."

So he went and gathered all of Ibonia's bones.

Then Joiner-together united the bones, so that they all came together again. And Life-giver made them live.

They continued invoking blessings until flesh grew and a little breath came, until he could eat a little rice, until at length he could eat as he had formerly been used to do.

When he was alive again, Ibonia prepared to go and fetch his wife away from Ravatovolovoay. He went off, and when he came to the village there was the prince playing a game above the gateway.

When he saw Ibonia, he asked, "Where are you going?"

Ibonia said, "To get my wife."

Then Ibonia struck him with the palm of his hand, and Ravatovolovoay became like grease in his hand.

So Ibonia got everything that had belonged to Ravatovolovoay.

Commentary: "Ibonia"

This story is in five parts: the first part depicts Ibonia's marvelous birth; in part two, Ibonia is given a name; part three pairs Ibonia against Fozanatokondrilahy; and, in part four, Ibonia fights Ravatovolovoay; part five dramatizes Ibonia's resurrection.[28]

The opening conflict of the story has to do with two barren women who go to a diviner, Ratoboboka, for advice; he gives them charms with the interdiction that they should go to a tree that does not speak, and follow its root. The women make a pact: if they bear a daughter and son, their offspring will marry. It turns out that one of them bears a girl, Rampelasoamananoro, and the other gives birth to a boy, Ibonia.

Ibonia has a supernatural birth. He speaks in his mother's womb, telling where he is to be born. He cuts himself out of his mother's womb, then heals her. He moves into the hearth fire; when his parents attempt to save him, their hands and feet are broken. In an identity pattern, Ibonia is named. In his song, he names himself, singing his praises. He claims that he is the earth, the universe. Now he moves to manhood. His first task involves his dog and Fozanatokondrilahy. Ibonia's father tests him to assure that his son is prepared for this challenge. Then Ibonia and Fozanatokondrilahy throw each other, and push each other into the ground. Ibonia wins, and takes the subjects of the vanquished. In an embedded image, Ibonia helps people who are skilled in various ways: a swimmer, one who can tie firmly, one who is able to see great distances, one who gives life. That is not the only embedded image; there is also a life-tree.

The struggle with Fozanatokondrilahy is only a preliminary to the major confrontation, that with Ravatovolovoay, a battle over Ibonia's wife. Again, his father tests him. Ibonia disguises himself, emphasizing the identity theme that is at the heart of transformation stories like this one. He takes the hair and skin of an old man who works for Ravatovolovoay, and goes to his enemy. They engage in contests. When the "old man" wins a throwing match, Ravatovolovoay's suspicions deepen. And when the "old man" wins a competition having to do with roping oxen, Ravatovolovoay's suspicions deepen the more. This contest pattern is intensified by Ravatovolovoay's patterned death-threats. After revealing his identity in a blaze of light, Ibonia and his wife are reunited, and then escape.

Ibonia tells his wife not to speak or beckon to him, or he will die. The house will not burn or be broken into. Then Ibonia causes all his enemies to sleep, and he and his wife leave. He awakens them, and they give chase. But his wife breaks the interdiction and he dies. Ravatovolovoay takes her again. Now the image embedded earlier comes to fruition: Far-seer sees what has happened, Strong-swimmer gathers Ibonia's bones, Joiner-together unites the bones, Life-giver gives them life. Ibonia is reborn, his identity as a man and a leader revealed. He gets his wife, destroys Ravatovolovoay, takes everything that belonged to his enemy, and establishes his kingdom.

This is the story of Ibonia's transformation to manhood, but there is an etiological element as well, having to do with the origin of marriage. Ibonia's experience is not his alone: he charts the way for all humanity.

THE EXPANSION OF THE TALE INTO AN EPIC, THE DEVELOPMENT AND INTERWEAVING OF THE TALE PATTERNS IN *THE IBONIA EPIC*

Stories are organized rhythmically, according to patterns. The patterns interact to reveal meaning. In the Ibonia epic, the tale patterns are evident. What is new is the inclusion of mythic and poetic patterns that weave into the tale narrative patterns. Note the patterns, and the way the tale patterns are developed, repeated, and added to.

The Injection of Myth into The Ibonia Epic, *All to Be Worked into Patterns*
[patterns 1 and 2 in the epic]

1. The five sons visit Father Sky: connecting the heavens and the earth.
2. Nature responds to the acts of Ibonia and his mother.
3. Ranakombe's supernatural abilities.
4. Rasoabemanana's ordeal takes her to the corners of the universe, to the heavens.
5. Etiological elements: various landforms come into being because of the actions of Rasoabemanana and Ibonia.

The Inclusion of Heroic Poetry in The Ibonia Epic, *the Material of Significant Patterns in the Epic* [patterns 7 and 9 in the epic]

1. Ibonia's self-praise.
2. The inventory of villainy.
3. The ritual of naming.

The Patterns in The Ibonia Epic

The epic-performer builds on the tale; by means of patterns, the tale is developed and given a deeper meaning.

1. *Pattern 1:* A visit to Father Sky. (1) Prince of the East, (2) Prince of the North, (3) Prince of the West, (4) Prince of the South, (5) Prince of the Middle visit Father Sky, who celebrates each family with cannons and food . . . but the Prince of the Middle breaks the pattern because his wife, Rasoabemanana, is barren, and they have no child. The cannon is therefore fired into the ground.

2. *Pattern 2:* Nature responds to the acts of Ibonia and his family: the grass dries up and the earth groans when the barren woman and her husband move by. This pattern runs through the epic.

3. *Pattern 3:* Ranakombe's prophecies and warnings. This pattern runs through the epic.

4. *Pattern 4:* Rasoabemanana's ordeal. The quest for the grasshopper and for the child-bearing talisman.

5. *Pattern 2 repris:* Nature responds to Rasoabemanana's ordeal.

6. *Pattern 3 repris:* Ranakombe's prophecies and warnings. "This child is burdened with a baleful destiny. . . . [T]his child is a misfortune."

7. *Pattern 5:* Ibonia's love for Iampelasoamananoro. "If Iampelasoamananoro dies, I shall not let the earth have her; if she remains alive, I shall let no one else have her."

8. *Pattern 6:* Inventory of villainy. The mother catalogues for her son "the dangerous men on earth," and creates their praises: Ikabikabilahy, Ifosalahibehatoka, Impandrafitrandriamnibola, Andriambavitolahy, Rainingezalahy, Imbolahongeza, Ingarabelahy, Izatovotsiota. Ibonia's routine reply: "They are children."

9. *Pattern 7:* Ibonia praises himself, "I am a deadly child."

10. *Pattern 8:* The child seeks a place to be born. He orders his mother to wander. She goes to (1) a slope on a far off rock, (2) a very high mountain, (3) all the forests of this world, (4) the water, (5) the city, (6) the farm—where he is born. Each time he rejects a place, his mother alters that place, bringing into existence a landform.

11. *Pattern 1 repris:* A visit to Father Sky. At last, when Ibonia is born, the cannons can be fired into the four cardinal directions, but only after the child insists upon it.

12. *Pattern 2 repris:* Nature responds to the birth of Ibonia.

13. *Pattern 9:* The ritual of naming. Ranakombe, saying, "Shout for joy," suggests various names, each time developing the name into a praise poem: Ipapangolahilavelatra, Andriamboromahery, Andriandambozoma, Andirafosalahibehatoka, Andriantolohoboboka, Andriamitomoamibotretraka, Andriambolosarotralinafamorandro, Andriankabikabilahy, Impandrafitrandriamanibola, Ingarabelahy, Andriambavitoalahy, Irainingeza, and, finally, Iboniamasiboniamanoro. Each time, Ibonia rejects the name: "I don't want it," and Ranakombe responds, "What a terrible child this is."

14. *Pattern 2 repris:* Nature responds to the naming of Ibonia.

15. *Pattern 10:* Raivato versus Ibonia. Raivato contemplates his future enemy.

16. *Pattern 7 repris:* Ibonia praises himself. "I am a creation of power." Ranakombe praises Ibonia.

17. *Pattern 9 repris:* The ritual of naming. Ranakombe adds other names to Ibonia's name: Isikinana, Isikindahiandriampapangolahilavelatra, Isikindahiandriantolohoboboka, Isikindahinandirampandrafitrandriamanibola, Isikindahiningarabelahy, Isikindahinandiandambozoma, Isikindahiandriambavitoalahy.

18. *Pattern 11:* Childhood games. As a part of his puberty rite of passage, Ibonia and his four slaves fight with the more numerous children of the village: cow pies, mud, clumps of earth, stones, jumping. Ibonia wins each battle.

19. *Pattern 10 repris:* Riavato versus Ibonia. Ibonia is warned not to seek Iampelasoamananoro: he is no match for Raivato.

20. *Pattern 7 repris:* Ibonia praises himself. "When I get up, the skies are rent."

21. *Pattern 2 repris:* Nature responds. With his foot, Ibonia causes the earth to reverberate.

22. *Pattern 5 repris:* Ibonia's love for Iampelasoamananoro. "If she dies, I will not surrender her to the earth; alive, I leave her to no one."

23. *Pattern 7 repris:* Ibonia praises himself. "I am the great male."

24. *Pattern 5 repris:* Ibonia's love for Iampelasoamananoro. "Were she dead, I would not leave her to the earth; alive, I will give her to no one."

25. *Pattern 3 repris:* Ranakombe's prophecies and warnings. What Ibonia must do to get his wife: move through a forest and get talismans, stay under water until daybreak. Ibonia does this.

26. *Pattern 12:* Ibonia as a trickster and a hero. He buries himself to his
    shoulders, then causes people's goods to fall into a ditch. His father is
    furious, his mother challenges him: fight a crocodile. Ibonia does, and
    kills it; fight an ogre: Ibonia does, and kills it; fight the monstrous
    Ikabikabilahy: Ibonia hammers him into the ground, and Ikabikabi-
    lahy joins him; fight the strongest of the strong, Andriambavitoalahy:
    Ibonia cuts this swallowing monster open, and releases the people
    from inside; the monster and the people follow Ibonia.
27. *Pattern 7 repris:* Ibonia praises himself as he overcomes the various
    obstacles set before him by his mother.
28. *Pattern 10 repris:* Raivato versus Ibonia. Ibonia is warned not to seek
    Iampelasoamananoro.
29. *Pattern 13:* Alternative brides are suggested to Ibonia: the daughter of
    the Prince of the South, the daughter of Andriantsifamaho. He
    rejects them, insulting Andriantsifamaho.
30. *Pattern 14:* Ibonia becomes Ikonantitra, Raivato's retainer. The
    pattern: Ibonia learns the old man's ways.
31. *Pattern 10 repris:* Raivato versus Ibonia. At Raivato's homestead, the
    plate and spoon used by Ibonia, who is now disguised as Ikonantitra,
    break; the mat he sleeps on flies apart; Raivato's charms rattle—all
    are warnings to Raivato that an impostor is in his house. Ibonia as
    Ikonantitra fights and defeats Raivato at chess, wooden crosses, oxen
    in the fields. Raivato repeats the earlier warnings, that Ibonia is too
    womanly to defeat him. Finally, having stolen Raivato's charms,
    Ibonia defeats Raivato by hammering him into the ground.
32. *Pattern 7 repris:* Ibonia praises himself: "When I go up a hill, I find
    new strength. . . ."

The separate stories having to do with Ibonia are reordered and thereby organized into epic form. The basis is the tale, the patterning is central to the epic
form, history is clearly in the background, and the trickster is a major characteristic of Ibonia.

The Inclusion of the Trickster into *The Ibonia* Epic

*Consider the twelfth pattern of the epic in order to discover the trickster qualities
of the hero. Ibonia is a trickster and a hero: "He buries himself to his shoulders,
then causes people's goods to fall into a ditch. His father is furious, his mother challenges him: fight a crocodile. Ibonia does, and kills it; fight an ogre: Ibonia does,*

and kills it; fight the monstrous Ikabikabilahy: Ibonia hammers him into the ground,
and Ikabikabilahy joins him; fight the strongest of the strong, Andriambavitoalahy:
Ibonia cuts this swallowing monster open, and releases the people from inside; the
monster and the people follow Ibonia."

Ibonia as a Trickster, 1

When Ibonia and Ranakombe finished their battle of wits, Ranakombe went
back home, and Ibonia was with his parents. Four women slaves of Ibemampanjaka (The-great-one-who-causes-to-reign, Ibonia's father) had had children
at the same time that Ibonia was born, and these were all boys. Ibemampanjaka
gave Ibonia these little slaves, who grew up and played with him. When the five
boys were old enough to be considered inhabitants of the village, they went to
play with the other boys in the fields.

When they were together, they played at throwing clods of cow dung at each
other. They divided up into two sides, but Ibonia refused, saying, "All of you
get together on one side, and I and my four slaves will be the other side."

But all the children answered, "You will not beat us, because there are too
few of you."

There were many children in Iliolava.

But Ibonia would not listen, and he ordered, "Go on over there to be on one
side, and we shall be on the other. It is decided."

They started to throw clods of cow-dung at each other. Of those who caught
Ibonia, the ones who touched him fell on the ground and the ones who did not
touch him staggered and were dazed.

And that is how Ibonia and his four slaves won over all the others.

In the evening, the children returned home to their villages and each told
his parents: "We have been beaten at cow pies by Ibonia. There was only Ibonia
and his four slaves on one side, and all the rest of us were on the other side, and
still we could not win."

The parents said, "That is just your cowardliness. Did anyone ever see five
boys beat all the children of Iliolava?"

Another day, Ibonia and the children were playing again in the fields. They
were playing and throwing mud at each other. Ibonia and his four slaves took
one side again, and the others did not succeed in winning this game either. In
the evening, when they went home, the children said: "We were beaten again by
Ibonia and his four slaves."

Their parents made fun of them. "You would think we never gave you anything to eat, if five people could defeat you!"

But the children said, "Go yourselves into the field when Ibonia comes!"

Another day, Ibonia went again into the fields with the children, and they fought with each other, throwing clumps of earth, but once more the children lost. The grown-ups who had come to watch were stupefied when they saw the clouds of dust raised where Ibonia's pitches reached.

Later, they were throwing stones, and Ibonia was the winner again. Towards the end, all the children of Iliolava fought in the fields against Ibonia and his four slaves, playing by-the-waist, or boxing. Finally, they competed at jumping. Some, trying as hard as they could, went as high as twelve feet; others, eighteen feet; and some, even twenty-four feet. Ibonia was the last, and he jumped over a hill that was three days walk from there. When the children arrived home, they told everyone there, "We were jumping with Ibonia, and he jumped last, and he went over that hill over there, and went over others, and we do not know where he landed!"

Hearing these words, the people were amazed, and they said, "We shall be in trouble if the son of the king is lost or dead over there."

But when his parents heard about it, they were not worried because they knew how their son was. Ibonia came back after three days. On the way back, he walked, having given up jumping.

Ibonia as a Trickster, 2

When he had arrived at Iliolava, he planted himself before the gate again. He dug into the dry ground, and buried himself up to his shoulder blades. People came and went from the town, carrying their loads. But Ibonia stabbed through their pots, their rice, or their faggots with his spear, and everything fell into the ditch. He spared only living creatures. So people went to tell Ibemampanjaka and Rasoabemanana: "Ibonia has arrived at the entrance gate, and now the people are besieged. There is no load coming or going that he does not poke a hole into with his spear, and everything falls into the ditch."

When Ibemampanjaka heard this report, he went to speak with Rasoabemanana: "There is your son, Rasoabemanana. But let me be the one to go, and I shall surely kill your devil of a son."

But she replied, "Well, how about that. Maybe I was the one to have him, but it took two to conceive him! In any case, if you kill him, it is not a crime."

Ibemampanjaka went out and shouted, "Let there be a meeting of all Iliolava."

People all came together. Ibemampanjaka gave them the order to gather stones, with which to stone Ibonia. But no one could get close to him. As soon as anyone got near the gate, he hit him with his spear. The people stoned him, but without any effect, even though they stoned him with the equivalent of a heap of stones. (They say that is how the cult of the stone-pile began.)

As Ibemampanjaka and his subjects could do nothing, they went back home.

Then Rasoabemanana went forth. She showed off her grand airs in the main square, then walked up to the entrance gate, her bearing proud and regal. She spoke thus: "How about it? Could it be that Ibonia is evil, or cowardly? Will you play us the comedy of the bull of Imozy (The-awkward)? Jeered at, he does not bellow; excited, he will refuse to fight; cut up, his meat will not become tender. Or will you present to us the comedy of the cow whose milk cannot be drunk? Here we are, not knowing what to do, as if we were struggling with rams. In vain can one yell at them, they still cannot be convinced to carry burdens. Leave them alone; and they will break each others' heads. I do not understand this business. You deserve the name The-dulled-one-of-iron. If you were really courageous, is not the great crocodile north of the town, leaving nothing of cattle and men who pass by there? If Ibonia is really a man, let him go and fight there."

Ibonia came out of the ground, shouting, "I am a creation of power. With you, I am kind; but with others, let it be known that I am not easy to get along with. I am the claws of the kite, the talons of the eagle. I get what I want when I am not given it, so much the better reason to give it to me! What I put in place does not escape by itself."

He called his slaves, Itiahita (The-one-whom-one-loves-to-see), Itsimi-asarobako (The-handsome-fellow-who-does-not-work), Imahalanatsaha (He-who-does-not-go-often-into-the-fields), and Itiaranovola (He-who-likes-rice-water), and said, "You, weave a rope, because I am going to fight the crocodile north of the town."

He went then to the water's edge, wound the rope under his arms, and declared, "If it is upstream that blood appears, pull me up, because I shall have been killed by the crocodile; if it is downstream, pull the crocodile up, because then, I shall have killed it."

At that, he jumped into the water. The crocodile closed its jaws around him, and after they had seized each other, in about three times the time it takes to cook rice, Ibonia killed the crocodile, and blood appeared downstream.

Imagine the joy of the slaves! They hurried to pull the rope which acted as signal. Ibonia came up, then they brought in the crocodile too.

The four slaves cried, "Our father is powerful! Our father is powerful! You see, Ibonia, it is lightning, our lord, he is a meteor. He is not to be numbered among humans."

The populace of the town rejoiced, because the crocodile that had swallowed up everything they had was killed.

Rhythm, Patterning: The Trickster Box

The engine that is fantasy includes the formal elements of the performance, the patterns or rhythm of story. The essence of metaphor is transformation, a move from one set of images to another, with threads of likeness connecting images that are unlike. Fantasy is not just the furniture of the parallel world: it is the means of connecting the parallel and primary worlds. In other words, it is the stuff of metaphor: it is both a part of the image of metaphor, with contemporary, real-life imagery, and most important, the engine of metaphor: form. Metaphor here, then, is defined as the union or the intersecting of the primary and parallel worlds, two worlds that are, in the language of storytelling, perceived as one. The patterns link the two worlds. In "Ibonia," the mythic Raivato and Iampelasoamananoro are the storyteller's way of revealing the two sides of the real-life Ibonia. The construction of the epic is the key, the way the patterns interact, the way the parts of the story are repeated early and late, pushing the story forward even as the basic materials from which the linear story emerges are routinely recalled by the storyteller, so that simultaneously the story repeats itself and moves forward. Other patterns emphasize identity, and the patterned movement is between those two identities. Certainly there are images about which we can agree that, if they are not fantasy, then they tug at the edges of the real. But the point is that, within the context of story, a variety of images can be found, running a scale from the starkly realistic to the mysterious to the strange and other-worldly to the monstrous and violent. Fantasy images by themselves tell us little. It is the coupling of those images with other images in the stories that creates meaning. The important thing is Ibonia's rhythmical movement to epic hero, with other events and patterns commenting on his developing identity as a man. There is a descent into hell, into the world of Raivato, as the hero becomes identified with his new societies, Ibonia through self-praises. It is a new world: Ibonia's is a new world, a world in which the role of women is protected.

Fantasy is complex, composed as it is of mythic images, patterns, relationship, within the context of artistic performance: mythic images and the emotions, mythic images and the resonance of tradition, contemporary images, form, rhythm, repetition, and patterning. Contemporary images are not fantasy until they are introduced into the parallel world: they retain their real-world significance, but are brought into relationships with fantasy images. All are encompassed in performance, which is, of course, fantasy: dance, music, relations with audience. So it is that we define fantasy as an image, an action, a pattern, a relationship that occurs within a tightly manipulated and controlled narrative environment that partakes of the real world but is itself a parallel world. That parallel world can only occur within the context and embrace of the real world, so that there is always an ironic encounter between them. But the relationship is only ironic: it is not a one-to-one relationship. The fantasy parallel world is fed by the real world: indeed, everything in the parallel world can be seen to have its origins in the real world. But it is not the real world in its organization, in the relationship between images, and in the images themselves when those images transcend in some way their real-life counterparts. This parallel world exists in its own right, with its own rules and laws. These rules and laws can be stated in broad terms, but they can only be worked out by an analysis of the individual narrative that exists within that parallel world. The tale within the epic remains vivid: it is not that the epic-performer drastically revises the tale, it is that the epic-performer constructs, mainly through patterning, the epic with the tale at its functional heart.

5

Sunjata/Sundiata

The Foundation of Epic:
Fictionalizing Historical Characters

To understand the West African epic *Sunjata* or *Sundiata*, one must understand other oral forms: the oral tale, the oral lyrical and panegyric poem, oral history, and oral myth. And one must understand the enormous energy, undifferentiated trickster-energy, that is unleashed during the formative time, the transformation or transition period, as the culture moves from one dispensation to another. That energy and that transformation are embodied in the epic hero, an ambiguous character possessed of god and human, vulnerable yet invulnerable, tied to the historical and cultural past, moving into a new vision that he personifies.

The tale is straightforward, with common motifs from the folkloric tradition. It is composed of motifs, which are at the center of patterns. The epic takes place within a network of praises. Oral poetry reveals heroic aspects of humans, positively, in the rush of pleasure in recounting the affairs of authentic culture heroes; negatively, in the comparison of the flawed contemporary leader with the great heroes of the past. The raw material of this poetry is by and large realistic, historical. But it is history made discontinuous, then placed in new and novel frames. Within this new context, the historical character is described, then judged. It is in the measurement of the poem's subject against the ideals of the society that the poem has its metaphorical power. It is clearly tied to historical events.

There are marvelous occurrences as Sunjata struggles with Sumanguru. The story unfolds in a context of praises and historical events, making plain Sunjata's

SUNDIATA

A Movement to a Union with Danharan and Soumaoro by Way of the Griot
Key Characters: Sundiata and Danharan/Soumaoro
The Basic Movement: Bringing Sundiata and Danharan/Sumaoro together
    as one
The Mechanics of the Movement:
    Myth: Soumaoro
    Tale: Sundiata's rite of passage
    Commentary: The griot (poet)
Trickster, the Engine of the Movement: Sundiata's mother, the griot
    Disguise: The mother's preparation of Sundiata; the griot as Soumaoro's
    bard
Hero: Sundiata (moves to union with Danharan and Soumaoro)
Physical Strength of the Hero: The fight with Soumaoro (and others)
Frailty of the Hero: The hero's dependence on the griot
A Diminished Nature: There is no Sundiata without the griot
New Possibilities: Sundiata moving beyond himself (by means of the griot's
    words)
Definition of Hero: A character whose abilities are given form by the griot

cultural universality and historical certainty. There is transformation, a betwixt and between period. This is the time of the trickster. Sunjata is attractive and unattractive. During the transformation period, he goes through various stages: miraculous birth, coming to manhood, magical acts, accomplishing impossible tasks that reveal him as a great man destined for towering achievement, the epic struggle with Sumanguru, discovering Sumanguru's secret, the destruction of Sumanguru. The story of Sunjata's companions is also told, especially that of Tira Makhang.

The tale and myth traditions link the epic hero to the gods of a society and to its traditions, both important linkages. But the epic hero goes beyond these. He is often a revolutionary, in the sense that he espouses change. Sunjata becomes the embodiment of the culture and its great historical turning point. In fact, the tale and myth contain bits of history, just as the heroic poem contains bits of fantasy: it is a matter of degree. The epic hero, partaking of both fantasy and reality/history, is in the process of changing things even as he changes, and that is where the traditions of the trickster, clown, and carnival

SUNJATA

A Movement to a Union with His Sister and Sumanguru
Key Characters: Sunjata and Sumanguru/Sunjata's sister
The Basic Movement: Bringing Sunjata and Sumanguru/sister together as one
The Mechanics of the Movement:
   Myth: Sumanguru
   Tale: Sunjata's rite of passage
   Commentary: The griot
Trickster, the Engine of the Movement: Sunjata's sister
   Disguise: Pretends to love Sumanguru, goes to bed with him
Hero: Sunjata (moves to union with sister and Sumanguru)
Physical Strength of the Hero: The tests of manhood, the fight with Sumanguru
   (Tira Makhang et al.)
Frailty of the Hero: The hero's dependence on his sister
A Diminished Nature: The hero is not an individual but a conglomerate
New Possibilities: On the backs of his sister, Tira Makhang et al., Sunjata
   establishes a kingdom
Definition of Hero: A hero has no existence by himself: he is the result of those
   around him and of his griots

---

come in. Tales, myths, and heroic epics all deal with shaky periods in the lives of individual humans, of the universe, of the culture. We see people who are in the process of transformation, who will assure that these shaky periods (the period of the trickster, the clown, carnival) will be successfully navigated. This is especially clear in the case of the individual in the tale. Here, we see a person standing on the threshold of a new event in his life. But it is earthshaking only for him: The culture remains steady, and his rite of passage is a part of that steadiness. This steadiness is not the case in the myths and epics. Here, the society is being altered drastically. In the myths, we stand on the threshold of human civilization; in the epics, we stand on the threshold of wholly new societies. Sunjata is heroically born, but he must experience a pattern of struggles to prove himself.

The hero fulfills heroic expectations as a warrior. As a warrior, he is undergoing a transformation: that transformation becomes that of a larger society. The period of change, the betwixt-and-between period, is a time when the hero is in a trickster-mode, when he is both creative and destructive. It is in this period that his identity is in question, and when he is free of affiliation with traditional institutions and expectations. This is also the period when he is most vulnerable, when his humanity is most in evidence. It is at this time that he most acutely feels his humanity, when he is therefore most introspective. During the betwixt-and-between period, he experiences freedom as he can never experience it on either side of this great transformational divide. This is when his spirit soars, when he is most troubled yet least encumbered by social restraints. It is therefore at this time when he is closest to the gods, a fact that frequently becomes evident by the very presence of the gods. In the end, the hero can never be the same: he becomes a composite of all that he has seen and met. Thus, Sumanguru becomes a part of Sunjata.

We shall consider two versions of the epic, *Sunjata* and *Sundiata*. The concept of a hero: he is typically born in a miraculous way. And his growth to manhood may be supernatural or strange. But he grows into a lion-child. He engages in a struggle of some kind. That struggle reveals both creative and destructive possibilities, within him and within the larger society or group within which or with which he struggles. He has an intensely personal struggle with his own infirmity, but rises above these early circumstances (a Cinderella motif). The hero undertakes a journey of some kind, a monomyth, which involves leaving home, struggling with a negative force that is often the other side of himself, then returning, changed. Identity is at the heart of the hero's story. A villain is at the center of his struggle. This is Sumanguru, the sorcerer king. The hero is never without helpers; here, they help Sunjata take away the magic of Sumanguru. Those helpers often become emblematic of him, aspects of his character, as is the villain. The hero's story involves the gods, and it involves the trickster, the latter in the form of the dualistic villain who is both creative and destructive. In *Sunjata*, the griots, sorcerers, and fetishes play the role of god. The hero is tied to the past: in *Sundiata*, griots and his mother tie him to the greatness of the past. Then there is the fracturing of that perfection by negative contemporary influences, and there is a need for rebirth, for a reinvention of the society, the need for a hero. There is a sense of history here: contemporary names of people and places, historical places and people. The hero has a vision of a future world, an Eden, a demi-paradise. He becomes at some point exemplary of that larger society or group. (See Sunjata, when the people claim him King of Mali: to them, he is an outsider, a pretender.) He may restructure the world.

There are often two motifs here: the Cinderella motif and the Messiah motif. And there are two forces here that are never completely resolved: the destructive forces are never wholly withdrawn or subdued, and the creative forces are never wholly without frailty. The poet manages these two seemingly antithetical motifs. The sinister element here, however, is the shadow of the trickster, because he too experiences journeys, monomyths, the things experienced by the hero. And he is the wild card here. There is hero in the trickster as there is trickster in the hero. Hero and trickster: the design of a society, the design of a human being. In the end, the hero has all destructive trickster elements under control, and he rules, but never without the possibilities of new disruptions.

Sunjata depends on his mother for his strength, his legitimacy, and he is finally on his own (she dies, at his insistence). Various secondary characters shadow Sunjata, including his sister, Tira Makhang, his brother (he feeds his calf to him), and his griots. All of these characters comprise Sunjata. His puberty ritual, the trousers test, boiling wax test, silk cotton tree test: all of these have to do with emphasizing Sunjata's legitimacy, along with the naming patterns and the griots.

HISTORICAL BACKGROUND: MALI AD 1230–1475.

During this period, Mande was the language of the Islamic Mandingo. Sumanguru was in control of their land, and Sunjata (Sundiata), courageous and able, would lead his people to victory. He became the national hero of the Mandingo. Sunjata, whose name means "hungering lion," was a prince of the Keita clan. He was not very promising when young, he was a least likely hero: he could not stand up or walk, and it was said that he could not be cured. Because Sunjata's father had died when he was young, control of Mali had fallen to the cruel Sumanguru who was widely feared and despised. He did not pay much attention to the sickly Sunjata because he did not consider him a threat. This was an error. Deeply suffering, Sunjata was able to walk with an iron cane. So it was that he became an expert horseman and hunter, courageous and skillful militarily. The Mandingo considered him the prince who would save them from Sumanguru. In 1230, Sunjata was proclaimed King of Mali. Sumanguru saw a full-scale revolt taking place. He had a huge army. The showdown was in 1235: two mighty armies collided in Karina. Sumanguru was said to have magical powers, but his army was crushed by Sunjata. Sumanguru escaped. In 1240, Sunjata was completely in control. Mali was now the most powerful state in western Sudan. His armies extended the empire's boundaries. He moved his capital to Niani, his birthplace. He controlled the gold fields. Agriculture was important. Sunjata died in 1255 while his empire was still growing and prospering. His son, Mansa Wali, the Red King, took over.

It is a story of the Manding empire, and Sunjata and Sumanguru are its extremes. Out of this struggle comes the Manding realm. Hence, we see the story being carved out of history, and in the end, history and geography and culture wholly reclaim it, as the story becomes lost. The story of Sunjata is really the story of the beginnings of the Manding society. The praise names, geographical places, historical events: all of these are the stuff out of which the story is carved, and the pulses and forces at work in the birth of a nation are the same pulses and forces that we see at work in the tale: Sunjata and his lengthy birth process, the move to manhood, the struggle with his evil side, assisted by his emanations, his sister and Tira Makhang, with the griots keeping the historical frame clearly in sight.

In the epic *Sundiata*, the struggle between Sundiata and Sumaoro is seen on several planes, with the griot (who controls identity, the identity of the king, the identity of Mali) moving between them. On the earthly plane are Sassouma, a jealous and ambitious mother, her son (whom she will see be king), and a daughter (who is used by the mother and son to further the son's career). On the ethereal plane is Soumaoro, the evil god (sorcerer). In the liminal region are Sogolon, a woman whose roots are in death and the mystical, her husband the king (he has a wraith), and their son, Sundiata, born in a wild and frenzied sexual relationship. He is liminal by his very birth, and then is forced to the boundaries by Sassouma. The move of the hero: the initial battle is that between Sundiata and Danharan (between Sogolon and Sassouma). This leads to Sundiata's exile and his rite of passage: his movement to the readiness to be king. The essential battle is that between Sundiata and Soumaoro: that will determine the future kingdom of Mali. Then Sundiata will move from the liminal region to the ethereal, and thence to the earthly.

If this is a heroic epic, why is Sunjata not at center stage at all times? He is at center stage as he undergoes his tests—iron rods, trousers, beeswax, silk-cotton tree—for here he shows his coming of age, his readiness and ability to fight for the throne, whether fighting his brothers or Sumanguru. His traveling, his odyssey, his journeying away from home, his isolation take him off on his own. He gains an identity (the etiological elements with the griots give him his name; and later, he gets his legitimacy). A long time is spent to establish his legitimacy and identity. This is his genealogy. But once his legitimacy and potency are established and Sunjata has prepared his horses and armies for battle with Sumanguru, something happens to the tale: we now shift our attention from Sunjata to two other characters, and they now take center stage, and the initiative seems to pass out of Sunjata's hands. Tira Makhang becomes essential: "Sunjata declared, 'The time for battle has not yet arrived. Tira Makhang has not come.'" This is followed by the gathering of soldiers. But the time is still not ripe for battle: "Sunjata told him, 'The time for battle has not yet arrived, Tira Makhang has not come.'" And again, "the important men" are called by the griot, but again, "Sunjata said to him, 'The time for fighting has not yet come. Tira Makhang has not come.'" When Sankarang Madiba Konte, Sunjata's grandfather, asks, "Is Tira Makhang better than all the rest of us?" Sunjata answers, "He is not better than all the rest of you, / But he fights a morning battle, / He fights an evening battle, / And we join with him in the big battle." And the pattern continues: "Sunjata declared, 'The time for fighting has not yet come, Tira Makhang has not arrived.'" And he gives the same answer to the question, "Is Tira Makhang better than all the rest of us?" This is followed by a lengthy praise poem and genealogical segment on Tira Makhang. Finally, after all this, Tira Makhang is seen coming, and he says, "Wrap me in a shroud, / Because when I see Susu Sumanguru, either I put him in a shroud or he puts me in a shroud." Then, instead of Sunjata showing his courage, there is a question of whether or not he is afraid. The next major section deals not with Sunjata's courage but with his sister's cleverness and courage, as she gets the secret of Sumanguru's strength and invulnerability from him. Then, when Sunjata does confront Sumanguru in battle, he is successful only because his sister had been successful in getting Sumanguru's secret. What do the Tira Makhang and sister sections mean for a definition of a hero? The hero is composed of Sunjata, and Tira Makhang and his sister. The helpers are a part of him, just as they are in the tale. It is not the hero *per se* who is important, but what the hero stands for, his vision of a new society, and his movement of the people toward that new society. If he has helpers, that is no problem; they stand for the same thing he does, and they become extensions of him and his character.

Within the context of the oral tale and the patterning of imagery within those tales, the epic performer brings history into the combination. Here, Sunjata himself is a historical figure, along with the litany of names of those whom he attacked and those who were on his side, including Tira Makhang. The final third of the Sunjata epic emphasizes this historical data, because much of it is not worked into the fictionalized Sunjata of the first two-thirds of the epic.

6

The Odyssey

THE FOUNDATION OF EPIC:
INJECTING THE TRICKSTER INTO THE HERO

In *The Odyssey*, the cycle of tales is obvious, along with the patterning of those tales. And the historical background of the Trojan War and other events remains at the forefront of the epic. Homer clearly and emphatically works the trickster into this patterned mixture of history and tale.

Odysseus is a trickster: consider the Trojan horse, the experience with Polyphemus, Odysseus's arrival home in disguise. Odysseus is a hero: we hear his heroic story in his own words (hence the elaborate flashbacks, not told in the third person but as first-person reminiscences by Odysseus).

Why tell the story in the first person? Why break the linearity of the story, for the lengthy flashback? The reason is heroic self-revelation. The stories are told by the characters themselves, at home by the participants, Odysseus by himself, etc. There is a rich interaction of past and present; we keep moving from the moment of the past (Odysseus's adventures) to the moment of the present (Penelope's plight), so that the play with linearity heightens the question of heroism, of Odysseus's heroism. Even with the flashback, we know the bearson tale, we know the monomyth, so even though the storyteller takes liberties with the flashbacks, we place events into their proper sequence. But why break the linearity?

The trickster energy and the developing hero: these occur simultaneously. The basic story: it moves from Troy to Odysseus's wife besieged by suitors, with a son who is unable to do anything about it. Myth: the gods take sides, especially Athena and Poseidon. Tale: the monomythic move to the nadir, to

Odysseus

A Movement to a Union with Penelope
Key Characters: Odysseus and Penelope
The Basic Movement: Bringing Odysseus and Penelope together as one
The Mechanics of the Movement:
  Myth: the gods
  Tale: Polyphemus, Circe, etc., the suitors (keep Odysseus and Penelope
    apart) (pattern)
  Commentary: Odysseus's sense of identity
Trickster, the Engine of the Movement: Odysseus' trickery
  Disguise: Odysseus as the old man
Hero: Odysseus (move to union with wife, his other side)
Physical Strength of the Hero: struggle with Polyphemus, Circe, etc., and with his
    exploits at Troy in the background
Frailty of the Hero: age; a sense of loss
A Diminished Nature: his age, his name, his home
New Possibilities: moving beyond these, a rebirth
Definition of Hero: a character who, in his movement to oneness with the
    woman he loves, reveals the possibilities of triumph over human infirmity
    (age, frailty, etc.)

Tiresias in the underworld where Odysseus learns his fate, death. The underworld: the dead he meets there; it is a grim place, without hope. Any hope is to be achieved on the earth. Is there heroism in Hades? There is a progressive movement of the hero to the point that his friends are gone, his ships destroyed, and, at home, his wife is under siege. He moves to the lowest point, and learns that death is to be his destiny. But he returns and plays out his role of hero, destroying his wife's suitors and recovering his wife and son. Telemachus is the microcosm of Odysseus: he is the future, and there is hope in that.

The sense of loss: Odysseus's glory days, the sense of gain; his free will, doing what he wishes to do. Odysseus is his own bard: he is the one who tells his story. He uses his trickster energy; this is his transformation, to move to Ithaca, to move to heroism, even with the images of the heroes of the past in Hades. Achilles wishes to be back on the earth. In the end, it may not be so much about free will as to make use of possibilities within one's life, which is also the conclusion of Gilgamesh. Gilgamesh's trip to the nadir, Utnapishtim, and Odysseus's trip to the nadir, Tiresias: the epics and the epic heroes are the same.

In "The Bearson,"[29] an oral tale, there is an incipient Odysseus (this summary is based on one hundred variants of the story in twenty languages). There is an extraordinary birth: a woman meets a bear in the forest, is taken to his cave, and she bears a son to him. The mother and son escape from the bear's den and return to the human world, where the human husband of the woman adopts the child as his own. And so the child grows up. Before starting on his adventures, Bearson acquires a marvelous weapon that he learns to wield with consummate skill. Then he sets out on his adventures. Bearson and his companions come to a house in the wood. It is the house of a demon, and it is filled with food. Bearson and his comrades eat and go to sleep. The demon returns, and accosts Bearson's companions, one by one, until it comes to Bearson, who overpowers the demon who then escapes to the underworld. Bearson follows him down a deep well, and finds great treasure in the underworld. Then, as Bearson returns from the underworld, his comrades attempt to prevent his escape. The tale can be seen in broad outlines in the epic, as follows:

In Ithaca, suitors vie for the hand of Penelope, Odysseus's wife, in marriage, and they have various plots. Penelope tricks the suitors and keeps them at bay. Her son, Telemachus, is powerless against the suitors, and he goes to Pylos, to visit Nestor, and then to Sparta in search of his father.

And the odyssey begins: Odysseus leaves Troy and is shipwrecked and has experiences with Calypso and Nausicaa and the Phaeacians. He tells his story to the Phaeacians, a story about the Cicones, the Lotus-Eaters, the Cyclops and Polyphemus, the country of the winds, the leather bag of Aeolus, the gigantic cannibalistic Laestrygonians, Circe the beautiful witch who turned men into swine, the Realm of the Shades (Hades) where he sought the prophet Tiresias, the island of the Sirens whose music made a man forget everything and then killed him, the passage between Scylla and Charybdis, and the Island of the Sun, Thrinacia, and the herd of the sun-god. Then the Sun causes a shipwreck, and Odysseus is cast ashore on Calypso's island and has to stay there for years.

The Phaeacian king will help Odysseus to return to his home. A ship is readied and Odysseus embarks. He does not recognize his own country. He is met by a shepherd, who is really Athena in disguise, and he is home, in Ithaca. Athena reveals herself to him, and they work out a plan. She tells him what is going on in his house: she will help him clear it of the suitors. He must spend the night with Eumaeus, his faithful swineherd; Odysseus is disguised as a beggar. Athena goes to tell Telemachus who has now returned home. Odysseus is reunited with Telemachus, telling him, "I am your father." After twenty years, Odysseus returns home, in disguise. His dog recognizes him. Odysseus is struck by one of the suitors. Penelope appears, sends for the stranger who had been struck. He does not reveal himself. His old nurse recognizes him, he quiets her. The next morning, the suitors return. There is feasting. Penelope's plan: he who strings her husband's bow and shoots an arrow straight through twelve axe-head holes in a line will be her husband. The suitors cannot bend the bow. Now Odysseus reveals himself to the swineherd and the keeper of cattle. His plan: find a way to get the bow and arrow into his own hands, and get the others to close the women's quarters. Odysseus strings the bow and shoots the arrow through the axe-heads. Then, with Telemachus, he kills the suitors. Athena helps. Now Penelope is told.

The gods are in the background, fighting their own battles. But we can see these as the shadows of the battles being fought by the real characters. And in fact the gods weave into and out of these real characters, but are in the end powerless to do anything about the activities of those real-life characters. They are the shadows of myth, mythically present but not actually affecting reality. The heroes are on their own: this is the power of this myth. The gods move and dance in the background, but the human characters must cope with fate and with their own characters themselves. Odysseus is moving into a new more realistic monomyth in which fantasy is present but does not really have much effect on human relations and actions. Realism is replacing the fantasy of the tale and the godliness of the myth, both of which exist as structures for the epic. But the epic deals with human heroes, heroes becoming agonizingly aware of a sense of loss, of a loss of that oneness, that unity with the gods: humans are on their own, and it is at this juncture, in this epiphany, that a definition of heroism is forged. The heroes are not supernatural, they are not gods, but they have the possibilities of the gods in them, and hence the movement of the gods constantly in the background. Heroes are becoming agonizingly aware of their limitations, of their humanity, and it is to the degree that they accept these limitations and this humanity that they are adjudged heroes. They struggle against their limits, and that is the key here.

The movement of *The Odyssey*: in the tale, a man moves toward home, slowly loses everything, all of his crew, ships, until he is totally alone. At the same time, he loses his identity. He is moving through a monomythic adventure, has many adventures, always moving to wrest life, Penelope, from death, the one hundred and twenty suitors. In the myth, the gods are in the background, especially Athena and Poseidon, fighting each other, fighting the mortals, but they, in the end, do not really affect the action. It is Odysseus's story, not theirs. Why, then, are the gods present? It is a rite of passage, of a man moving to fullness, moving to identity, a man struggling for his humanity, finding his limitations, struggling against these. Slowly, the man is bereft of everything, name, wealth, friends, support. He is alone, on the boundaries, liminal, peripheral, moving across the earth and into the bowels of the earth, touching his past, struggling against forces greater than he, depending on his wit (Odysseus as the trickster), slowly moving to the end, his goal, his wife, his life, his name. At the same time, his son, Telemachus, is struggling for his own identity: his movement takes place with that of his father, appropriately.

A hero is a human moving through change and carrying the identity of the society with him. The hero epic is really a story of the social being writ large. Gilgamesh and Odysseus are both moving to an understanding of their limits, both are fighting this. With Gilgamesh, the second pattern is the epic pattern: his quest for Enkidu / immortality is equivalent to Odysseus's quest for Penelope / identity. Along the way, they learn and refuse to give up. At the heart of the epic is the story, the Bearson story. There is a struggle for life during which a man moves to the boundaries, is alone, and through his wit in the end prevails. It is the monomythic adventure, with a movement into the bowels of hell in all cases, where strange and otherworldly characters are met, their psyches unfettered. And in these contexts, the hero struggles, with himself, with his world, his desires, his limits. Always, there is something drawing him: Enkidu, Penelope. But our eye is on the struggle: that is where we find our definition of "hero." So it is not that Gilgamesh becomes our spokesman, our prototype for our own movement to mortality, so much as that he struggles against all odds for an elusive goal. That is where the heroic epic is to be found—not in the goal but in the struggle.

In working toward a definition of a hero, there are various considerations, including the trickster as an essential aspect of the hero, the amoral trickster energy in the many trickster tales crucial to the hero because it constitutes the energy that is necessary for the heroic charge. More than that, the trickster contains the potential for good or for ill, and a hero must make that choice. Once the choice is made, the hero shapes the trickster energy that can also easily shape him: he shapes it into his own particular brand of heroism. But he cannot be a hero without the trickster: the trickster gets his fame from shaping his world. In that newly shaped world, the hero is the one who shapes the trickster. A hero, then, may be defined as one who transforms or shapes his world: he cannot do so without the trickster within him.

If the tale character charts the way for the hero, if the gods provide the hero with celestial marching orders, it is for the trickster-in-the-hero to provide the energy that will drive the idealism of the heroic figure. The monomythic design is one that we all experience, as we move through the stages of our numerous rites of passage. What elevates this monomythic design to heroism? The trickster in his cycles moves through the monomyth and the stages of the rites of passage as well, but in his own clownish, often humorous, often ruinous ways. What can this mocking monomyth have to do with the hero? When we read or hear about the hero, he is already defined. We have not seen what it is that conspired to form this hero. The ingredients must surely include the tale character, because that will be our means of recognizing the hero as one of us. Those ingredients must contain the gods, because the lofty heavenly beings provide a mythic context for the hero. Most important, the ingredients involve the trickster and his low-level antics. Between the tale and the myth is the heroic epic. What places the hero between everyman and the gods is the trickster.

Consider Troy and Odysseus the trickster: seeking to gain entrance into Troy, clever Odysseus with the aid of Athena ordered a large wooden horse to be built. Its insides were to be hollow so that soldiers could hide within it. Once the statue had been built by the artist, Epeius, a number of the Greek warriors climbed inside with Odysseus. The rest of the Greek fleet sailed away, to deceive the Trojans. One man, Sinon, was left behind. When the Trojans came to marvel at the huge creation, Sinon pretended to be angry with the Greeks, stating that they had deserted him. He assured the Trojans that the wooden horse was safe and would bring luck to the Trojans. Only two people, Laocoon and Cassandra, spoke out against the horse, but they were ignored. The Trojans celebrated what they thought was their victory, and dragged the wooden horse into Troy. That night, after most of Troy was asleep or in a drunken stupor, Sinon let the Greek warriors out from the horse, and they slaughtered the Trojans. Priam was killed as he huddled by Zeus's altar and Cassandra was pulled from the statue of Athena and raped.

Odysseus the trickster now moves to a liminal area, as he is tricked by the gods, Poseidon and Athena. Poseidon tricks Odysseus as the Trojan hero moves toward his home in Ithaca, creating various distractions and impediments that slowly result in the dismantling of the hero, until in the end he is alone and powerless. Then Athena tricks him into moving to Ithaca and becoming involved in his wife's domestic quarrels. The trickery of the gods moves Odysseus from immortal hero to domesticity, to a husband caught in a wife's dispute. Small wonder that the final acts of Odysseus are so vicious. The storytellers are the trickster-gods Poseidon and Athena: Odysseus merely reads the script.

Part Three

The Hero, with the
Trickster at the Center

THE HERO'S JOURNEY

The hero's journey, the ancient monomyth, is the great paradigm. It clearly is so for Gilgamesh, for Mwindo, Sundiata, Beowulf, Odysseus . . . But it is also the model for Legba, for the Winnebago Hare. Or are they the paradigm for the hero? Legba is a god with such disgusting trickster qualities. Hare is a trickster with decidedly heroic potential.

The hero's journey figures into this paradigm. Sunjata, born a least-likely hero, unable to walk, moves into his monomythic transformation to hero when he leaves home with the two emblems of his identity, his mother and his griots. Together, the mother and the griots provide Sunjata with an identity that becomes fulfilled and complete in the characters of his sister and the villain Sumanguru: these are the warring sides of Sunjata, and in the competition between them Sunjata is able to put down the Sumanguru within him and move to the sister . . . in precisely the same way that Mwindo, in his journey, struggles between the Shemwindo and Iyangura within him. Along the way, they are tested, and along the way they move into myth . . . Sunjata with the sorcerers and the supernatural qualities of Sumanguru, Mwindo with the various supernatural characters he meets along the way and especially in the end with the gods in the heavens.

The hero's journey: and this journey moves on the earth but it has mythic overtones and consequences. Odysseus moves into Hades, and is constantly placed within the context of gods warring for his soul . . . Athena and Poseidon, who, in the end, are no different from Iyangura and Shemwindo, from the sister and Sumanguru. Each has tests along the way, Mwindo with the people of

Tubondo, with Muisa the aardvark, Sheburungu the dragon; Sunjata with his brothers, the iron rods test, the trousers and beeswax and silk-cotton tree tests. And Gilgamesh with Enkidu, Humbaba, the Bull of Heaven.

Transformation, the hero's journey, the monomyth, the rites of passage: the movement of the hero is through a difficult terrain marked by tests and tasks, by villainy and traps, by various experiences that test his heroism and shape him . . . a journey, in short, through the trickster energies within him. In John Gardner's 1971 novel, *Grendel*, roles are reversed, the villain becomes the hero, the hero the outsider . . . but the movement remains the same: difficulties, possibilities of heroism, ideals, experimenting with possibilities.[30]

The hero's monomyth[31] is also that of the tale character, of god, of the trickster. What does this mean? What, then, differentiates the hero from these other characters, from God and mere mortal and the trickster? It is this: the hero is the grand embodiment of all of these, as the epic is the gathering-together of tale and myth and history. The hero is the summary and the sum of the oral tradition: he reveals the interplay of characters in the oral tradition, he exposes the alchemy of the griot, the poet, the bard: take the hero apart and you have equal parts God, tale character, historical character, and trickster. Put these together and you have a mortal tale-character who is tormented by the basest aspects of his psyche and exalted by the most sublime. Put these together and you see the hero in an epic confrontation with his grossest elements and with his purest. The fact is that one cannot understand the hero without taking the demon into fullest consideration, and one cannot comprehend the nature of the hero if one omits the factor of God. The monomyth is nothing more nor less than the hero's movement to the great battlefield of his psyche, where the epic confrontation occurs, the struggle between a mortal and his demons as that mortal seeks to touch the heavens. It is this combination of creative and destructive forces that characterizes the hero . . . and, interestingly, the trickster as well. And it is at that moment, when he is locked in combat with the demons and angels of his being, that the hero is, paradoxically, most free.

Freedom plays a crucial part in epic. The part of heroic epic that most excites and attracts is not the heroic end—that is, the messianic part of the hero. Nor is it the least-likely-hero beginning, that is, the Cinderella part of the hero. Rather, it is what goes on in between. This is the area of the heroic epic that is the place of the trickster, therefore the place of the gods and the place of the demons: it is the area where the hero's destructive and creative potentials are bared, where he is most liminal, most vulnerable. The energies have not yet been enlisted for good or for ill, and perhaps they never will be: they are being formed here, in this neither/nor place, this betwixt-and-between place. The hero is at that moment on the boundaries and, as a liminal character, he is for that moment, and no other, free. It is a fearful time, an exhilarating time, a time when one feels most harrowingly alive. If we avoid that moment of exhilaration, that quintessential sense of freedom, we end up like the man in Nadine Gordimer's story, "The Soft Voice of the Serpent" (see Epilogue): seeking to avoid reality, seeking to create a world safe from reality. That is the effort, but the trickster intervenes . . . and suddenly, fearfully, the man experiences freedom. This is what defines the hero: he is most fulfilled as a human being during this time that he is most fragmented, most incomplete, most vulnerable, when he is, paradoxically, least fulfilled. That is the enigma of the hero, that is what defines him, that is what brings hero and trickster into unsettled union, that is where freedom lies. And, if we accept Grendel's argument that the bard's epic productions are all lies, this may also be the place where our only truth can be found.

It is in John Gardner's *Grendel* that the role of the bard is seen most obviously. That role is also seen in the *Sunjata/Sundiata* epics and in *Beowulf*. The poet is the "memory scraper." The grand mead-hall, the hall of Heorot, was built "by the power of his songs." We see the "old Shaper" through the eyes of his enemy, Grendel's eyes: the poet was "a man I cannot help but admire." It was the poet who "would sing the glory of Hrothgar's line and gild his wisdom and stir up his men to do more daring deeds." Even to Grendel, he "made it all seem true and very fine." Grendel watched "men gone mad on art." When the poet spoke, "They would seize the oceans, the farthest stars, the deepest secret rivers": such was the power of the bard. "[R]inging phrases, magnificent, golden, and all of them, incredibly, lies. What was he? The man had changed the world, had torn up the past by its thick, gnarled roots and had transmuted it, and then, who knew the truth, remembered it his way—and so did I." Grendel was "torn apart by poetry." When "The Harper sang . . . I listened. I knew very well that all he said was ridiculous, not light for their darkness but flattery, illusion, a vortex pulling them from sunlight to heat." Grendel observes, "He reshapes the world. . . . So his name implies. He stares strange-eyed at the mindless world and turns dry sticks to gold." The poet was "always transforming the world with words—changing nothing. . . ." And Grendel was converted: "I was addicted. The Shaper was singing the glorious songs of the dead men, praising war. He sang how they'd fought me. It was all lies." And Grendel was impressed: "It was a cold-blooded lie that a god had lovingly made the world. . . . Yet he, the old Shaper, might make it true, by the sweetness of his harp, his cunning trickery. It came to me with a fierce jolt that I wanted it." Or does a sense of heroism go beyond the bard? Hear Grendel once more:

"Heroism is more than noble language, dignity. Inner heroism, that's the trick! Glorious carbuncle of the soul! Except in the life of the hero the whole world's meaningless."

What the bard does is take our demons and our angels and create an epic out of them. In the process, he sees a halcyon ending, he sees Nirvana, heaven, Eden, Valhalla, the achievement of an end that is at once positive and filled with promise, that is, in short, heroic. But in the process, the battlefield is littered with corpses, with the flotsam and jetsam of the struggle. Moving away from this carnage, the hero walks defiantly into the sunset. But make no mistake about it, those corpses, that flotsam and jetsam, the detritus of battle are a part of the hero, a part of heroism, a part of the epic adventure, a part of the monomyth. Shemwindo, Soumaoro, Grendel, Polyphemus: these are forever a part of those who vanquished them, just as surely as Enkidu is forever a part of Gilgamesh. In the epic, we have seen our demons, and they are us. It is left to the bard to orchestrate this great struggle and to give it the gloss that gives us hope. The reason we will not, cannot, let go of the hero, of the hero's epic, is because to do so would be to admit to one of our deepest fears: that we really are no better than the demons in us, that the demons are inexorably a part of us. We laugh at the trickster, knowing full well that he belongs to us. We hiss at the demon, realizing in our deepest being that we hiss at ourselves. The epic confrontation brings these characters that we harbor into struggle, and the epic assures us that we can triumph over these inner forces. It is, as Grendel says, all lies . . . but it is all we have. We cannot do without the poet: he gives us the illusion of victory.

At the same time, the poet gives us a more promising message, and that is the message of the battle itself. We may indeed be possessed of demons, the trickster is indeed characteristic of us. But the struggle, the battle, the epic confrontation: we can find our hope in that. If the end is an illusion, the struggle is not, and it is in the struggle that we can escape the reality of our demons and the illusions of the poet: it is in the struggle that we can find our freedom. . . .

What does the rite of passage have to do with the heroic epic of Beowulf? or with Mwindo? Epics grow out of the narrative traditions, grow out of an epic matrix, an epic framework; the artist creates a single image from this epic or two or three. The epic will be seen in its rich context and will be constructed within the context of other narratives that cluster about this particular hero or heroic attitude. In *The Mwindo Epic*, a variety of parallel image sets occurs leading to and from the central event in the performance, that event in which the three (father, son, and sacred aunt) are elevated on chairs before their subjects. As the narrative proceeds, details of marriage and other cultural activities are included, but there can be little doubt that the emphasis is on Mwindo's assumption of the chieftaincy and what this chieftaincy means. Also involved in this central thematic movement is the transformation of Mwindo from a boasting trickster into a responsible chief. Two transformations occur, then: that of Mwindo, and that of the chieftaincy, for Shemwindo the father obviously stands for a certain kind of chieftaincy, and Mwindo the son stands for quite another. The shaping influences on Mwindo are Iyangura his aunt and the various forces of Nature but especially Nkuba Lightning. Mwindo changes, chieftaincy changes, and these perceptual processes are as usual caught up with the developmental; Mwindo's subduing of his father also means the changing of the meaning of the chieftaincy. When Mwindo pursues his father, he does so as an already altered man, this change represented by the cord that is tied from this hero to his aunt. And the change is dramatized; Mwindo destroys, and that is the old order, but Mwindo gives life, and that is the new. Mwindo takes property, but he restores it. Slowly, an ideal kind of chief is being externalized here. That ideal is dramatically juxtaposed against the old kind of chief, the father, Shemwindo. It also contrasts with what Mwindo himself is at the beginning, and remains to a certain extent throughout, for the narrative represents a learning experience for Mwindo. The killing of the dragon, which occurs at the end of the epic, is as much a part of this lesson as his earlier destruction of the underworld characters and their property. The parallel sets reflect similar activities, but there is a gradual movement toward awareness on the part of the hero, and also of course on the part of the members of the audience.

7

Mwindo

THE MWINDO EPICS[32]

C. M. Bowra asserts that poets in Africa "seem unwilling or unable to construct songs of heroic action which are enjoyable for their own sake and not some kind of summons to action or an instrument of personal use." He writes of "some African peoples, who delight to honor victorious achievements but address their poems to single real persons and compose especially for them." Such poetry, he contends, comes "from people who have no heroic poetry and have never advanced beyond panegyric and lament. The intellectual effort required for such an advance seems to have been beyond their powers." He refers to the Zulu oral tradition, labeling the poetry "simple and primitive, the expression of an immediate, violent excitement." This poetry, while expressing "a heroic ideal of an advanced kind," is nevertheless "still confined to panegyric," which "does not often attain any length and certainly does not compare in scale with long heroic poems." The poet "does not conceive of great events in an objective setting. Indeed," Bowra concludes, "this restriction of outlook may be why African tribes have in general no heroic poetry. The present so absorbs and occupies them that they feel no need to traffic with the past and the imaginary."[33] That both of these judgments fell short of accurately describing the realities of African artistic achievement has been underscored dramatically in the past four decades by the publication of a range of epic performances, available for the first time to audiences outside Africa. "The time when Bowra . . . or Finnegan . . . could question the existence of the epic genre in Africa," writes Daniel Biebuyck, "has long ended."[34] Even allowing for the relative scarcity of African epic texts in the West at the time that Bowra wrote his book (1952), however, there were materials that might have given him pause, an excellent version of the Malagasy epic *Conte d' Ibonia*, for example, published in 1939 in French translation and presumably available to him.[35]

Ironically, in this version of the Malagasy epic, panegyric and imaginative heroic narrative interweave: the section in which Ranakombe considers names for his son rhythmically moves between the father's eloquent and prophetic eulogies and the child's pompous refusals to accept the names. The panegyric segment is an integral part of the heroic action of the epic, one genre (which Bowra mistakenly concludes was the African equivalent of epic) merged with another. This blending is not, of course, restricted to African oral traditions; Bowra observes that it existed in the traditions of "the Greeks, the Germanic and Slavonic peoples, the Asiatic Tatars, and some peoples of the Caucasus,"[36] oral traditions that, because of the presence of both genres, he considered more advanced than those of African peoples. Recent research and a growing amount of oral epic material now in print have clearly established African epic as a form comparable to that of Homer, the Gilgamesh and Beowulf bards, the Popul Vuh and Mahabharata poets. Versions of the Sunjata epic, for example, have been collected by Gordon Innes and D. T. Niane, performances by Bamba Susu, Banna Kanute, Dembo Kanute, and Djeli Mamoudou Kouyate;[37] and the Ozidi saga as performed by the Ijo bard Okabou Ojobolo has been transcribed and translated by the Ijo poet and playwright John Pepper Clark.[38] Much significant research on the epic has been carried out in Central Africa, in Rwanda and Zaire, by such scholars as A. Coupez, A. de Rop, G. Hulstaert, John Jacobs, Alexis Kagame, Th. Kamanzi, Patrice Mafuta, and Jan Vansina. Similar work has been done among the Soninke, Swahili, Adangme, Fang, and Xhosa.[39]

Few scholars have been more active in this area of research than Daniel P. Biebuyck, H. Rodney Sharp Professor of Anthropology and Humanities at the University of Delaware. His work on the Nyanga epic, begun almost as an avocation ("During my extensive field research among the Nyanga, I had no intention of setting the detailed study of their oral literature as my major goal," [ix]), has become important in the analysis of African oral performance and the study of epic generally. A Nyanga narrative performed by Candi Rureke, *The Mwindo Epic*, published in 1969 and edited by Biebuyck and Kahombo C. Mateene, is a symmetrically designed work describing the movement of a self-serving hero to humanistic chieftaincy.

Hero and Chief is an invaluable counterpart to Rureke's work; it contains three variants of the Mwindo epic by three Nyanga poets, Shekwabo, Nkuba Shekarisi, and Sherungu. In addition to the full epics, there are summaries of other versions of the Mwindo story in a section entitled "The Bards" and in the appendices. Biebuyck brings to this volume the same painstaking scholarship that he and Mateene brought to the first.

To enable the reader to experience the epics in a rich cultural and artistic context, Biebuyck supplies useful data about the cultural content of the epics, about the characters and places, about formulas and stylistic qualities of the narratives.[40] There is also a study of the bard, Mr. Sherungu. Biebuyck asked him to "dictate his memoirs" to assistants, and the result was an autobiography that "covers 3,456 closely written pages." Biebuyck adds, "To my great surprise it was in this context that he provided me with the text of epic IV" (12).

Of the many questions raised by these variants of a single epic, one of the most persistent for Biebuyck is the relationship between the images in the epics and the realities of Nyanga history and culture. Biebuyck returns to the subject often. Initially, he seems to have unequivocal views about this linkage. In *The Mwindo Epic*, he and Mateene argue that "The content of the epic is a rich survey of customs, institutions, activities, behavior patterns, values, material objects that are of main significance to the Nyanga. It is, in fact, a synopsis of Nyanga culture."[41] Biebuyck later makes this point even more forcibly: "The content of the epic constitutes an encyclopedic inventory of the most diverse aspects of a people's culture." He contends that "There are direct and indirect statements about the history, the social institutions and social relationships, the material culture, and the system of values and ideas."[42] But the images are refractory, prismatic, metaphorical; they are also fragmented and selective, so mingled with fantasy and the fabulous that their historical and cultural value becomes questionable.

In *Hero and Chief*, Biebuyck seems to narrow the earlier comparatively bold statements about the relationship: "The Nyanga epics are vast storehouses packed with diverse cultural information," he repeats, but "such an inventory," he cautions, is "far from complete. . . . Nyanga culture is too intricate to be synthesized in a single set of literary documents. Like all other texts, the epics are selective: the information they give is limited, incomplete, and imprecise." Not only that, "Certain broad aspects of Nyanga culture are lacking. The epics contain no reference to the elaborate circumcision rites or to the multiple initiations into membership in voluntary associations and cults," for example. Furthermore, "Because the epics describe some aspects of Nyanga culture more elaborately than others, they tend to give an unbalanced view of its constituent parts." Finally, "despite their pervasive cultural significance, the epics would not provide enough information for a detailed and balanced ethnography of the Nyanga people" (34–35). The epics, he argues, "are not designed as rigidly accurate treatises" (68). They do "tell much about Nyanga history," but they do so "indirectly, and in symbolic form" (41). If the epics do not recreate history or provide an encyclopedia of culture, they do evoke an attitude toward history and culture, and the position that they take on change in human affairs becomes a definition of heroism. Two categories of imagery exist in all imaginative tales: the real and the fantastic, representing respectively the present and the past. If there is to be a hero, he becomes representative of both categories of imagery. In the tale, there is no contradiction between his existence in the two worlds; in the epic, however, there is. The tale frequently has a hero potential; when that potential has been achieved, tale becomes epic. But no matter what its label, epic is always created within the tale tradition of form and image. The linkage between epic and reality evolves from these concepts of hero and heroism, and from the formal arrangement of the imagery having to do with them.

As with panegyric (which is usually shorter than epic and in which historical linearity, at times apparently totally absent in epic and even when present not the cardinal organizing device, plays a crucial part), the performer of epic by taking a position determines the theme of the narrative. By subtle alterations of non-epic tale composition, epic poetry generates a heroic view, often provocative and sometimes uncomfortable, about the nature of culture and history. Utilizing images from the familiar real world, performers bring their audiences to re-experience these images in new and unfamiliar environments, a fantasy world of dragons and underworld demons, of impossible deeds and coincidences that tax credulity. Oral narrative and poetry are part of the myth-making capacity of the oral traditions: real-world experiences are placed into an artistic form, and in that novel context are given new meanings. The tale frequently focuses on moments of stress in individual human lives, rites of passage, for example, during which people undergo significant changes of identity. It falls to the epic to reveal such changes on a more monolithic scale, and in the process to celebrate the culture's sense of the heroic, and to invest that quality in the loftiest position humans can hold in the society. Among the Nyanga, this is the chieftaincy.

The solution to the problem of the relationship between real-world images and those of an art tradition begins with the formal characteristics of non-epic tale and their continued influence on the composition of epic. Rhys Carpenter sees "An underlying and all-pervasive folktale" in Homer's epic, giving the work "a narrative tone through all fictional adornment and epic development." He concludes, "If we excise from the Odyssey all that is borrowed from the heroic trappings of the Tale of Troy, we shall have a folk tale ingeniously converted into a novella, a story of quasi-contemporary human incident."[43] Denys Page notes, "The theme of the Odyssey . . . is an adaptation of a folktale—the common and widespread tale of the husband who returns home after many years;

finds that his wife has been faithful despite trials and temptations; and is now so changed in appearance that he must prove his identity by tests and tokens."[44]

The close ties between tale and epic have also been noted in African oral tradition. Christiane Seydou, writing of the Peul epic *Silâmaka et Poullôri*, observes,

> On y reconnaît une exploitation judicieuse de la technique théâtrale et de celle du conte, du récit, habilement combinées. . . .
>
> Si cette épopée commence comme un conte les personnages antagonistes étant présentés dans la situation qui porte en germe tout le dénouement—, une fois posées les données, la technique du conte fait peu à peu place à celle du théâtre avec la scène du combat contre le serpent.[45]

Biebuyck comments that Nyanga *karisi*, or epic, is distinguished by the Nyanga people "from other, well-isolated categories of literature such as the tales with or without a mysterious content (*uano*, *mushinga*), the 'true' stories (*kishambaro*), the narration of extraordinary events that happened to particular individuals (*nganuriro*), and other genres."[46] The *uano*, Biebuyck and Mateene write in the introduction to *The Mwindo Epic*, "is a tale in general," while the *mushinga* is "a tale where the supernatural element, produced by the intervention of divinities, celestial bodies, monsters, and forest specters, stand in the foreground." These stories "are narrated, partly sung, mimed, and partly dramatized on a great variety of domestic, legal, ritual occasions to entertain, to instruct, to explain, to moralize" (9–10).

But *karisi*, the long epic narrative, is unique: it is not *uano* or *mushinga* grown large. The "epic texts are few in number and are known to only a small number of men." This select group will "participate in the performance, transmission, and preservation of the epic form" and the "patterns of transmission of epic are . . . determined by kinship and friendship" (11–12). Still, although epic is a distinct category, it "incorporates most literary forms known to the Nyanga, in both poetry and prose. . . . The protagonist is a human hero . . . but he is surrounded by almost all categories of dramatis personae found in the tales" (14). The distinction blurs: epic is a unique genre, yet it partakes of the imagery and the forms of the tale. *The Mwindo Epic* echoes through many African tale traditions, the quest for a bride, the suitor test, and the duel with the bride's father. Its bewildering blend of trickster, culture hero, and hero in a single character can also be seen in the San saga of Mantis, a character who embodies both destructive and creative energies.[47] The tale of the contrasting good brother (or sister) and the bad, common throughout Africa and beyond, is the basis for Epic IV. Such tales have the potential of being worked into longer narratives with heroic themes. The various Mwindos who move through the four epics provide a valuable set of clues to the relationship between epic and tale, which seems as close in African traditions as, for example, among the Greeks. The link, a complex one, seems to hinge at least partially on the concept of heroism.

Biebuyck's model of the Nyanga hero is a demanding one, and the Mwindo character in the four epics does not always fit that mold. "The hero," he argues in *Hero and Chief*,

> is more than an audacious and vigorous youth . . . ; he is a performer of perplex-ing deeds. . . . He is a producer of wonder . . . as common people are not. . . . The hero is constantly plunged into difficulties and hardships . . . ; he is tested and tormented . . . ; he is capable of escaping dangers . . . and of safeguarding himself. . . . He possesses the plenitude of manhood . . . ; he is conscious of his power; his only aim is to be victorious.

Heroism among the Nyanga also has a moral component, and the hero bears a message of "progress toward social order, peace, good living, and the resulting glory and fame." His "ultimate status is that of 'eternal savior of people'" (93–94).

The hero of Epic I does indeed fit this demanding description. Those of Epics II, III, and IV, however, seem unable to meet this heroic measure. Biebuyck argues that the hero is invulnerable, "in control of his own death," yet he can also be defeated, even killed, and he is unable at times to control his enemies and to retain the allegiance of his followers. He is now heroic, now a boasting and even repulsive trickster; he is shrewd, but also stupid. "The hero," Biebuyck concludes, "displays many contradictions of character" (103). The contradictions of the epic hero emanate to some degree from an apparent merg-ing of trickster and hero characters from the tale tradition. Epic heroes are not as strongly defined as central characters usually are in tales; they are ambiguous, strong yet weak, heroic yet guileful. Is it possible that one so lofty, noble, and virtuous can merge with one so low, so crafty and scurrilous? The foolish antics of Trickster, even when he is being a creative culture bringer, never really dupli-cate the courageous actions of the hero as he confronts dragons and other vil-lains. Like the hero, the trickster is, as noted, a slippery character, now behaving meritoriously, now shamefully decadent; he is a god, a savior, he transforms and creates, but he also destroys. He is most often indifferent to the suffering that he causes, yet he can also be compassionate. Both the trickster in the tale and the hero in the epic are ambiguous, contradictory, and at the outer limits of their ambiguities and contradictions, the borderline between them grows indistinct and they become one.

The Nyanga Mwindo hardly seems a swashbuckling hero, even in Epic I. To be sure, he kills a dragon and releases a captive people. He subdues his recalcitrant father and overwhelms his father's allies, and he earns the admiration of his stern aunt, Iyangura. But much of his martial success is achieved with his magical conga scepter, an external supernatural aid. And when he kills the dragon, an apparently heroic act, he is immediately severely criticized for it, and his heroism assumes puny significance.

It is a rather unlikely gaggle of heroes: there is arrogance, bluster, rodomontade; there is cowardice, trickery, knavery. More important, there is vulnerability, mortality. Do these figures, with feet so obviously formed of clay, truly represent the best that their societies can boast?

Are we to accept the indifferent rake of Uruk as a subject of heroic adulation?

Vulnerability seems in fact to be a necessary characteristic of the hero in the epics, even a requisite qualification for heroism. Mwindo plays the role of the trickster in most versions of the story, the boasting scrapper not even seeming to evolve heroically in some of the versions, in others maturing and developing, always with the assistance of others. As long as he remains the trickster, he is within the tale tradition. As much as anything, it is the quality of vulnerability that distinguishes the epic hero from the central character of the tale. Both have agents or extensions that render them invulnerable, but in the epic these forces can always be overcome. Even with such supernatural aids as the conga scepter, there must always be the chance that the hero can lose, the hero can die.

Is he then a hero? Biebuyck thinks not. He argues that the hero is guided by a form of fatalism: "The hero never dies. His highest destiny is to become a chief, and he cannot escape it" (105). Earlier, he insists, "The hero is not a man of hatred; instead, he is usually forgiving and conciliatory. Physical excesses are not his hallmark. . . . He is neither a brute nor a vile killer" (103). Yet Mwindo is all of these at times. Biebuyck contends,

The contradictions in character are understandable in terms of Mwindo's dual personality (epics I, II, III): as a hero he is rough, unpolished, and, in Nyanga terms, uninitiated; as the heroic son of a chief he carries within himself the destiny to become a chief, that is a person who is purified and a true initiate. It is this counterbalancing of opposites which leads him to purification and makes him acceptable as a chief. (104)

But it seems difficult to make this point with any confidence for Epics II, III, and IV. It works well for Epic I. What to do with these other untidy epics? Biebuyck attempts through his footnotes to nudge their errant Mwindo into the Epic I heroic mold, but the trickster will not stay there. Yet all four narratives are said by the Nyanga to be *karisi*.

In a San narrative, Mantis unleashes a malignant force, the All-devourer, in much the same way that Mwindo in Epic II brings a deadly bird to life from an egg and nourishes it. The evil force is in both cases a product of the hero, a force that must then be brought under control by the very person who released it (in the San narrative, the children of Mantis must accomplish this task). These destructive and creative powers are as much a part of the contradictory nature of the hero as the trickster and heroic qualities in which they have their genesis. The trickster hero, the audience learns, can go either way, destroying or creating; he is a volatile figure, and it is the forces that operate on him from outside that will determine his destiny. That destiny, and the central character's heroism, grow out of his frailty and vulnerability.

The hero is involved in a struggle, and in the Mwindo epics, while it is ostensibly a move toward the chieftaincy, it is as much a struggle with the hero's internal nature, this energy that knows no direction, as with external forces. These latter sometimes seem to be the dramatic embodiments of Mwindo's internal struggle, and tensions between them result as the one seeks to mold the other. As Mwindo subdues the Shemwindo outside himself in Epic I, for example, he tames and channels the dangerous trickster qualities within himself; the two, Shemwindo and Mwindo's nature, become one. It is the same metaphorical combination that operates in many African literary works that have been influenced by the oral tradition. Thomas Mofolo's *Chaka*[48] is a work of literature that grows out of the oral tradition of the Sotho and Zulu people of southern Africa. This novel has as its main character a historical figure, the Zulu king Shaka, who is surrounded by supernatural companions. Again, the artist blends images reflecting reality and fantasy. The historical personage is vulnerable, the supernatural comrades are not; together, they become a virulent team, invincible as long as their aims remain common. The one becomes a part of the other. But when deviations of purpose occur, when the hero's character begins to move away from identification with the unnatural powers, he is doomed. The hero is fully fleshed, the supernatural characters are allegorical; the combination does not adversely affect the experience of the tale because of the unity achieved between the human hero and the fantastic forces of the supernatural team. They are perceived by the audience as a single entity, purely evil powers and purely positive influences, facets of the human character's psyche and world.

The blending of allegory and realism operates in Nyanga epic also; and, because the causes, allegorically expressed, of Mwindo's heroism or anti-heroism are worked into his nature, the possibilities for tragedy are always present. The external characters act on the hero to alter his character in one direction or another at the same time that they graphically express his dual nature. Iyangura and Shemwindo are the opposing forces in Epic I, as Isanusi and Noliwe are antagonistic forces in the character of Shaka. It is not so much Mwindo as the epic struggle that is heroic. The distinction is an important one. The three new versions of the Mwindo epic in *Hero and Chief* generate uneasy questions about the nature of epic, of the hero, and of heroism. When compared with Epic I, they seem disconcertingly unheroic. Mwindo seems altered, sometimes even leaving the narrative for lengthy periods. In Epic II, for example, after his expedition to the buffaloes, his follower, Shekaruru, becomes the major character, and, while his relationship with Mwindo is maintained, and while it may be argued that in this sense he is but an extension of Mwindo, we nevertheless follow his activities, his hunting expedition, not Mwindo's. Moreover, when the dragon, Kirimu, is destroyed in the same version of the epic, it is conquered not by Mwindo, as in Epic I, but by a young trapper who is avenging the death of his brother. That event is followed by another hunt, again led by the trapper and not by Mwindo. Then we turn to Shekaruru's further activities. In the end, Mwindo is installed as chief, but fully half of the epic has been given over to his followers and their adventures. In Epic III, this imbalance takes another turn: it is not Mwindo but his followers who deal with his enemy, Chief Mutero Murimba, and they do so by giving that chief their allegiance. In Epic IV, the theme of heroism seems to emanate from Little-one-just-born-he-walked rather than from Mwindo.

Epic I reveals a theme of humaneness, describing the movement of a hero who begins as a swaggering character with enormous energy but with little social conscience: "Look!" Mwindo cries, "You are impotent against Mwindo, / Mwindo the Little-one-just-born-he-walked. / He who will go up against me, it is he who will die on the way" (66). This is the early Mwindo. Ahead of him lie his aquatic journey, his subterranean quest for his fleeing father, and his celestial journey. Each of these adventures repeats the theme of the epic, and that lesson that he learns on the earth, in the water, and beneath the earth is summarized for him in the heavens. He is told that "there is no room for your heroism . . . there is no room for your pride." He is given a final order by Lightning, Rain, Sun, and Star: "never a day should you kill an animal of the forest or of the village or even an insect" (138). This theme is revealed early, in Mwindo's relationship with Iyangura, his aunt, who imbues him with her qualities of gentleness and understanding, and a sense of reverence for living creatures. She becomes Mwindo's other self, as the greedy, egotistical Shemwindo is for a time reflective of the trickster, Mwindo.

The centerpiece of this version of the epic occurs when Shemwindo, Iyan-gura, and Mwindo appear "in the middle of the gathering of the assembly" on chairs lowered from the sky by Nkuba Lightning (121–22). The triumphant, symbolic scene suggests the interlocking relationship of the three characters, already suggested in the first part of Epic I in the tensions between Mwindo and his wicked father, and the rapport between the hero and his virtuous aunt. This triumvirate embodies the theme of the epic and anticipates the didacticism that Mwindo must endure in the celestial region. The lesson, learned a number of times in the narrative, seems curiously lacking in Epic II.

In the second epic, there is no change in the nature of the hero, and the quality of heroism so crucial to all epic seems to be lacking. Mwindo is absent from much of the narrative, and significant events in Epic I do not appear in Epic II; the relationship, for example, between Mwindo and Lightning in Epic II is simply that between a character and his supernatural agent, much as happens in the tale. In Epic I, Lightning is Mwindo's friend and protector, but he is also a stern teacher. With other manifestations of natural phenomena, Lightning teaches Mwindo the first lesson of Nature, that it is not to be tampered with. In Epic II, Mwindo remains to the end a trickster-hero characterized by bravado and self-adulation:

> he made a proclamation, saying, "You, Masters-of-the-subterranean-world, you who are on earth and you who are in the sky, and you who are in air, come to appear here with me where I am; give me heroism and much force and honor to surpass the other so-and-so chiefs who are next to me" (*Hero and Chief*, 151)

There is little echo here of the cautionary "there is no room for your heroism" of Epic I.

It is true that in Epic I Mwindo brings his people back to life, he rebuilds their houses. But he remains the boasting trickster: "he said to himself that he, Mwindo, had not yet arrived at the place of God, being fully alive; that he was not himself, that it was befitting for him to first go and see God, so that he might meet with him. . . ." (152). Mwindo's ties in Epic II are with his hunting dogs, instruments of slaughter, a significant symbolic change perhaps from the humanism of Epic I.

The first epic ends with a series of statements about the chieftaincy, a sort of grand summation of the events of the narrative that has now come to an end:

> Heroism be hailed! But excessive callousness either pushes a man into a great crime or brings him a great one. Mutual agreement brings about kinship solidarity. . . .

Even if a man becomes a hero (so as) to surpass the others, he will not fail one day to encounter someone else who could crush him, who could turn against him what he was looking for. (*Mwindo Epic*, 144)

Epic III ends with similar statements:

He who is not advised among the people of the world is (like) a dead person. . . . If you hear that the land of a particular chief is famous, (it means) that he (the chief) is in harmony with his people. Lo! The land that has no chief, has no people, it dies; it is finished without hope of salvation. (*Hero and Chief*, 232)

But in Epic I the images themselves certify and underscore these didactic conclusions. This is not at all the case in Epic III, in which Mwindo remains the blusterer that he was from the start. He tells his follower, Meshemtuwa, not to spear a wild boar "without my having preceded you in striking it. Do you surpass me . . . ? I have finished killing and killing many, many animals: shall this wild boar outdo me?" (193–94). Even when Mwindo is to be punished by Nyamurairi, the chief of the subterranean world, "because he had killed masses and masses of animals," the similarity to Epic I, in which the hero is disciplined for his actions, is not sustained. Nyamurairi as the chief of the subterranean divinities might be expected to assume the educational chores that Lightning undertakes in Epic I. But this is not to be, as Mwindo seems not to learn. In the end, Nyamurairi does give Mwindo his daughter, and some advice, but he only warns Mwindo not to go against the rules of hunting (202–3). "Later, Mwindo continues his vaporing: 'I am the one, my mother! I have finished (the work) where I have gone. I have killed masses and masses of people and animals where I have gone'" (204n86). These are hardly the words of a chastened hero.

A follower refers to Mwindo as "chief, Mr. Rejoicer-of-people, who does not foster hatred—the conciliator, the good speaker who does not rest," a panegyric to the chief (205). Yet this is not the Mwindo we see in Epic III, and even though he shows, as Biebuyck notes, "the humility and fairness that are expected of a true chief" after Nyamwindo his mother has urged him to kill his followers, he will later abandon them (206n86). The self-praise so repugnant to the celestial beings in Epic I persists in Epic III as Mwindo confronts Mutero: "Surely, Mutero, you are not capable (of fighting) against me; I will cleave you into two parts." He sings "to praise himself: 'I have overcome the enemy / Where I have gone. / He who wants to die rapidly, / Let him climb upon me'" (213). He is a braggart even in the presence of Lightning, and in fact first insults and then actually fights and defeats Lightning (215), not at all like Epic I. Mwindo and Lightning then go off together to war against Nyakatwakari.

Mwindo decides not to kill Nyakatwakari; Biebuyck argues that he "belatedly shows generosity and humility by not killing her," implying "that in this way he saved his chieftaincy" (224n134). It is difficult to see that Mwindo has grown, that he has changed, that he is moving from the status of hero to that of chief. In fact, Mwindo's own followers now desert him because of his abandonment of them: "Look! our chief has gone. He hates us, saying that we are the reason he failed to marry a maiden" (22). They seek another chief, and find one, ironically, Mwindo's enemy, Mutero. "We no longer want to stay with [Mwindo]; we will go to settle with another chief." And Mutero shrewdly commiserates with them: "Come . . . to build where I am, so that you may no longer be accused of a big thing that you have not done. . . . And, if you stay close to me, I will know the one who would vex you, the one who would kill you for no reason" (226). And, for a time, as in Epic II, we leave Mwindo completely, and follow the activities of the more generous (and more heroic) chief, Mutero Murimba. Many details are lavished by the performer on the honoring of this chief. The movement toward chieftaincy is from Mwindo to Mutero, and Mutero gives to Mwindo's erstwhile followers the right to put their own chief on the throne. Only in the end do we return to Mwindo. As for the heroism of Mwindo and his fitness for the throne, that is merely suggested in the text and in Biebuyck's footnotes, but the images of the epic do not support this contention as they do in Epic I.

In Epic IV, there are no pretensions that Mwindo is heroic. He inherits his mother's hatred in this version (compare this with the love that he inherits from his aunt in Epic I), and is not fit to become a chief. He is regularly contrasted with his brother, Little-one-just-born-he-walked, who, as Biebuyck notes,

> exhibits the characteristics of a great leader: he does not act callously; he is generous in words and deeds; and he respects the seniority principle (for his brother [Mwindo] is automatically the senior as child of the ritual wife). (250n31)

Little-one-just-born-he-walked says, "Even though the ritual wife [Mwindo's mother] hates my mother, I am not with it [hatred]" (250). But Mwindo does not want the animals deferentially presented to him by Little-one-just-born-he-walked: "Return his animals! We do not want the animals from the child of a despised wife" (250–51). In a note, Biebuyck comments, "Mwindo shows signs of impetuosity, rashness, and thoughtlessness which are not indicative of true leadership and seniority" (251n32). And Little-one-just-born-he-walked himself later seems to offend tradition when he violates the rules of seniority by marrying before Mwindo does (252n36). In fact, Little-one-just-born-he-walked is the shrewd brother, Mwindo the stupid one, in a narrative formally based on a popular African tale about a pair of siblings with opposite characteristics.

The people can see who is the wiser of the two, and they select Little-one-just-born-he-walked as their leader:

> This Little-one-just-born-he-walked will become chief even though Mwindo is saying that he is going to fight with him. This Mwindo will be incapable against him. Your companion, the one who was born and who was walking, is not a weak person. (254)

There is something of the trickster in Little-one-just-born-he-walked, as he robs Mwindo of all his support. But he also has qualities of the hero: when Mwindo confronts his father with the question, "Who is the (true) son of the chief?" his father responds, "You are the chief designate. . . . However, he who will surpass his companion in intelligence, he is the one who will become chief" (255).

In Epic IV, there does not seem to be a movement of a central figure from hero to chief; instead, the performer presents two brothers engaged in a struggle for the chieftaincy. Mwindo remains the lesser of the two throughout the narrative: the jealous one, the impatient one, the pretender. It is not Mwindo's epic. The chief counselor comments that "a chief is not brought forth, that he to whom he likes to give it (the chieftainship) is chief designate" (249).

Epics I and IV have obvious heroes, Mwindo in the first, Little-one-just-born-he-walked in the second. Epics II and III seem less epic and less heroic. There is, to be sure, the requisite miraculous birth, and there is a quest. The quest for the father in Epic I becomes a quest for a bride in Epics II, III, and IV. The underworld relationship with Kahindo seems in Epic I incidental to the more significant search for Shemwindo. That hunt is only faintly echoed in Epic II: Mwindo, we are told, "was looking for his father, because Nyamurairi had hidden Shemwindo" (157). But that is the first we learn of the search for the father, and, once stated, the quest seems at once forgotten. Biebuyck notes that "the reasons for Mwindo's father being hidden by Nyamurairi are not spelled out in this epic," and concludes, "The Nyanga listener is not at all disturbed by such apparent inconsistencies" (157n67). But are these inconsistencies? Epic I is not, after all, the model for the other epics. Each of the four epics

has its own reason for being, its internal logic. One of these elements, for example, is not a quest for the father. The search for a wife forms the center of the
underworld movement in three of the epics: Kahindo̧ is present in all four,
related to a leader of the underworld with whom and for whatever reason
Mwindo must struggle—whether for a father or a bride seems not to be significant. It seems that the object of the struggle is not as important as the struggle
itself. Moreover, a mere adventurous cycle involving miraculous birth, quest,
success in the quest followed by accession to the throne is not enough to build
an epic. By itself, the cycle does not assure heroism; these four variants of *The
Mwindo Epic* would seem to indicate that.

The theme of heroism must be built into the various parts of the cycle and
into the structure. Consider these characteristics of the four epics: Mwindo's
praise name in Epic I is "Little-one-just-born-he-walked"; in Epic IV, the two
names become two characters. In Epic I, Mwindo's dual character is given form
in the separate distinct characters, Iyangura and Shemwindo. In Epic II,
Mwindo is absent for long periods of time, his place taken by his agents or
extensions. In Epic III, Mwindo is replaced in the loyalty of his followers by his
opposite, Mutero Murimba.

This is a significant formal characteristic of these narratives: characters strip
off one another, they merge, they move into and out of each other. Shemwindo
and Iyangura are, in one sense, parts of Mwindo; as separate characters, they
act as dramatic devices for our comprehension of the meaning of the central
character's movement from the one to the other, a set of concrete images that
dramatically reveals the heroic theme of the epic, the move from trickster to
hero to benevolent chief. Epic IV, then, can be seen as a further fragmenting
of character: Little-one-just-born-he-walked and Mwindo a single character in
Epic I and becoming two characters in Epic IV. If Iyangura and Shemwindo
are the embodiments of the destructive and creative potentials in Epic I, then
Mwindo is the neutral source of energy being acted upon. In Epic IV, Iyangura
and Shemwindo are replaced respectively by Little-one-just-born-he-walked
and Mwindo.

There is no pre-set Mwindo epic, except in one important respect: all versions of the epic generate a theme of potential heroism and chieftaincy. Many
of the same characters people the several epics, some becoming compound
characters, others fulfilling a variety of necessary roles that support the dualism from which the theme grows. Each epic reveals the theme in a different
way, but all of them utilize the basic oral narrative technique of fragmenting
the central character so that the critical parts of the thematic conflict themselves become characters, moving before the members of the audience in full

dimensionality but with such clearly defined qualities that they become almost allegorical.

If these four versions of the epic are any indication, the Nyanga performer has considerable latitude in the construction of the heroic narrative, taking as his basic raw material images and form from the tale tradition, with one of the tales usually acting as the spine and an organizing set of matrices for the working of the separate parts into a unified story. But the epic moves the materials that it shares with the tale to a new level of experience, merging the separate polar characters into a single character and thereby creating heroic themes. Fragmenting, characteristic of both tale and epic, links the four epics in the Biebuyck collection; though the characters seem at times to be anything but epic heroes, in the complex language of the epic the performer is dealing with sublime material.

If Epic I seems the most heroic of the four narratives, it is because Mwindo is so clearly invested with qualities of heroism in that version. If we concentrate on the character of Mwindo alone, Epic IV seems thoroughly unheroic, Mwindo being so ordinary and stupid as to be no opponent at all for the clever Little-one-just-born-he-walked. Similarly, the Mwindo of Epic III seems heroically inferior to his enemy, Mutero Murimba, and is certainly not heroic in the eyes of his disillusioned and abandoned followers.

Why are these Mwindos apparently inferior to the Mwindo who moves so heroically in Epic I? The answer to this question is to be found in the relationships of the various Mwindos to other characters. In Epic II, Mwindo begins to attain a stature thematically that he may not have in fact. In Epics II, III, and IV, the combinations become crucial: Mwindo and Shekaruru and the young trapper in Epic II, Mwindo and Mutero Murimba in Epic III, Mwindo and Little-one-just-born-he-walked in Epic IV. As we come to understand the significance of these combinations, we also can see why the Mwindo of Epic I is a character with such reverberating qualities: he does not act alone, his character can be seen only in its relation with Shemwindo and Iyangura. The theme of a heroic Mwindo, or a theme of heroism in which Mwindo is somehow involved (not necessarily as a hero, but as a catalyst to heroism), is revealed in those dramatic relations between characters who have been the same character all along.

Both tale and epic require polarized characters, good and evil, who, as noted, border on the allegorical. Mwindo is both creative and destructive: he moves from the one to the other, the basic movement in each of the four epics. When other cultural considerations become attached to these polarities, the narrative gains in complexity, and the theme of heroism broadens. That movement is achieved in different ways, with Mwindo always somehow involved. This movement is not the same as the cyclic actions of the narrative; it parallels the cycle, giving its images their resonance and meaning.

Always, we see the questionable character of Mwindo: the trickster. Inevitably, the narrative provides a foil to this negative Mwindo: Iyangura, Shekaruru and the trapper, Mutero Murimba, Little-one-just-born-he-walked. In the one case, Epic I, the polarities exist outside Mwindo, in Iyangura and Shemwindo. In the other three epics, Mwindo remains one of those polarities, always the negative, with other characters dramatizing the positive. Although Mwindo is not always heroic himself, then, the theme of heroism could not be achieved without him. He is a device, the means whereby the theme is revealed. His character is frequently a catalogue of social ills: the braggart and insolent leader, the egotist, the indiscriminate slaughterer of people and animals (with the mistaken notion that such actions are heroic). It is possible to use Epic I as the model for the other three narratives if we take as our measure not Mwindo, but Iyangura-Shemwindo; this combination becomes Mwindo-Shekaruru/young-trapper in Epic II, Mwindo-Mutero Murimba in Epic III, and Mwindo-Little-one-just-born-he-walked in Epic IV.

In all four of the Mwindo epics, the duality of Mwindo is expressed by a Mwindo fragmented into more than one character. An "old" Mwindo and a "new" Mwindo reveal the past and future concepts of the chieftaincy: in Epic I, the old Mwindo is Shemwindo and the new is Iyangura; in Epics II, III, and IV, the old Mwindo is contrasted with Shekaruru and the trapper with Mutero Murimba, and with Little-one-just-born-he-walked. Narrative action depends on the contrast between two or more characters, but the theme of heroism requires that the audience experience them as a single entity.

The fate of Mwindo is not necessarily tragic, but the negative Mwindo must give way so that the creative Mwindo can thrive. The central character becomes heroic because of his contradictions, whether expressed in a single character or in fragments of his character; and because the contradictions are so integral to epic, they represent the major break with the tale. The hero is necessarily vulnerable, for he is doomed: he must be able to die, or at least a part of him must be able to die, so that the new can be born.

Now, within the context of the preceding discussion, let us take a closer look at Epic I.

THE MWINDO EPIC BY SHÉ-KÁRISI CANDI RUREKE (NYANGA)

The Mwindo Epic depends for its effect on serially produced image sequences rather than simultaneously generated sequences.[49] This is the structure of the performance: two opening image sets (the father's attempts to destroy his son; the son's gradual movement toward his aunt) and a final set (the dragon, the trip to the heavens) paralleling one another in complex ways, with three parallel sets involving Muisa, Ntumba, Sheburungu mirroring the others. What holds these six image sets together in cohesive argument is the central axis, the polar mediation. The opening sets establish the pattern or model for the other four image sets in the performance, three of which (those dealing with Muisa, Ntumba, and Sheburungu) are developed before the initial sequences have worked themselves out. The two opening sequences and the final one are the primary image sets of the work, and the three intervening sequences are secondary.

We must consider these image sets at some length. The hero's unnatural, marvelous birth is not a part of any parallel imagery; it primarily sets the tone for the actions that follow and provides initial insight into the character of the hero. The first image set details Mwindo's relations with his father; the second with his aunt. Shemwindo violates natural law by callously ordering the destruction of all male children born to his wives, apparently to prevent the birth

---

MWINDO

A Movement to a Union with Iyangura
Key Characters: Mwindo, Shemwindo, and Iyangura
The Basic Movement: Mwindo's movement to a sense of his own humanity
The Mechanics of the Movement:
   Myth: the gods
   Tale: the story of Mwindo's struggles with his enemies
   Commentary: the gods
Trickster, the Engine of the Movement: Mwindo is initially the trickster, but the
      ultimate tricksters are the gods
   Disguise: Mwindo as godly
Hero: Mwindo, coming to a sense of his own humanity, moves to the Iyangura
   in him
Physical Strength of the Hero: the struggle with Shemwindo and his allies
Frailty of the Hero: the lesson of the gods
A Diminished Nature: his loss of immortality
New Possibilities: understanding that his achievements as a human will be his
      most important legacy
Definition of Hero: what Iyangura comes to represent for Mwindo

---

of an heir who might challenge his chieftaincy. On the other hand, Iyangura is a gentle woman, generous and compassionate, thoughtful, toward whom Mwindo gravitates both symbolically and physically.

Even before he is born, Mwindo causes to appear before his mother fire-wood, water, and vegetables: representations of fire, water, and earth. The father seeks to destroy his son in various ways—by throwing spears at him, by forcing him into a grave, by putting him into a drum and depositing the drum into the water. When the father accomplishes this final deed, heaven and earth react, the torrents of rain joining the heavens to the earth. Mwindo is from the start identified with the elements.

Mwindo's maleness is betrayed to Shemwindo by a cricket, and this sets the father in action. At this point, the opening image sequence is interrupted by the second, also a principal set—the one in which Mwindo, in the drum, makes his way to his aunt, beginning at the source of the stream, working his way through several obstacles, including the testing by Iyangura and the encounter with Kasiyembe. Mwindo is aided by a spider. And when Kasiyembe attempts to bring Lightning to destroy the hero, Mwindo's own words have greater force. By an act of his will, he sets Kasiyembe's hair on fire, again demonstrating among other things his mastery of fire. Mwindo dries up all water supplies, revealing his control of yet another element (one that Kasiyembe, as a disciple of Mukiti, should have under his own influence). But Mwindo, at the urging of his aunt, heals the burned Kasiyembe, and returns the water, earning the salute and blessing of Kasiyembe. Moreover, when Mwindo prepares to re-turn "'to fight with his father,'" Iyangura urges him not to do so. The lonely path, she warns, "never fails to find something that could kill" a man. So they return to Tubondo, and the second image set ends as the narrator again takes up the threads of the first sequence, that dealing with Mwindo's relations with his father.

The second image set has as its purpose the regularizing and cementing of relations between aunt and hero, as the aunt imposes a series of tests on Mwindo which he must pass before she chooses to join him in his quest. The first sequence continues to explore the father-son tensions, and the assault on Tubondo is a dramatization of that conflict. Mwindo first demonstrates his ability to best his father by compelling everything that is in Tubundo to join them on the outskirts of the village. Then, when the hero's uncles stand against him, they are destroyed. With the help of Lightning, Mwindo annihilates all of Tubondo's citizens and razes the village. Shemwindo escapes, then Mwindo causes all of the things of the village to be restored to their former places. The pattern of life / a cleansing death / renewal is thus crucial to each of the two opening image sets.

That opening sequence is again interrupted, this time by the series of three subsidiary parallel image sets. In the first of these sequences (actually, the third such set in the performance), Mwindo successfully accomplishes the series of tests set him by Muisa. With the assistance of Lightning and the conga-scepter, Mwindo destroys the deceptive Muisa. In the second of the subsidiary sequences, Mwindo, again with Lightning's help, causes the destruction of Ntumba's cave and his lands. And he curses the aardvark. The final set of the trio (and the fifth of the six image sequences) deals with Sheburungu, who challenges Mwindo to a game that the hero loses again and again, wagering his belongings until he has nothing left but his conga-scepter. When he wagers that, his luck turns, and he wins all of Sheburungu's possessions.

Mwindo finally catches his father, seizes him and returns with him. As he retraces his journey, the three image sets concerned with the underworld creatures are revisited. Mwindo restores Sheburungu's possessions to him; he speaks kindly to Ntumba, thereby reversing his curse; and he brings Muisa back to life. In the process, he obtains the blessings of all three erstwhile enemies, much as he did with Kasiyembe earlier. Meantime, as he has done constantly during this underworld adventure, he keeps informing his aunt above the earth of his health and progress.

When Mwindo returns with his father, the three are reunited in the village of Tubondo. At this juncture, the first image sequence is again taken up. Mwindo forgives his father, generously provides him with hospitality, and refrains from his customary boastfulness in his relations with the subdued father. Then, at Iyangura's urging, Mwindo brings the people of Tubondo back to life. As the first image set finally comes to a close, the audience is presented with a picture of the three of them, Mwindo, Iyangura, Shemwindo, sitting on airborne chairs. The kingdom is split in two, Shemwindo publicly acknowledges his perfidy, and Iyangura speaks to him:

> You, Shemwindo, acted badly together with your counselors and nobles. If it
> were a counselor from whom this plan of torment against Mwindo had emanated,
> then his throat would be cut, here in the council. . . . You have acted badly, you
> Shemwindo, when you discriminated against the children, saying some were bad
> and others good, whereas you did not know what was in the womb of your wife;
> what you were given by Ongo, you saw it to be bad; the good (thing) turned into
> the bad one. So, there is nothing good on earth! But nevertheless we are satisfied,

you notables, (because of) the way in which we are up on our feet again here in Tubondo, but this Shemwindo has committed an iniquitous deed. If the people had been exterminated here, it is Shemwindo who would have been guilty of exterminating them.

And these are the words of Mwindo:

> As for me, I, Mwindo, man of many feats, the Little-one-just-born-he-walked, I am not holding a grudge against my father; may my father here not be frightened, believing that I am still angry with him; no, I am not angry with my father. What my father did against me and what I did against my father, all that is already over. Now let us examine what is to come, the evil and the good; the one of us who will again start beginning, it is he who will be in the wrong, and all those seniors here will be the witnesses of it. Now, let us live in harmony in our country, let us care for our people well.

So the ritual and paraphernalia of kingship are conferred on Mwindo, and the performance moves to its climax.

But the performer now adds yet another, a final image sequence to the narrative. This sequence builds on what has come before, in the sense that Mwindo, now the chief, puts his courage to the test once again, going into battle against the dragon that has destroyed a hunting party sent out by the hero. The capping of a complete performance by yet another image sequence is not foreign to African oral traditions. Messages are experienced, not delivered in homilies or moral tags. Such messages are aesthetically perceived by the members of audiences by means of full image sets that become, in effect, thematic adjuncts to otherwise complete narratives.

Mwindo destroys the dragon, and hundreds of people are released from within it. Because Lightning had a blood-pact with the dragon, Lightning takes the hero on the celestial journey: "I come to take you," says Lightning, "I want to go and teach you because I am very vexed with you, my friend, since you dared to kill Dragon, whereas Dragon was my friend; so know that you are doing wrong." Mwindo's world is upside down, the normal order of things has been reversed: "That *ntiriri*-liana has become *mubanga*-rope, / And *musara*-liana has become *mukendo*-bag." Says Lightning to Mwindo, "I have rescued you many times from many dangers, so then you show me that you are equal to me" by destroying the dragon. And Mwindo now realizes that "This time I am in trouble in every way." The things that he had valued as being heroic are really nothing to Nature; they are therefore meaningless. Nkuba-Lightning "made Mwindo ramble everywhere through the sky." Mwindo spent one year in the sky, and finally,

> Rain and Moon and Sun and Kubikubi-Star and Lightning . . . forbade me to kill the animals of the forest and of the village, and all the little animals of the forest, of the rivers, and of the village, saying that the day I would dare to touch a thing in order to kill it, that day (the fire) would be extinguished; then Nkuba would come to take me without my saying farewell to the people, that then the return was lost forever.

Mwindo then returns to his people with certain commandments, and the epic is brought to a close.

These, in brief, are the six paralleled image sequences that make up the performance, through which the theme flows and by means of which it is experienced. Each of the six sequences reveals a similar structure, the pattern established in the first set acting as a model. These identical aesthetic experiences of the initial model make possible the revelation of theme.

It might be useful to provide a set of summaries of the six image-sequences. First, consider the separate conflicts:

in the first set, Shemwindo attempts to kill Mwindo;
in the second, Kasiyembe attempts to kill Mwindo;
in the third, Muisa seeks to kill Mwindo;
in the fourth, Ntumba attempts to deceive Mwindo;
in the fifth set, Sheburungu attempts to destroy Mwindo;
in the sixth, the dragon threatens to exterminate Mwindo and all his people.

Mwindo is the victim in all of the sequences, with a father or an extension of the father the villain.

In the first image set, the father seeks to deprive Mwindo of his rightful place as heir to the chieftaincy;
in the second, Kasiyembe seeks to annihilate Mwindo and thereby keep him from his rendezvous with Iyangura;
in the third set, Muisa sets tasks for the hero which test Mwindo's agricultural abilities;

in the fourth set, Mwindo is faced with the duplicity of the aardvark;
in the fifth, Sheburungu would dispossess Mwindo of everything he
     owns;
and in the sixth, the dragon would destroy all of Mwindo's people.

In a variety of ways, Mwindo would be the loser, each image set exploring one
of those ways.
     The hero receives assistance in various forms in each of the sequences:

in the first, Lightning is his prime assistant;
in the second, it is the spider;
in the third, the hawk and Lightning help him;
the hawk and Lightning also help him in the fourth;
in the fifth, it is the hawk and the sparrow;
and in the sixth, his conga-scepter assists him (as indeed it does
     elsewhere in the performance).

The initial resolutions of the six sequences follow similar patterns:

in the first set, Mwindo captures his father;
in the second, he burns Kasiyembe's hair, and thus injures and subdues
     him;
in the third, he kills Muisa;
in the fourth, he destroys the aardvark's cave (but because the aardvark
     did not attempt to harm Mwindo, the hero does no harm to him
     other than to curse him);
in the fifth image-set, he wins the gamble and thereby brings
     Sheburungu down;
and in the sixth, he destroys the dragon and releases the people.

In each of the image sets, there is a further resolution that diminishes the
significance of the initial resolution (usually involving death or injury) and
brings each of the sets into harmony with the general theme of the work. In
fact, it is the second resolutions that generate the theme of the epic:

in the first image set, Mwindo forgives his father, Shemwindo blesses
     the hero and gives him half of his kingdom;
in the second set, Mwindo heals Kasiyembe, who thereupon blesses
     him;

in the third, he brings Muisa back to life, and Muisa not only blesses the
    hero but wants him to marry his daughter;
in the fourth set, he rebuilds the aardvark's cave, and the aardvark then
    blesses him;
in the fifth, he returns the wagered possessions to Sheburungu, who
    then shows his affection for the hero;
and in the final sequence, he is brought to an understanding that he
    must never again destroy a living natural thing, even a dragon.

Slowly the sequences begin to show their affinities.

Consider again the parallelism of the six image sets. The first two follow
similar patterns, the second reflecting the first in the sense that the efforts of
Kasiyembe to destroy Mwindo parallel the attempts of Shemwindo to kill his
son: they are the same thing. Mwindo's urge for life and the chieftaincy in his
struggle with his father is paralleled by the search for his aunt in the second
sequence. The father stands between Mwindo and his goal in the first set;
Kasiyembe stands between Mwindo and his goal in the second. The goal in the
first set is life itself, and the chieftaincy; this is equated structurally in the second set to Iyangura and what she stands for. Thus, two poles are set up in these
initial images, Mwindo moving from Shemwindo/Kasiyembe (the same thing)
to Iyangura/life/chieftaincy (also the same thing). Since Iyangura is early identified with life and the chieftaincy, her character will become identified with
Mwindo's goals. Shemwindo and what he represents become symbolic of evil,
of tyranny, of a society at odds with itself.

Those initial parallelisms established, the narrator now moves to an ex-
ploration of that polarity, an examination of the father's evil, by means of the
three closely related parallel image sets, all of which take place under the
ground, all of which are developed during the quest for Shemwindo. Each of
these sequences includes a character who places obstacles between Mwindo
and his father. It is necessary that the hero capture his father and bring him
under control before he can take his place as leader of the people. With the
assistance of Nature (in the forms of Lightning, the hawk, and the sparrow),
Mwindo subdues those who would stand between him and the object of his
quest. In his actions involving Muisa, Ntumba, and Sheburungu, Mwindo
simultaneously reinforces and develops the theme of the performance; the
essential movement of these three subsidiary sequences is identical to that laid
down in the opening image sets: the attempts to kill Mwindo, Mwindo's triumph, his compassion and generosity, a renewed harmony at the end of each
sequence. Mwindo's maintenance of contact with his aunt acts as a narrative

device, binding the diverse subsidiary images together and linking them to the second image sequence. It also underscores the relationship between Mwindo and the aunt. The central narrative movement from son to father (Mwindo's quest for Shemwindo) and from hero to aunt continues to assert itself throughout the performance.

Finally, in the sixth image set, the dragon that would destroy Mwindo and his people obviously parallels the father, and Mwindo's triumph over the dragon corresponds to his subduing of his father; in a more complex way, his generosity to his father, as to Kasiyembe, Muisa, Ntumba, and Sheburungu, finds a parallel in the celestial journey.

The hero moves from his origins to the assumption of the chieftaincy. This is the linear movement of the narrative. But the structural relationships, not tied to chronological time sequences, emphasize the *meaning* of the chieftaincy.

The vital narrative conflict in this performance is simply the placing of an obstacle between Mwindo and his father and aunt; the resolution is discovered in the way that Mwindo overcomes the obstacle. The production achieves its complexity by bringing six of these simple conflict/resolution relationships into conjunction one with the other. But the linkages are not simple. The first image set is interrupted by the Iyangura set, and the two then blend into a single sequence. They are developed to a point at which they are interrupted by the three subsidiary image sets. Then they move ahead once more, until they are interrupted by the dragon sequence. When that sequence comes to an end, the dual image sequence is transformed into that describing the celestial journey. There is really no distinction between the dominant sequence and the celestial image set, so that in a sense the argument will have come around full circle with the final dramatic restatement of the argument first encountered in the opening two sets.

The theme is generated largely by the activities that take place between the poles, between characters who become symbols. The father, the aunt, the obstacles are brought together not only by a linear plot; more important, they reveal an affinity with one pole or the other, and so align themselves in the gradual revelation of the theme of the narrative. Hence, two activities are in operation here. On the one hand, the arrangement of the six image sets, complex but based on simple conflicts and resolutions, allow the movement of a single plot from the beginning of the performance to its end. The other operation depends on the plot only for the provision of elements and characters. Similarities and differences are experienced by the members of the audience, and so a felt sense of polarity is established. In *The Mwindo Epic*, Mwindo moves symbolically from one pole to the other, from the excesses represented by his father to the gentleness and humaneness embodied in his aunt. What is initially a physical movement in the linear plot becomes a symbolic movement aesthetically experienced because of the relationships constructed between images.

But if that were the only thematically significant movement in the epic, then there would be no reason to continue the narrative beyond the end of the second image set. Once Mwindo has reached his aunt and allied himself with her, once the two of them with the assistance of nature have destroyed the village of Shemwindo, the performance could come to an end, because Mwindo has now apparently achieved those qualities represented by the aunt. But more must be done: the father must be captured, he must be brought under control, for he remains a threat to the harmony of the society. What all this means is that we are dealing here not with three characters, but with a single character. We are considering not Mwindo as a culture hero; rather, we are experiencing a theme of Nyanga heroism, of chieftaincy. This theme is dramatically, concretely worked out in the three characters, each representing some aspect of the pilgrimage toward perfection. "Shemwindo and Mwindo and Iyangura went in a line," the performer tells us,

> while appearing in the middle of the gathering of the assembly. Mwindo beseeched his friend Nkuba, asking him for three copper chairs. Nkuba made them come down. When they were close to the ground, being close to the ground, they remained suspended in the air about five meters from the ground. Mwindo and his father and his aunt climbed up onto the chairs; Iyangura sat down in the middle of both, Shemwindo on the right side and Mwindo on the left side.

It is Iyangura who sits in the middle and not Mwindo, for she represents the essence of heroism and the kingship. These three characters are a single character, and the polar mediation of Mwindo between Shemwindo and Iyangura is a dramatization of the odyssey of Mwindo as he prepares himself for the chieftaincy. It is a spiritual as well as physical odyssey, an initiation, an education that takes the hero into all of the elements, taking him finally into the sky itself, for lessons administered by the heavenly bodies and natural phenomena. But that education actually takes up the entirety of the epic; it is capsulized in those first two image sequences.

Mwindo is a trickster-hero. In the opening part of the performance, he is very much the trickster, born boasting and laughing, still the unpolished, unchanneled man, "an excessive boaster, intrepid, arrogant, verbose, highly self-conscious, and ruthless." All are qualities of Trickster, and in the early images Mwindo lacks the qualities of a hero. But the hero grows out of the trickster.

Like Blake's tiger,[50] the trickster is undifferentiated force, and the trickster must be brought under control, his enormous energies must be trapped for the good of the community: it is then that the hero emerges from the trickster. In a sense, that is the odyssey that Mwindo travels in this narrative. In his efforts to capture and control his father, his father representing in their most unbridled and therefore most dangerous form the blind and self-serving energies of Trickster, Mwindo is symbolically bringing those same qualities in himself under control. As he controls his father, so he controls himself, and we can see the changes in his character as the epic progresses, as he moves from his own self-consciousness, his self-centeredness and indifference, to a concern for others; as he moves, in short, from Shemwindo to Iyangura. Compassion is the Iyangura in Mwindo's character asserting itself, as he moves from the callous egoism of his father, most brutally symbolized in the father's efforts to destroy his own son, to the generosity of Iyangura, symbolized at its most sublime in the aunt's urging of Mwindo to bring the people of Tubondo back to life. This polar movement is experienced in each of the parallel image sequences.

The dragon image set is the most complex in the narrative, but it flows naturally and logically from the base that has been established. But why should the dragon not be killed? After all, the destruction of the dragon means life for many people. Surely the elimination of the dragon does not violate the generally humane theme of the narrative. Why should Lightning intervene? The dragon set follows the pattern of the earlier images: the dragon is Shemwindo, and it stands between Mwindo and his aunt's goal of humaneness. As in the earlier destruction/re-creation image sets, the dragon is killed and from that destruction comes life, the people who move out from inside the beast. But this is not sufficient, and Lightning (Nature) informs Mwindo of this. It is proper to bring civilization to his people, to see harmony, but not through death and deathlike curses and other forms of destruction. There must be a better way for man to deal with man and with Nature. Thus, though Mwindo brings forth life in the dragon episode, he also destroys Dragon. And the dragon's blood-pact with Lightning establishes its relationship with Nature. Mwindo has clearly upset Nature's balance by killing the creature.

It is the same lesson that Mwindo learns in relation to his father. When he finally does capture Shemwindo, he does not kill him. Instead, he treats him humanely and justly. He has brought his father under control, and death is unnecessary. The dragon must be controlled, but not killed. Destruction is at the root of tyranny in the first place, and a new ruler does not build on bloodshed, no matter how seemingly fruitful this may be. On the symbolic level, the father is the dragon, and as the dragon swallows people, so Shemwindo as a tyrannical ruler swallows the people by diminishing them, making their society a dissonant one through his self-serving machinations. Like the dragon, the father is not natural; his actions are not in tune with the natural order.

Mwindo is made to ramble through the sky for a period of a year, where he sees all the good and bad things in the sky, good and bad things / Iyangura and Shemwindo things that exist together. Mwindo is taught by the rain and the moon, by the sun and the *kubikubi*-star and by Lightning, his friend and protector. It is here in the sky that he learns the basic lesson of Nature, that he must not tamper with Nature, that he must not destroy the creatures of Nature, that to destroy any part of Nature is to unbalance it, to disrupt universal harmony. As Mwindo is told by the celestial bodies, on the day that he dares to touch a thing in order to kill it, "that day (the fire) would be extinguished"; that is, on the day that Nature is disrupted, on that day civilization, too, represented by fire and its civilizing consequences, will be destroyed. The two are dependent one on the other, the one cannot be damaged without having an effect on the other. This is the lesson that Mwindo must learn, it is the lesson of nature, the meaning of chieftainship.

But it is also a lesson that he has been learning throughout the performance. In bringing the father in him under control, in allowing the Iyangura in him to gain ascendancy, he learns that lesson; he moves from the destructiveness and recklessness of the father (trickster) to the creativeness of the aunt (hero), the aunt who urges him to bring people back to life rather than destroy them. Thus, Mwindo destroys, and follows his father's model: Kasiyembe, Muisa, the world of Ntumba, the possessions of Sheburungu, the dragon. But in each of these cases save the last, he brings them back to life and restores them. The dragon episode leads to the lengthy lesson in the sky. But that final image set can be seen to be not so much an education of Mwindo as a reflection of the education that has been taking place all along.

The ties with Nature are obvious, and form a secondary axis in the epic, complementary to the primary axis. The dissonance is depicted in various ways: Mwindo's betrayal by the cricket, by the hawk, the contest with Lightning, the killing of the dragon. But the hero's harmony with Nature is also emphasized: he has the active assistance of the birds, the spider, the elements. He cures the girl's yaws, frees the people; he moves about with ease through the water, the air, on the earth. He controls fire, as the symbol of civilization. The relationship between Nature and society is very close indeed in this performance, harmony in the one being tied to harmony in the other. Mwindo moves through the water to his aunt, through the earth to his father, through the air to the heavenly bodies; the purpose of all this is to defend and nourish Nyanga civilization, represented by fire. Through the elements, he comes to terms with his father, his aunt, himself, his society. Master of the elements, master of his father, of Iyangura, finally of himself and Nature, all are bound together. The movement is toward harmony with Nature, a movement duplicated in each image sequence: disequilibrium to equilibrium, destruction to renewal.

Heroism does not mean the destruction of people, it means their preservation. Chieftaincy does not exist for the unchecked self-indulgence of a man; it exists for the people, to bring the people into a sustained and productive harmony with Nature. The epic acknowledges the positive and negative potential of man's nature; the final triumph of Nyanga philosophy is of the compassionate and moderate qualities, the qualities of the hero.

Mwindo begins as something of a trickster, torn between his father, Shemwindo, and his aunt, Iyangura. He and his father struggle. They struggle on the earth, the drum in the water, destruction of the society ensues; they struggle under the earth, through three confrontations with his father's cohorts; Mwindo is always held on the earth by the ties to his aunt. Finally, he captures his father, and they are suspended on chairs. They come to terms. Now, the liberated Mwindo kills the dragon, releases the people, but he now has a struggle in the heavens, with the gods, who inform him that he is not a hero, not until he recognizes the sanctity of all lives, even the hated dragon. Then he returns with these commandments, like Moses coming down from the mount, and he rules his people. He leads them now into a new dispensation.

"Hero" has a new definition. Mwindo does everything that a hero should do: there is a miraculous birth, there is the struggle with the father, the overcoming of tyranny, the movement into the underworld where a struggle with the father/death figure occurs, a movement to life and compassion in the form of his aunt who shapes him. He demonstrates his mastery over the four elements, fire, water, air, and earth, and he takes his place as leader of his people. As he supplants his despotic father, Mwindo's political and cultural vision is of a leadership that is compassionate, that has the needs of the people as the foremost concern. To demonstrate this, he moves off against a dragon that has swallowed members of his kingdom. He destroys the dragon, and releases the people inside, and all sing his praises. Surely, this is what any self-respecting, swashbuckling hero should do. But the gods have other ideas. They waft the heroic Mwindo to the heavens, and, on a celestial journey, they teach him and reshape him. "Here," they tell him, "there is no room for heroism," at least the heroism as defined by Mwindo. As they teach him, the hero is reduced to a passive, suffering subject. He is exposed to icy winds, intense heat, thirst. He is taken to the realms of the forces of nature. Before being permitted to return to earth, the hero receives a commandment that he then carries to his people: he must never again destroy any living being. All beings are related, no matter how seemingly odious, and it is not for humans to make a judgment that a life can be taken.

We can begin to see the outlines of a possible definition of hero.

8

Gilgamesh and Beowulf

Both *Gilgamesh* and *Beowulf* are structurally and temporally in two parts: one at the height of the heroes' lives, the second during their declining years. In *Gilgamesh*, part one deals with Gilgamesh and Humbaba and the Bull of Heaven; in *Beowulf*, part one consists of Beowulf's struggles with Grendel and Grendel's mother. Part two of *Gilgamesh* focuses on Gilgamesh and Utnapishtim; part two of *Beowulf* reveals Beowulf's struggles with the dragon. "Hero" is defined by the relationship between the two parts of each of the epics. That definition emphasizes a being who is not godly, not eternal, but one who is mortal. "Life is transitory. . . ."

GILGAMESH

The poems that make up the Gilgamesh epic were found on clay tablets discovered in the nineteenth century in Nineveh. The origin of the epic was Sumerian. In the Sumerian king list, Gilgamesh is identified as fifth in the first dynasty of Uruk. He reigned for one hundred and twenty-six years. The epic poems "antedate Homeric epic by at least one and a half thousand years."[51] In the early parts of the story, the focus is on Enkidu. There is a story-within-the-story: the account of the flood. But mainly, the center of attention is Gilgamesh. He is a mature human at the beginning of the epic, in the sense that his position as king of the city of Uruk is already secure, and one of the works for which he was to be remembered, building the walls of the city, is already in the past. In another sense, his physical maturity and his status are only the background for his education, which takes place in two distinct stages. In the first half of the epic, Gilgamesh must establish a name for himself, a process of individuation that demands preparations for an initiating encounter with the demonic Humbaba. In the second half of the epic, Gilgamesh, having lost his friend and brother, must pass through stages of melancholia and dissolution of the self, a dark night of the soul, from which he emerges intact but profoundly different from the boisterous and arrogant champion who made up riddles about his name after he defeated the Bull of Heaven.

Gilgamesh is also the story of the double. If Gilgamesh is two-thirds god and only one-third human, his double, Enkidu, seems to reverse the ratio. If Gilgamesh is outwardly the same at the beginning and end of the epic, the story of Enkidu everywhere emphasizes change. For Enkidu, it is a story of birth, development in the wild, a step-by-step initiation into the life of a civilized man, courageous acts, and death. It is the story of everyman. It is also the story of the emergence of humankind from the wild, a parable of culture, Mesopotamian speculation about the First Man.

The epic is the tale of a hero. The hero, a part of the old, a part of the new, changes the society. The hero is leading his people into a new dispensation. To do this successfully, he must be a part of both worlds. He represents the people,

---

GILGAMESH

A Movement to a Union with Enkidu
Key Characters: Gilgamesh and Enkidu
The Basic Movement: Bringing Gilgamesh and Enkidu together as one
The Mechanics of the Movement:
  Myth: the gods
  Tale: Humbaba and the Bull of Heaven (pattern)
  Commentary: Siduri et al.
Trickster, the Engine of the Movement: the gods and Enkidu
  Disguise: Enkidu as Gilgamesh
Hero: Gilgamesh (move to union with Enkidu)
Physical Strength of the Hero: fight with Enkidu, Humbaba, Bull of Heaven, gods
Frailty of the Hero: overweening pride and arrogance, mortality; a sense of loss
A Diminished Nature: his loss of immortality
New Possibilities: confronting and moving beyond his limitations (mortality),
    a rebirth, finding stature in that
Definition of Hero: a character who, in his movement to oneness with Enkidu,
    reveals the possibilities of triumph over human infirmity (age, frailty, etc.)

---

but his vision takes him, and his people, into the new world. He is vulnerable, he could die, again emphasizing the transitoriness of life. During the course of the epic, he learns the fact of his mortality. The theme is communicated through dualism: Gilgamesh and Enkidu, the one part god and part man, the other part man and part animal. There is a movement of the one from god to human, of the shadowing other from animal to human. They meet in the center, their humanity affirmed, their mortality assured. Epic deals with the hero confronting his own limitations. To be sure, fantasy swirls on all sides of him. He is aided by fabulous and miraculous agents, donors, and helpers, but that is the point: these exist outside of him. They are not a part of his character: he is not invulnerable, invincible. Godlike though he may be, there is an Enkidu side to the character, an Enkidu shadowing of Gilgamesh. In *Gilgamesh*, it is the Enkidu side of the hero with which Gilgamesh is attempting to come to terms. Epic occurs within the framework of fantasy, but its focus is the humanity of the hero. In all oral narrative, fantasy and realism exist side by side: those are the two basic reservoirs of imagery. In oral narrative, there is a vision, a model, a pattern, and that guides the characters in the narrative: their world can only be based on already established models. They are therefore caught up in a predetermined pattern, and can only pattern their own affairs and actions on it. It is vulnerability that is at the center of epic, and it is for that reason that epic often seems brooding, fatalistic, tragic. In the epic, the oral narrative character has lost his fabulous qualities; the move is toward humanity.

Is the epic hero a trickster? In *Gilgamesh*, the gods are tricksters, Enkidu their instrument for duping Gilgamesh. And as Gilgamesh transforms from god to man, the energy unleashed is represented by the struggles with Humbaba and the Bull of Heaven, as Gilgamesh and Enkidu merge: this activity of struggle and merging is the betwixt-and-between period, as Gilgamesh moves from one state (god) to another (man). During this period of transformation, Gilgamesh moves through a period of chaos to order, from one state to another: he moves through a period when normal rules are not operating. This is the time of the trickster. It is not so much trickery as amorality during this crucial betwixt-and-between period. Can Gilgamesh be considered a hero?

This is a hero whose dealings are with the gods. Gilgamesh has never looked at death before. Enkidu sees in him a helplessness to understand or speak, and he knows that he should teach Gilgamesh. But his sickness makes him helpless. All he has is weakness and rage about the kings and elders and animals. Gilgamesh knows that his friend is close to death; he remembers their life together, and there are tears. He appeals to Ninsun, his mother, and to the elders to save his friend who had once run among the animals, the wild horses, the panther, had run and drunk with them as if they were his brothers. Just now he went with them into the forest of Humbaba and killed the Bull of Heaven. Enkidu is a part of nature. Gilgamesh hears Enkidu murmur: everything had life to me, the sky, the storm, the earth, water, wandering, the moon, salt, even his hand had life. It is gone.

Where is the justice in *Gilgamesh*? What have the gods wrought? The death of Enkidu is my death, laments Gilgamesh. If a heavenly justice seems to have been lost, a new and more challenging justice is proffered here by the gods: humans are now on their own. Now justice is for humans to weigh, now the human image is for humans to measure, now the life cycle is for humans to traverse. The gods showed the way, but now humans are on their own. What seems to be the ultimate act of injustice by the gods to humans is in fact the greatest justice: so the eating of the fruit of the forbidden tree was an act of freedom, not an act of enslavement. It was a gain and not a loss. If justice is human rectitude, the quality of being righteous, if justice is sound reason and validity, if justice is the quality of righteousness, then the *Gilgamesh* epic is the greatest epic of them all, for it places justice in the hands of humans. Humans are on their own; they must now deal with the trickster forces within them, to determine right and wrong.

Gilgamesh and Enkidu fight, they become friends immediately. The relationship is tested and confirmed again and again, and expressed in one of the most moving elegies to have come down to us from the ancient world. The love of Gilgamesh and Enkidu is likened to that of husband and wife, and to the bond between brothers. Indeed, Enkidu is brought into the family of Gilgamesh, adopted by the goddess-mother of Gilgamesh, Ninsun. If the Enkidu trickster story shadows Gilgamesh's heroic epic, what does the addition of the trickster contribute to a definition of hero and the heroic epic?

Enkidu, an everyman, goes through the life cycle: separated from the animals, he becomes a cultural being, up from biological being to cultural being. Enkidu's story is the model for the story of Gilgamesh, a movement from godhood (immortality) to humanity (mortality). It is the story of the first human; it is the story of the coming of death, the loss of paradise, the loss of everlasting life. The loss is first told through Enkidu, who clings to life. It is told through Utnapishtim, and the flood. The flood is the separation of humans from the gods, a story of impermanence.

That is also the story of Gilgamesh. It is Gilgamesh's primordial rite of passage. He is in a betwixt-and-between position, semi-god and semi-man, moving toward mortality, toward humanity. It is the story of the creation of humanity. A god becomes a man. How is this done? Through twinning: The gods, the ultimate tricksters, create a man, a clone of the god Gilgamesh. And then they link the god's destiny to the destiny of that man.

Gilgamesh and Enkidu bond through their common struggles, and they become more and more bonded. Gilgamesh, when it is too late, understands what the gods have done to him. But he has already crossed the threshold. He is Enkidu, and he cannot get out. This doubling or twinning relationship is the key to the pattern and, hence, the theme. Related to it is Gilgamesh's frenzied search for immortality, his encounters with the various people on his way to Utnapishtim's land, a pattern of rejection and deepening sorrow. Also a pattern: the struggles with Enkidu, Humbaba, and the Bull of Heaven, but these are related to the doubling pattern. Another pattern is the dream-portents; these emphasize the mortality/immortality struggle in which both Gilgamesh and Enkidu are involved. These are the major patterns. They form two categories: the Gilgamesh/Enkidu relationship, and the aftermath: Gilgamesh's quest for Enkidu, which means his quest for immortality. It is an ancient quest, and here it is a quest for Enkidu, for what Enkidu represents for Gilgamesh. It is a movement into the dark side of the soul, a frenzied coming to terms with one's own mortality. This makes the epic a realistic psychological struggle. The fates of Gilgamesh and Enkidu are linked, their destinies bound. This is twinning.

Enkidu is the trickster: he is undifferentiated energy, betwixt and between, liminal, he is on the boundaries, in-the-process of becoming, not yet formed. This is Enkidu, he becomes Gilgamesh.

The trickster becomes a dangerously unpredictable character, amoral, obeying no laws except those of his own wants; the trickster-like clown-like character is present at the rites of passage, when change is occurring. There are no laws at this time: the trickster embodies this. Enkidu fits into this trickster position. Gilgamesh is betwixt and between. Enkidu becomes the embodiment, the personification of this state of being betwixt and between. He is Gilgamesh, he is Gilgamesh undergoing great change, undergoing differentiation. Enkidu is being formed, he is in the process of becoming. His formation into manhood from an original state is Gilgamesh's formation into manhood from an original state. It is crucial that Enkidu's "original state" be mortal (hence his animal beginnings), as it is crucial that Gilgamesh's "original state" be immortal (hence his godlike beginnings). Enkidu is the mechanism for Gilgamesh's change. He is the force that exists during this period of betwixt and between, and in that sense he takes over the role of the trickster. The gods are manipulating all.

Gilgamesh's heroism is to be found in the struggle. Gilgamesh is a very modern hero. He struggles against impossible odds, certain to lose, but his heroism is to be found in the struggle itself. He refuses to accept the loss, he will not go gently into that good night, and that is where we identify with him. The vulnerable hero will die, and in his struggle against death, we find heroism.

BEOWULF

Much has been said about the Christian elements of the epic *Beowulf*.[52] Some argue that they represent the rather stylistically crude interpolations of monks who wrote the epic down; others insist that the Christian elements are very much a part of the epic. The Christian details in the narrative are not interpolations, but involve the action and the theme of the epic. They represent a new element in the world of Beowulf, as becomes obvious in the struggling throughout the narrative between fate and a more Christian assessment of destiny. The Christian and the non-Christian elements are in the background of this epic throughout, and Beowulf seems almost self-contradictory at times, as he contemplates his destiny from one vantage or the other. He speaks "with words of thankfulness to God the king of Glory, our eternal Lord," at the same time that he tells how "Fate has swept away the courageous princes who were my kinsmen." In fact, there *is* a conflict between these two larger forces, and these two conflicting worldviews are expressed dramatically in the person of Beowulf, as he seeks to adapt to the one while still very much a part of the other. And the performer, too, moves from a dependence on one to a dependence on the other, as he comments on the actions of the drama. Against this background of change is Beowulf himself, and he does not escape this broader conflict. His own heroism has different meanings, depending on which of the two faiths it is based. "Whichever of us is killed must resign himself to the verdict of God," he says, then moments later, "Fate must decide." Against a largely bleak fatalistic background is placed the last judgment "and the sentence of almighty God." And Hrothgar speaks to Beowulf in the same way that the dream speaks to Gilgamesh, "Be on your guard against . . . wickedness, my dear Beowulf! Choose the better part, which is eternal gain. Avoid pride, illustrious hero. For a little while you will be at the peak of your strength; but it will not be long before sickness or the sword, or the hand of fire, or the raging sea, a thrust of the knife, a whizzing arrow, or hideous dotage . . . or failure and darkening of the eyes, will plunder you of your might; and in the end, brave soldier, death will defeat you." Beowulf sighs, as he is about to die, "I speak with words of thankfulness to God the king of glory, our eternal Lord, for all the wealth that I see here, and because I was permitted to win it for my people [i.e., by defeating the dragon] before my death." But during the actual battle, the narrator notes, "For the first time Beowulf had to fight without success, because

Fate refused to grant it to him." And in the background, throughout the epic, are the stories told by warrior and by bard, about the great heroes of the past, the heroes of the ancient traditional ways, for there is an awareness throughout that things are changing, and the heroism of Beowulf reflects this change and the contradictions that change espouses.

The action of *Beowulf* takes place in Scandinavia after the founding of Denmark's Scylding Dynasty by the mythological Scyld Scefing. The epic is divided into three sections: the hero's mortal fights with Grendel, with Grendel's mother, and with the dragon. Chronologically, it is divided into two sections: the hero's daring adventures as a young man, and his exemplary deeds as an old king. From a narrative point of view, the epic is divided into three parts: the hero's adventures in Denmark, his own account of these adventures, and his deeds as King of the Geats. The section concluding with Beowulf's return to his homeland handles time in a basically linear manner. The remainder of the poem repeatedly plays on a sense of time by intermingling past, future, and present, as when both Beowulf's past exploits and the future catastrophes resultant from his death are brought to bear upon his present sacrifice to reveal the tragic dignity of the event.

BEOWULF

A Movement to a Union with Wiglaf
Key Characters: Beowulf and Grendel
The Basic Movement: Beowulf's move to a new identity
The Mechanics of the Movement:
    Myth: Grendel and his mother
    Tale: the story of Grendel, the story of the dragon
    Commentary: Wiglaf
Trickster, the Engine of the Movement: Beowulf's age; he is his own trickster; and
    the dragon
    Disguise: age
Hero: Beowulf, struggling with age
Physical Strength of the Hero: fight with Grendel and his mother, and the dragon
Frailty of the Hero: his ultimate defeat, because of advancing age
A Diminished Nature: his loss of immortality
New Possibilities: confronting and moving beyond his limitations (mortality), the
    decision to fight the dragon
Definition of Hero: Beowulf's struggle against his own vulnerability to age

---

The tale-part of the story has to do with Grendel, Grendel's mother, and the dragon, swallowing monsters all. The myth deals with Scyld, Beowulf's death, Beowulf's travel to the underworld, the struggle with Grendel, and history and heroic poetry; it also incorporates the stories of the past. Broad themes include man against death; the hero defending mankind against its enemies; he fought for kings, now his people will not fight for him. Heroism in this epic involves the transcending of human limits, and the responsibilities of a lord to his people. The mythic aspects of the story also involve the Christian element and the element of the pre-Christian past as represented by the now-folkloric characters, Grendel, Grendel's mother, the dragon. History includes the stories of Sigemund, Finn, and the Scandinavian background.

The narrative traces royal succession down to King Hrothgar, who decides to advertise the might of his realm by erecting near the modern town of Lejre a magnificent hall, which he names Heorot. Here, the king and warriors spend much time feasting at night, until a troll-like and cannibalistic creature of darkness named Grendel, descended from Cain, takes such vehement exception to the constant uproar of revelry that he submits the hall to a series of murderous attacks that end all nightly occupancy by human beings for the next twelve years.

Apparently nonplussed by the monster's irresistible savagery, Hrothgar finds no better solution than to bear his grief and hold apparently fruitless meetings with his advisors. Somewhere in the land of the Geats, a physically powerful young man identified as a retainer of King Hygelac, whose name we shall later learn is Beowulf, hears of this situation and immediately sets sail for Denmark with fourteen companions to free the world of Grendel's depredations.

The Geats make land the next day, and, with the boar-like crests on their helmets shining in the sun, they march to Heorot, where Beowulf announces the purpose of his visit and his determination to fight Grendel alone and without weapons, though he will wear a corselet made by Weland himself.

Hrothgar invites the Geats to sit at a banquet during which Beowulf is in turn taunted by a retainer named Unferth and honored by Queen Wealhtheow's gracious attention. The Geats are then left alone to wait for Grendel, who soon breaks into the hall and succeeds in devouring one of them before grappling for life with Beowulf, from whom he escapes mortally wounded, leaving an arm behind. The next day is devoted to celebrations, during which a poet entertains the company by singing a song about Beowulf's exploit, which he likens by implication to the marvelous deeds of the Germanic heroes, Sigemund and Fitela, and contrasts to the crime of a wicked king of old named Heremod. During the sumptuous banquet that follows, Hrothgar bestows priceless gifts upon Beowulf, and the poet sings once again to tell of the death of Finn and Hnaef, before Wealhtheow presents Beowulf with a necklace as valuable as the one that Hama once stole from Eormanric.

That night, a contingent of Danes remains in Heorot, but Grendel's mother attacks them to avenge her son and carries off a warrior named Aeshere, who is Hrothgar's dearest companion. Early the next morning, Beowulf is asked to help with the new peril and is taken to a pond where Grendel and his mother presumably have their lair. On this pond's shore he receives a valuable and tried sword from Unferth, who has now forgotten his earlier antagonism. He dives into the pond and enters an underwater cave where he kills Grendel's mother beside the body of her dead son, although Unferth's weapon fails him, and he must use an ancient sword that seems to have been waiting for him there. Back in Heorot, his accomplishments are praised by Hrothgar, who again contrasts him to Heremod and seizes upon the occasion to deliver a little sermon on the sins of pride, sloth, and covetousness.

On the fourth day, the Geats sail back to their homeland, where Hygelac expresses some surprise at the success of the expedition. Beowulf tells a slightly different version of his adventures, mentions that Hrothgar has promised his daughter, Freawaru, in marriage to Ingeld, and gives Hygelac and his queen some of the gifts that he received in Heorot.

Beowulf had been considered somewhat worthless in his youth, and the narrative jumps over half a century to a time when Beowulf has been king of the Geats for fifty years. When a dragon, enraged at the theft of part of a treasure he has been guarding, begins spewing fire at the Geats and their dwellings, Beowulf decides to fight him single-handed. The narrative flashes back to Hygelac's death on a battlefield in the Rhineland, his son Heardred's death at the hands of the Swedish usurper, Onela, and Beowulf's subsequent accession to the throne, then back again to the occasion when Beowulf hugged a Frankish warrior to death during Hygelac's last battle.

In front of the dragon's lair, the aged Beowulf now addresses the eleven retainers who have accompanied him and orders them to keep away from a fight that he describes as nobody's responsibility but his own. As the fight begins and Beowulf's sword once again fails him, his retainers run for cover to a nearby grove, with the exception of his nephew, Wiglaf, who gives them a brief lecture on the nature of duty to one's lord and comes to his uncle's rescue in time to help him slay the monster.

Beowulf, however, has been mortally wounded, and he dies thanking God that he has been able to win the dragon's treasure for his people, asking that a barrow (grave mound) be erected for his ashes, and bidding Wiglaf to continue acting in a manner befitting the last of his family. Wiglaf has the event announced to the Geatish nation by a messenger who predicts forthcoming trouble with the Franks and Frisians. This takes us back once again to the Geatish raid in the Rhineland and to the Swedish king Ongentheow's killing of Hygelac's brother, Haethcyn, at the battle of Ravenswood before the Swede falls into the hands of one of Hygelac's retainers. Finally, the messenger warns that the Swedes will set out against the Geats as soon as they hear of Beowulf's death.

The poem comes to an end by the sea, on a promontory where a woman sings a song of sorrow by Beowulf's barrow, around which twelve mounted retainers mournfully ride while chanting a lament for their dead lord, whom they praise as the mildest, the gentlest, the kindest to his people, and the most eager for fame of all the kings in the world. The balance of *Beowulf*: the opening (Scyld) and the closing (Beowulf) tie Beowulf to myth. Aspects of this myth include the struggle with Grendel in youth, the struggle with the dragon in age, and the sword that fails in both instances. They continue with the magical sword, the one that seems to have been waiting for him, in part one, and for Wiglaf, in part two (he is the new generation, he will carry on for Beowulf). The first sword that failed results in the ancient sword: this ties Beowulf to the ancestral past. The second sword that failed results in Wiglaf coming to Beowulf's rescue and slaying the dragon: this ties Beowulf to the future.

It is the dragon that reveals to Beowulf that he is human. The dragon could be Beowulf's Enkidu, because the dragon is his match and shows Beowulf that he is mortal by killing him. Beowulf fights this dragon in the end as an old man, because it is his destiny. He knows he has to. And when he kills the dragon, he is at peace with himself. The dragon makes Beowulf realize that he is no longer powerful as he was when he was young. It forces him to realize that his youthfulness and strength do not go on forever and that he will die. The dragon serves as a metaphorical trickster in that it seals Beowulf's fate, which is necessary to make him a hero. The dragon makes Beowulf realize that he is mortal at the end of the story, as Enkidu makes Gilgamesh realize that he is mortal. The death of the dragon leads to the inevitable death of Beowulf. Even before Beowulf kills the dragon, he realizes that it could very well be his day to die.

Grendel is the trickster. By destroying him, Beowulf is bringing Grendel's energy, and by analogy the untamed trickster energy of Beowulf as a youth, under control. Grendel is like Enkidu; he is the spark that initiates Beowulf's change from swashbuckler hero into something more. The Enkidu in *Beowulf* may be Grendel at Hrothgar's hall, the trickster character of Grendel and the land that Beowulf ventures to where he wins acceptance. He is then left with feelings of being indestructible, only to be let down in his old age by the dragon.

The Enkidu of Beowulf is old age, time. It eventually brings him face to face with his mortality. However, as in *Gilgamesh*, Beowulf's heroism lives beyond his mortal body in the form of a society and in epic. The Enkidu in *Beowulf* is not a character but a process; it comes from Beowulf growing old and realizing that he is no longer as great and powerful as he once was. Beowulf is his own Enkidu. With time and age, he comes to realize that first of all he cannot do everything on his own, and second, that he is not the supreme being. These are realized in the battles with the mother and the dragon.

The Enkidu in *Beowulf* could, as noted, be Grendel, Grendel's mother, and the dragon. They all bring out the trickster elements inside him. In the acts of defeating each opponent, he has to use his trickster abilities. Enkidu could be anyone around Beowulf, be it friend or foe. who either helps or hinders the hero: Grendel, the thanes, the kings or the dragon. The king plays Enkidu, convincing the hero in the first half that he will meet an unpleasant death as all heroes do. The prophecy seems to bring about Beowulf's demise. The Enkidu of *Beowulf* is manifold. In terms of being a foil, Grendel is Beowulf's Enkidu. The dragon in the second part, however, is Enkidu when he shows the hero's mortality. There are other aspects of Enkidu that are provided by the various Danes in *Beowulf*.

There is a new sense of hero, and the Achilles heel dominates.[53] The hero exists within a context of history and myth. In the first part of *Beowulf*, the hero is the trickster, as he tricks Grendel and Grendel's mother to their deaths. In part two of the epic, the hero is also the trickster, but in an ironic way: the trickster used so effectively against external adversaries in part one of the story now turns against the hero himself, as old age becomes his trickster, and draws him to his death. There was the illusion of greatness: Beowulf will fight the dragon himself. But in the end, his own sense of heroism becomes his fatal enemy, the trickster within. The hero thought himself to be invulnerable, as indeed he was in part one of the epic. But now, the invulnerability is gone, and he must die. There are other ironies here: his people do not come to his assistance. Only Wiglaf does, and Wiglaf assures a new generation of heroism.

But the fact that in both parts of the epic the people are content to allow the hero to risk his life while they risk nothing raises issues about the concept of the hero. In this epic, the hero exists as one who is above the people, but there is little here to suggest that Beowulf stands for, embodies, the people. The people are selfish: they will sing the hero's praises if he wins, but they seem uninterested in him if he fails. In part one, the mythically appearing sword saves him. But that mythic sword cannot save him in part two. The first sword connects Beowulf to his ancestral past, as the second sword connects Wiglaf to his ancestral past. And so the sense of the hero continues through the generations. But we now know enough to recognize the theme of the melancholy hero.

There is much history in the epic of Beowulf, but the hero seems to exist in a way that makes history superfluous. In the end, the hero does not stand for his people, nor does he stand for a change in the history of the people. He is a momentary blip on the horizons of history, there for a moment, then gone. Why then do we keep telling the story of Beowulf? For that reason, to emphasize and explain that the hero is less an embodiment of the culture than a being on the periphery. Beowulf remains liminal, a boundary being, and the concept and definition of hero remains external, not an integral part of the people's history.

The gods in this story are the foes of the hero: Grendel and Grendel's mother, the dragon. The gods do not intervene as metaphors of the hero; they are the beings against whom the hero struggles, in a history that pays no attention to these struggles. So it is that the hero and his relations with myth and with history are revealed to be devoid of the exalted definitions that we give to our heroes. The epic of Beowulf raises questions about the hero and his links to myth and history.

Tragic Destiny

The hero has possibilities but, in the cases of Gilgamesh and Odysseus, their greatness as heroes was in the past. Now they must come to terms with a diminished nature. Ibonia begins as a lesser character and moves to greatness. Wherever the diminished capabilities are imposed, there is a movement to overcome limitations, and the definition of hero must have its starting point there. How does the trickster enter here? He reveals the inner strength of the hero, a strength that could move in either direction, towards order or chaos. He inevitably chooses chaos. The trickster energy is a risk but it is all the hero has.

The hero is in the process of becoming: consider Odysseus, gaining his stature and character as he moves through the folk-tale-like characters; and look at Ibonia, moving into his new identity, struggling against all known identities, moving into his own uniqueness. They are on the boundaries; they are like the Winnebago trickster driving himself and his world into a new identity. Gilgamesh resists as he shifts into his new identity. Penelope draws Odysseus on, Enkidu draws Gilgamesh on, Iampelasoamanoro draws Ibonia on: Penelope, Enkidu, Iampelasoamananoro: they are the new identity, but they have no existence outside the one hundred suitors, outside Raivato, outside the Bull of Heaven and Humbaba and the gods. The villains define the hero as much as that for which he yearns. There is always something of the past in this move into the future. But perhaps the most exciting thing is the freedom that the hero finds out there, in the struggle.

In *Gilgamesh*, Enkidu is created by the gods as a duplicate of the unruly Gilgamesh. "I have come to change the old order," Enkidu announces, "for I am the strongest here" (66). Although Gilgamesh defeats Enkidu in their first violent encounter, Enkidu is ultimately the stronger, for he brings with him the assurance of mortality: he has death in him. Enkidu is to Gilgamesh what the flood is to the rest of the world; the inclusion in the epic of Gilgamesh of a lengthy account of the flood is not an idle appendage.

Gilgamesh is interested only in the satisfaction of his desires: "'his arrogance,'" the men of Uruk mutter,

> "has no bounds by day or night. No son is left with his father, for Gilgamesh takes them all; yet the king should be a shepherd to his people. His lust leaves no virgin to her lover; neither the warrior's daughter nor the wife of the noble; yet this is the shepherd of the city, wise, comely, and resolute." (60)

So the gods create Enkidu, the equal of Gilgamesh. "Let it be as like him as his own reflection, his second self, stormy heart for stormy heart" (60). But there is a difference between the two: Enkidu is flawed. In the fatal dualism that dominates the structure of this narrative, Enkidu's flaw becomes Gilgamesh's flaw.

If Gilgamesh is like "a savage bull" (63), the world around him "bellowed like a bull" (105), and the great god, Enlil, finds the "uproar of mankind" intolerable, so "the gods in their hearts were moved to let loose the deluge" (105). Only Utnapishtim survives.

The physical and thematic movement of this narrative is from life to death, with the frenzied, tragic efforts of both Enkidu and Gilgamesh to stave off its inevitability. Enkidu is, as he promised, imposing a new order, because he contains within himself the certainty of death. The introduction of Gilgamesh's double, Enkidu, into the narrative is a dramatization of Gilgamesh's loss of divinity, his fall to mortality. Enkidu is identified not with the gods but with earth, with nature, and he slowly differentiates himself from nature, and, with the help of a woman, evolves into a full man. In formal terms, Enkidu is Gilgamesh, Enkidu's humanity becomes Gilgamesh's humanity, his mortality becomes Gilgamesh's mortality. Oral tradition is filled with tales of messages sent by the gods to earth to inform humans that they are mortal.[54]

The first part of the epic details Enkidu's development, his life in the wilderness, his separation from the animals, his emergence into wisdom. Hovering about throughout this first part of the story are dreams, most of them ominous, underscoring the certainty of death; these dreams envelop Enkidu and Gilgamesh ever more hopelessly in the web of mortality. After their initial struggle, the two embrace, and so "their friendship was sealed" (67). And so also was sealed Gilgamesh's fate.

The epic of Gilgamesh ponders his humanizing in an atmosphere that is sad and nostalgic. He is unable to accept his imminent death as foreshadowed in the death of Enkidu. Gilgamesh wanders far on his quest to find eternal life and thus escape his fate. He finds Utnapishtim, the only immortal man, who tells him the story of the flood, which is really the story of the coming of death. This tale of the coming of death is told three times in Gilgamesh's narrative: in the fate of Enkidu, in the parallel fate of Gilgamesh, and in the retelling of the archetypal flood story. In this establishment of a new order, and as he becomes aware of his mortality, Gilgamesh seeks a means of ensuring his immortality. In the end, he becomes a leader who is no longer the darkness of his people: "without him there is no light" (115). This is the meaning of the dreams, and the hope of the flood . . . and the epic. Gilgamesh's immortality is to be found in the manner in which he has ruled. He no longer abuses his power, he deals justly with his servant, and all people lament his passing. A mortal Gilgamesh grows out of the lusty tyrant, reversing course and becoming the ideal ruler. This new sense of leadership, revealed in the heroism of Gilgamesh, is the ultimate motive of the epic.

The heroic epic of Gilgamesh is similar to that of Mwindo. The prodigy in Epic I moves from childhood to his assumption of the chieftaincy, and along the way he subdues his father and comes into a close and symbolically significant relationship with his aunt. He has a unique relationship with the gods, with nature, as he moves toward the acceptance of power and the assumption of chiefly responsibilities. The two transformations that occur in Epic I have Mwindo changing from boasting trickster to heroic chief, and the institution of the chieftaincy moving from self-serving leadership represented by Shemwindo to a humane leadership represented by the later Mwindo. The shaping influences on Mwindo are his aunt and the forces of nature, but especially Nkuba Lightning. Mwindo changes: the Nyanga conception of chieftaincy changes. Mwindo's taming of his father reveals both. When Mwindo pursues his father in the underworld, he does so already as a changed man. And change is dramatized in Epic I in other ways: Mwindo destroys, and that is the old order; but Mwindo brings life, and that is the new. Mwindo takes property, then restores it. The thematic movement of this epic occurs many times, in large ways and small; slowly, an ideal kind of chieftaincy is being externalized, an ideal that is dramatically thrown against the old order, his father, Shemwindo, and what

Mwindo is himself at the beginning . . . and remains to a certain extent, for the narrative represents this learning experience, and the killing of the dragon at the end of the epic is as much a part of this lesson as the earlier destruction of the underworld figures and their property. The parallel image sets reflect similar themes, but there is simultaneously a gradual movement toward awareness through all these sets.

SHIFTING ALLIANCES

In the Icelandic epic *Njal's Saga*[55] there is an interweaving of relationships that is constantly in flux, repeatedly shifting as new alliances are established and old ones broken off. Against that activity is Njal, the peaceful Njal who, with others, is seeking to channel into legal molds the great energy involved in and released by these alliances and the feuds that fuel the alliances. The society is shaped by the shifting linkages occasioned by the blood feuds and the resultant alignments. Throughout the saga, men manipulate the system and attempt to make it work for the perpetuation of the alignments, seeking to make the new legal system a part of the blood feuding patterns instead of allowing that legal network to gain hegemony and thereby bring the blood feuding under control and transform the society. The feuding and linkages are ancient; the legal system is a fairly recent effort to harness these disastrous spates of violence that prevent the development of any other kind of society.

Against this bleak, violent, ever-shifting background, the tale of Njal is spun. There are other tales in the saga but Njal's is the principal one. His allegiance is to the legal system; with like thinkers, he attempts to persuade others to adopt it. Njal wants to bring men together, reason with them. In the legal marketplace, relationships are marketed, bought and sold, as the feuding system adapts itself to the legal system that now attempts to weave itself into the blood feud system.

The tragedy of *Njal's Saga* is that Njal himself cannot remain outside the feuding arrangements. For his own ends, he moves into the patterns of shifting alliances, and once he has done that he can never extricate himself, can never again become the disinterested intermediary at the legal marketplace. Caught up in the intrigues and counter-intrigues, as are members of his family, he is doomed, and goes to his death nobly and with full knowledge of what has occurred. He has sought to manipulate the blood feuding system and to move it toward legal ends; he then manipulates it for his selfish ends, and his tragedy is caught up in that. Njal is both product and captive of the one system even as he attempts to champion the other. In this case, the new world is postponed.

In the stories of Mwindo, Gilgamesh, and Njal, all is change, transition. The old order is passing, a new order beckons. The hero is tied to that past even as he is a part of the approaching new order. In *Gilgamesh*, Enkidu announces that he presages the new world, in which the self-willed and despotic reign of Gilgamesh must give way to a more enlightened chieftaincy; that new order is brought about by the introduction into Gilgamesh's being of death, with its consequent effect on his concept of the chieftaincy. In *The Mwindo Epic*, I, the transition is also in the conception of the chieftaincy, a new order brought about or revealed by changes within the character of Mwindo. In *Njal's Saga*, there is also change, a tortured movement toward a new social dispensation that will transform blood feuds to a new rule of law.

The three epics deal with major social upheavals that both create a hero and are revealed in the actions of the hero. He is a part of the change, in fact personifies these traumatic transitions. In a dramatic way, the theme is reflected in his character as it is simultaneously acted out in more historical or realistic images in the background; historical and imaginative images come into conjunction in the epics, and the fictional establishes the attitude toward the historical.

Mwindo, Gilgamesh, and Njal are heroes, but the tales eschew the swashbuckling hero. All three of the epics provide dramatically negative examples of such heroics, in favor of the tragic figure who comes to symbolize the change, a transition that is disjunctive and even revolutionary. The hero brings his society into the new order, but inevitably loses something of himself in the process: that is heroism, and it is often tragic. To make this work dramatically, the hero must contain both past and present within himself: Mwindo and Shemwindo in Epic I, Gilgamesh and Enkidu, Njal the advocate of the new and Njal the captive of the old. The implied contradiction characterizes the epic hero and gives him resonance, caught as he is between two worlds but always destined for the new and unknown realm.

Other epics have like obsessions. In *Beowulf*, a hero struggles with two faiths. Christian and non-Christian elements are in the background throughout the epic, and Beowulf seems also contradictory as he contemplates his destiny from one vantage or the other. A conflict exists between the two forces, expressed dramatically in the person of Beowulf as he attempts to adapt to the one while he is still very much a part of the other. And when Hrothgar speaks to Beowulf, it is an echo of the dream speaking to Gilgamesh, of Nkuba Lightning speaking to Mwindo. The two forces are involved in Beowulf's final confrontation. The epic is punctuated by the stories told by warrior and poet about the great heroes of the past, of the ancient traditional ways. There is an awareness that things are changing: the one survivor of the dragon laments,

"Earth, hold what men could not, the wealth of princes. . . . The holocaust of battle has claimed every mortal soul of my race who shared the delights of the banqueting hall. I have none to wield the sword, none to polish the jeweled cup. Gone are the brave. . . . There is no sweet sound from the harp, no delight of music, no good hawk swooping through the hall, no swift horse stamping in the castle yard. Death has swept away nearly everything that lives." (80)

And Wiglaf sadly says to the dead Beowulf, "You are the last survivor of our family" (93). Beowulf reflects the change and the contradiction that change entails.

It is not a coincidence that these large changes are reflected in the oral tradition, and have an impact on the tale. The construction of oral narrative, tale, or epic involves the past and the present, in two main types of imagery and in the blending of myth and reality. This is how the contradiction is worked into the very form of the narrative. Images are drawn from the past, from a repertory of fantasy, in which the culture's experiences are condensed in artistic and emotionally evocative images; and from the present, these images selectively representing a contemporary world known to all members of the audience and routinely experienced by them. When these images are in harmony, the central character, standing for the continuity of the society, bridges them, as in the tale. But when they clash, as during periods of historical and social change, when images from the past are no longer keyed to those of the present, he cannot bridge them and becomes instead the center of conflict. The contradictions between present and past are expressed symbolically in the central character because he is a part of both. This leads to his ambiguity; he continues to adhere to the past, to his trickster-like ways, yet he has a vision of and destiny in the future. This explains his dual nature, his destructive and creative energies. Because he has his roots in the culture's past, and because he is fated to lead his people into the new world, he is doomed, for he cannot exist in both worlds simultaneously. The contradiction built of conflicting categories of imagery leads to heroism and epic form. It is because his destiny is a tragic one that the destiny of his society is not. Change is revealed but never resolved in his person. At the same time, because the images of the past are the roots of the culture, and because the images of the present represent the contemporary reality of the society, the members of the audience become emotionally involved in the fate of the hero, as he becomes for that audience the repository of its own hopes, fears, and uncertainties during periods of change. It is a rich emotional experience, for even as the audience laments the hero's defeat, it perforce savors it.

Conclusion

In heroic poetry, history and imaginative image come into conjunction to create these epics, and the fictional helps to explicate the impact and the meaning of the historical. These are moments of historical transition, from old ideas of leadership to new enlightened ideas, from ancient beliefs to new faiths, from bloody patterns of existence to less violent sets of rules and laws. Mwindo, Gilgamesh, and Beowulf are heroic not because of their deeds; they are heroic because of what they represent, because they are the dramatic manifestation of significant events. The entire narrative tradition, or at least major portions of it, comes to bear on these moments of historical and social transition, and they are elevated into epic.

There is evidence to suggest that this is the structure of other epics as well. There is much, for example, in *Njal's Saga* that echoes the structure and themes of the *Mahabharata*, the vast Sanskrit epic, the longest epic known. In this massive and sprawling set of heroic adventures, the rivalry between the cousins (the Pandavas and the Kauravas) is treated in great detail and in scores of episodes. Vicious battles, bloodshed, accounts of great violence lace the developing then degenerating relations between the cousins, and set against the profound violence is reconciliation, the possibilities for peace. *Njal's Saga* is also filled with episodes of violence and fury, and these too are counterpointed with the hope of peace and reconciliation in a different kind of social organization, the diminishing of the blood feuds that preoccupy the Icelandic society and which threaten whatever delicate fibers are holding the society and the shreds of legalism together. In both of these epics, there is something that seeks, threatens, to break through, a new era with a hope for creativeness that is not a part of the old society, and men are at great pains to make it possible for this to occur. But it cannot happen because of the array of unfinished battles and unconsummated hatreds.

Mantis is a bridge to the trickster. With Mantis, there is the consciousness of change, of the passing of the old order, transformation and reorganization. That is what Trickster Mantis reveals as he himself is taught. Most certainly that is what is involved in the complex themes of the narratives in which Mantis is the transformer. The sense of change is ever-present, and there is also in the Mantis narratives the blend of nostalgia for what is passing mingled with anticipation for what is to come, a conservatism that mixes with a sense of future creativity. And Mantis knows that for the new age to be born, he must die. In these narratives, there is a coming to awareness of Mantis, who is in a sense the teacher of the San as yet unborn. Mantis through his stupidity and his trickery is learning and he is also preparing the way for the new age; he is amassing the material artifacts of the San people, he is ordering life as the San will know it, he is learning the necessities for getting along in San society, and all of these will be communicated to the San, as Mantis's age passes and the new and glorious age of the San appears.

It is almost as if, at critical moments in the history of the ancient societies, the oral tradition provides the wherewithal for great poets to bring elements of the tradition to bear on these significant and dangerous transitional periods. The hero is a product of the old society, but he is making the movement to the new. In the contradictions in his character and background are the contradictions that we sense at the passing of the old, the inauguration of the new. But the hero is more than a reflector, he also organizes elements of the two ages, blends them within his own character, and that fusing is a part of the transition. He is a product of the old, and sometimes succumbs entirely to the dictates of the old; but he is also an advocate of the new, and, as such, he seeks to channel useful elements of the old into the new, to make the transition possible. For there is no abrupt change here; the epics deal with change, and the heroes stand for change, but they have feet in both worlds, and they will ultimately have to die, once the transition has been made. In their death is the transition complete.

They are indeed heroes, but not necessarily in a Herculean sense, though they do commit deeds at times which are Herculean. But they are heroes not because of these deeds, and this should be the first clue that traditional approaches to the epic heroes may not be productive avenues of approach. Heroism is defined in a much different sense. Narratives, whether performed singly or together as in epics, concentrate, as we have seen, on change, on major shifts within the society, whether these shifts are rites of passage from adolescence into adulthood or from blood feuds into a rule of law. The narratives are a part of the transition itself; because of their ritual nature, they are active in assisting humans to make these difficult transitions through periods characterized by instability and self-questioning, individual or cultural. The narrative traditions have the materials to enable humans to make these important shifts without major dislocation of values and historical depth; indeed, an analysis of these epics from this point of view will show that they are kept intact. What we are dealing with, then, in some senses, is a social and historical device that is geared to potentially disruptive change. Heroism is not to be defined on the basis of the individual's confrontation with dragons, beasts, and the others in the pantheon of villainy. The hero is to be defined as the precursor and the carrier of social change. And this ties in with the haunting quality of these narratives. The narrative tradition has built into it the possibilities for unifying structures and themes, and in fact these developmental unities flow into the perceptual unities.

This, then, is the argument: the heroic epic is a grand confrontation between creative and destructive forces. These forces, in the story found in two distinct characters, are actually the opposing sides of a single character. The epic is the poet's way of revealing this inner struggle, a struggle that has a cosmic range, from our lowest impulses to our highest, from Hades and Middle Earth to the Heavens. Those dual forces can be found, in the oral tradition, in a single character, the trickster . . . difficult to understand, ambiguous, the essence of heroism. The hero's conquest of the demon is a bard's way of revealing the results of such an inner struggle, but that happy result is not always our reality. We continue to contend with these struggles. But the happy outcome crafted by the bard may not be the happiest part of this contest anyway. There is something to be said about the confrontation itself, a struggle that takes us to our authentic selves, a conflict during which we are tied down to no one's edicts, when we are, as we have seen, most free, most liberated. It may, in the end, be the trickster who is our salvation rather than the hero. Ideas are important in these stories, of course. The characters and the images are the carriers of the ideas. And the bard is the one who shapes and communicates those ideas. Whether the hero existed, actually, historically, or not is insignificant: it is what the bard and the society make of the hero that is important: it is the ideas he stood for: a new compassion in government (for Mwindo and Sunjata), a new marriage code (for Ibonia), for example.

The characters as historical characters are unimportant. It is what they stand for that is the important thing. They become convenient incarnations of forces, institutions, changes. But they are not very real, even if they are based on history. As the dragon says: all is illusion, illusion created by the shaper, the bard. So it is not the characters, the events, it is the ideas that flow through them that command our attention. Nor should we look for simple surface morals. These are indeed present, but these are not what the stories are really about. Mwindo thought that he had his moment: the destruction of his father, the taming of the underground denizens, the destruction of the dragon. But the gods think otherwise about heroism. Moon tells Mwindo that it is more complex: one must have a reverence for life.

We create our moments in the sun ("The moment has come," says Sogolon to her son, Sundiata. "I have finished my task and it is yours that is going to begin, my son. . . . Everything in its own good time"), and then they are quickly gone ("All things have to have an end," says Hare's grandmother. "Everything will have an end. I also will have an end as I am created that way"). If 'twere done, then 'twere well 'twere done quickly ("For a little while you will be at the peak of your strength," Hrothgar tells Beowulf, "but it will not be long before sickness or the sword, or the hand of fire, or the raging sea, a thrust of the knife, a whizzing arrow, or hideous dotage, or failure and darkening of the eyes, will plunder you of your might; and in the end, brave soldier, death will defeat you"). Given that fact, one must live one's life fully: "Where are you hurrying to?" Siduri asks Gilgamesh. "You will never find that life for which you are looking. . . . Fill your belly with good things; day and night, night and day, dance and be merry, feast and rejoice." Or, as the prophet Tiresias says to Odysseus, "You must then set out once more upon your travels." Traveling is the thing, the struggle itself, the quest itself.

Mwindo dispatches a dragon, and controls a father, and creates a form of government. But there is a larger scheme here: it has to do with the gods who are eternal. So Mwindo creates his world, but that world is not only evanescent, it may not be wholly proper: we are limited. And in fact the gods are saying that there is a higher order, higher than the hero. Says the god, Rain, to Mwindo, "here, there is no room for your heroism." So is the hero put in his place.

The hero means transformation. But in his boundary state, he is dangerous. He is in the process of change, as is his world. They shape each other. The hero is energy, untamed energy, energy located at the limits. Out there, it is dangerous, it is alien, it is new. The hero moves away from human existence, to the underworld, to the heavens, to the mountaintop, to the places of Raivato and Soumaoro, to the places of Grendel and the dragon. Here, he is energy, dangerous energy, because he is in the process of reshaping illusions.

In that sense, Mwindo is like Legba. They are both denizens of the boundaries, both unleashing enormous and perilous energy because something momentous is in the process of becoming. But it is not just ideas. If that were all, one would hardly need performance, all of the accoutrements of epic production. It is the ritualistic experience that we have as we become unified with the hero, with the trickster, as our own emotions are shaped by the poet. If we can accept that ideas can be emotions, then indeed, ideas are all-important. But it is the emotional experience that reveals ideas that we concentrate on here.

The Winnebago hare cycle is a template for the heroic epic. The shaping of Hare and Grandmother is equivalent to the shaping of the hero. There is a structural likeness with *The Odyssey*: the frame and the interchangeable episodes within that frame. The trickster tales begin with the unformed Hare and Grandmother, then move progressively to the final shape of the hare along with that of the earth. Compare this with the shaping of Odysseus and Gilgamesh. The trickster hare plays the usual trickster antics and, in the process, heroically shapes the earth, his own trickery evolving into compassion.

In South African writer Nadine Gordimer's short story "The Soft Voice of the Serpent,"[56] the locust can be compared to Enkidu, and to what keeps Odysseus from returning to his home. The gods lie in wait (the locust), and the rhythm of the story has to do with the man and the Garden of Eden. The breaking of that rhythm is the province of the locust. The trickster leads to inevitable fate, the hero facing his limitations: out of trickery comes something positive. In the Legba and Winnebago trickster hare stories the trickster moves to hero: the move begins with Legba's breaking of the rules and then establishing new ones. In the Legba story, a trickster lives his world of amorality, but then he transforms that amoral world into a wholly moral one, and emerges a shaper of the new, a heroic shaper. But he remains a trickster, and he is restricted. Legba shows the two sides of the trickster and therefore the two sides of the hero, but then so does the profane trickster. The two sides of the hero are revealed in the monomyth and the rites of passage. The curbing of one side, the releasing of the other, both shape the same energy within the hero. The rite of passage joins hero and trickster. Both Odysseus and Gilgamesh move to the nadir, Hades and Utnapishtim, and there learn of their limitations: they will die. But each moves heroically within those limitations.

The structure of *The Odyssey* and *Gilgamesh* involves a frame and a cycle of tales. *The Odyssey* has a frame at the beginning: Odysseus sets off on his quest. Home and Penelope are constituents of this frame, within which is a cycle of tales. The frame is completed at the end: Odysseus returns. Penelope is found; the quest is at an end. Odysseus returns home chastened by his experiences with Calypso, Circe, Polyphemus, and aware of his limitations, thanks to Tiresias and others in Hades. His flaming heroism of the Trojan War has been channeled into his love for Penelope and for Telemachus, but what is

more important, perhaps, is that he has come to an understanding that the crucial part of heroism is not an end but the process. *Gilgamesh* similarly has a
frame beginning: Gilgamesh as king (not a very good one), within which is a
cycle of tales: the fight with Enkidu, Humbaba, the Bull of Heaven, the friendship with Enkidu, the quest for immortality, Siduri, Urshanabi, Utnapishtim.
And there is a frame ending: Gilgamesh returns, a changed king, now contain-
ing the trickster, Enkidu. Gilgamesh has come to face his limits, and from that
altering experience he has evolved into a more heroic leader.

Within the frame is a cycle of tales. This is the flexible part of the epic.
Odysseus tells his tale to the Phaeacians. In the end, the king will help Odysseus to return to his home. Penelope is found, the quest is at an end. Athena
and Poseidon, the warring gods, provide this frame for the warring humans.
The gods do not influence action much in this epic. Their presence suggests the
hero's possibilities on a heavenly scale, a mythic level. The gods shadow the
humans, and especially Odysseus. They test Odysseus, they hover about him
as he makes his decisions, and his education at the hands of gods and men
moves him to a sense of his human limits and also his human abilities. In the
end, having returned to Penelope, he is once again prepared to move out to
sea, to new adventures, new tests. Odysseus as a hero is ever being tested. He
is by no means perfect. He is a master of disguise, he can be heartless to his enemies, he loses his name. It is the humanity of Odysseus that attracts us, that
and his eternal wandering, his struggles with others and the parallel struggle
with his own identity. The trickster element resides more lastingly in Odysseus
than in Gilgamesh.

The epic deals with human heroes, heroes becoming agonizingly aware of
a sense of loss, a loss of that oneness, that unity with the gods: humans are
on their own, and it is at this juncture, in this epiphany, that a definition of
heroism is forged. The heroes are not supernatural, they are not gods, but they
have the possibilities of the gods in them, and hence the movement of the
gods constantly in the background. Heroes are becoming agonizingly aware of
their limitations, of their humanity, and it is to the degree that they accept
these limitations and this humanity that they are adjudged heroes. They struggle against their limits, and that is the key here.

The mythic frame of *Gilgamesh* has to do with the gods and Enkidu /
the gods and Utnapishtim. Before Enkidu, Gilgamesh is a forgettable king,
to be remembered mainly for his overbearing use of his kingly powers. With
the advent of Enkidu, Gilgamesh progressively, in his struggles with Enkidu,
Humbaba, and the Bull of Heaven, and caught between contending forces of
the gods, moves to a sense of his humanity, his limits, but also his possibilities.

And his destiny, we are told, is fulfilled: "In nether-earth the darkness will show him [Gilgamesh] a light; of mankind, all that are known, none will leave a monument for generations to come to compare with his. . . . You were given the kingship, such was your destiny, everlasting life was not your destiny. Because of this do not be sad at heart, do not be grieved or oppressed; he has given you power to bind and to loose, to be the darkness and the light of mankind." The darkness and the light represent the sides of the trickster. There is much of Legba in Gilgamesh.

The taming of the divine tricksters: Legba becomes legitimate, Hare becomes compassionate. The divine tricksters move to the cusp of heroism. Is this the essence of the trickster in the epic? Is the divine trickster really tamed? Witness the locust. It is in the untamable trickster that we most effectively see the hero, because the trickster gives the hero his human frailty, reveals the hero's internal struggle between contending forces. And for better or worse, the trickster element in the hero can force that hero into more appropriate self-identity.

The tale, then, and the trickster story, the divine and profane, and the myth, and history: these are the raw materials of the epic-maker. In the end, there is no hero without the trickster. The hero is neither god nor Lucifer: he is both, and that is his glory and his difficulty. But if the trickster is the hero's Achilles heel, he is also his sublime nature. But there is no hero without that heel.

The birth of the hero, the hero's departure, the hero's preparation, the nadir, wresting the elixir from the nadir, flight, return: this is also an outline for a rite-of-passage tale, with its separation, ordeal, or initiation, and return phases. It is during the ordeal that trickster energy is most evident in heroic epics and in tales. In the heroic epics, the struggle becomes clear. But the difference now is in the way the central character deals with the limitations. To the extent that he rises above his limitations, the hero receives his adulation and definition.

Gilgamesh goes to battle against Humbaba, and first humbles and then destroys the arrogant guard of the cedars, but not without considerable supernatural assistance. When cowardice and discretion overcome him, touched with humanity as he is, the encouragement from his comrade, Enkidu, is essential. Gilgamesh seems on occasion frail, vulnerable, far from heroic. Perhaps because of his mortality and his fevered quest for eternal life, he is not responded to in the same way as one might respond to a tale character. Is he a hero? Does he accomplish anything heroic on his journey? After Humbaba, he does not really engage anyone in heroic combat.

And is Beowulf at his heroic height when he is wrenching the limb from the devilish Grendel? Does the audience respond differently to the warrior when he draws his sword against the gold-hoarding dragon? Like Gilgamesh, Beowulf is vulnerable: we see the end of heroism, the terrible price of mortality. Beowulf seems more the trickster-hero after the first battle, when he sings his own praises. He is more revered in the final battle, when he is weakened and vanquished. Beowulf is apparently more the hero in defeat than in victory.

Icelandic Njal, who so skillfully manipulates the complex legal threads that keep the feuding factions of his homeland from slaughter and disaster: is he heroic when he is being most manipulative? Can this peaceful man sustain our admiration even as he himself becomes the trickster, as he begins to operate the machinery for his own ends? Or is he more heroic, his heroism more authenticated by our compassion, when he goes nobly to his death?

It is the trickster in the hero that renders the hero mortal. *Gilgamesh* reveals this essential truth about the epic hero, when we see the tricksters (the gods and their instrument, Enkidu) planting within the hero his sense of mortality. The god in the hero will forever be warring against the trickster in the hero. But it is the trickster with his duality who will eventually win out.

And so the separation of the hero is when the hero sets out to reclaim his immortality (and everything implied by that): that is the essence of the ordeal, the nadir. In *The Odyssey*, we see a physical, an actual, nadir, as Odysseus moves to the underworld, sees the shades of the dead, and receives his intimations of mortality. It is the amorality of the trickster that is essential to this discussion. The hero molds that dualistic force, and renders it positive, getting the negative forces under control, if only, as we see in *Beowulf*, for a moment.

When one looks, therefore, at the African epics, *Mwindo, Ibonia, Sunjata*, one sees the same materials, the same contending forces, and essentially the same definition of the hero. In African myth, one sees that same hero that one sees elsewhere in the world, but with clear indications of the limitations of the hero. The hero receives two definitions, one based on his own possibilities, the other based on his reduced possibilities within the framework of myth. The hero receives a definition that is fictional, created by the bards. It becomes clear that the nature of the trickster is communal, as Sunjata's sister plays her role, as Tira Makhang plays his role. The hero lives within the reality of the world, and he never acts independently: he acts within the mythic system and within the community.

The trickster can be seen in obvious ways in the cleverness of Odysseus, the cunning activities of Mwindo, the deceit of the gods. But there is a more important element of the trickster in the hero, a more integrated trickster woven into the character of the hero, and that explains the hero's melancholy, his sense of loss, his uncertainties. The nature of the hero is such that the trickster element has to be seen as an essential, perhaps the essential, aspect of the heroic character. So whatever the final definition of the hero may be, it cannot be developed without a consideration of the dualistic trickster. It is the insertion of that little trouble-making trickster that gives the hero his fascination, his humanity. It is his ability to organize the one and control the other that culminates in the definition of hero. But both must be present. There could not be a hero in the absence of either of the two forces.

Epilogue:
The Trickster Lives!

Chinua Achebe injects an oral tale into his 1958 novel, *Things Fall Apart*, as a comment on the contemporary story of Okonkwo: a character in Achebe's novel recounts a trickster tale, a story about Trickster Tortoise who, during a period of famine, disguises himself as a bird with the help of feathers loaned to him by the birds, and flies into the sky with birds who are going to a feast. At the feast, he renames himself, calling himself All of You, and he becomes the spokesman for the birds. When the food is served, he asks for whom the food has been prepared, and is told "All of you." Tortoise thereby gets all the food for himself, leaving only scraps for the birds. The angry birds then take back the feathers they had given to Tortoise, and they return to the earth, leaving the trickster behind. Trickster has no choice, he has no wings, so he leaps from the sky and his shell is shattered when he touches the earth.

The ancient stories do not die; storytellers regularly return to them. Consider next a story collected by Harold Scheub in 1967. Nadine Gordimer also reaches back to the storytelling in the Book of Genesis to make a comment about a contemporary man.

A Hlubi Storyteller: "A Fatal Misunderstanding"[57] *(Xhosa)*
Now for a story.

There was a great famine in the country, and one man went out to hunt. He left his wife and children behind at home.

He traveled, he traveled, this man traveled, he traveled, he traveled and traveled.

When he was far away, he saw a herd of elands in the distance. Elands are creatures that are milked.

This man traveled on, he traveled, he traveled and traveled.

He arrived, he arrived at a place where there was an eland and a calf. This man approached them. He struggled to seize this eland and its calf, he came along there and struggled with them, he struggled and struggled, and finally he seized the eland. And when he had seized it, he pulled it along and went home with it. The calf followed behind, the man traveled on.

When he arrived on the cliffs, his homestead was down below, he called out loudly.

He said, "Wash the pails!"

The children were in the yard, playing.

They said, "Mother! Come out here! Father says that we should break all the dishes!"

So, with their mother, the children broke the dishes.

The man again shouted, he said, "Wash the pails!"

The children said, "Mother, do you hear Father? He says we should burn the homestead down!"

Then the mother and the children burned the homestead down.

The man descended, he arrived. He arrived, and the homestead was already burned down, the dishes were broken. He beat them, that man killed them, and then he was alone. He remained there, milking that eland.

The story has ended, it has ended.

A South African Story: "The Soft Voice of the Serpent," by Nadine Gordimer

A twenty-six-year-old man has lost his leg. He is in a garden, not allowing himself to realize the fact of his leglessness. A locust is in the garden as well, looking "curiously human and even expressive." And one of its legs is gone. The man sees the parallel between his situation and that of the locust. The man watches the locust intently as it struggles to move. He calls his wife to watch. "I can see it feels just like I do!" His wife says, "Funny thing is, it's even the same leg, the left one. . . ." "'I know,' he nodded laughing. 'The two of us. . . .'" And then, suddenly, "the locust flew away. . . ." They had forgotten that locusts can fly.

The Eden story (the title suggests this). "Perhaps there was something in this of the old Eden idea; the tender human adjusting himself to himself in the soothing impersonal presence of trees and grass and earth, before going out into the stare of the world." He sits in the garden, his garden of Eden, coming to terms with his state. And he is tempted by Satan, as Eve and Adam were in the original garden, and the soft voice of the serpent leads him to do what he wanted not to do: "He felt that he had no leg. . . . He never let the realization quite reach him; he let himself realize it physically, but he never quite let it get at *him*. He felt it pressing up, coming, coming, dark, crushing, ready to burst—but he always turned away, just in time, back to his book. That was his system; that was the way he was going to do it. He would let it come near, irresistibly near, again and again, ready to catch him alone in the garden. And again and again he would turn it back, just in time. Slowly it would become a habit. It would become such a habit never to get to the point of realizing it, that he never would realize it. And one day he would find that he had achieved what he wanted: he would feel as if he had always been like that. Then the danger would be over, for ever."

"The Soft Voice of the Serpent" is structurally a story that depends for its effect on the mythic parallel: the soft voice of the serpent in Eden, the soft voice of the serpent in the contemporary South African garden. Original sin in Eden: the horrid realization of his physical loss in the modern world. The locust is the physical parallel, and the temptation to see the locust as a fellow sufferer is the soft voice of the serpent. At the last moment, Satan has his way: the locust flies off, the human cannot do that, he is earthbound, he has lost his leg forever. It is a dreadful thing, for the parallel with the locust has brought him to do what he had not wanted to do, consider his plight. The comparison with the locust brings him to do this: "Or maybe he could be taught to use crutches."

"The two of us . . . ," he says. "The two of us."

The story of the fall of man is in Genesis, chapters 2 and 3; the main motif is that Lucifer causes the fall of man. This motif of the divine trickster, Lucifer (Satan), the devil, is a durable one appearing under various guises in the oral and literary traditions of the world. "The Fall" is a myth, describing cosmological change. As with all tricksters, Lucifer tempts his dupes (Adam and Eve, in this case) by creating a world of illusion. Patterning in such tales is established in the tensions between the illusory world created by the trickster and the real world (in which the dupes invariably and inevitably awaken, rudely): the two worlds are never the same, though for a brief moment they seem to be one. They are sufficiently similar that it is possible for the trickster to create his illusion out of fragments taken from the real world. Because the world of illusion contains elements of the world with which the dupe is familiar, that dupe is the more easily seduced into the trickster's world, his web. And the trickster makes his world seem splendid: he purrs about its attractiveness. Look, he says in this instance, on the day that you eat of the fruit of this forbidden tree, your eyes shall be opened, you shall be as the gods, you shall know good and evil. It is a magnificent promise, and the woman falls for it, becoming the trickster's dupe. The result of the trickster's antics is never pleasant to the dupe, but in this case it is particularly dreadful; the result is the fall of humanity, a cosmological change. The trickster has seduced the human into his web of illu-sions, and only when it is too late do Adam and Eve realize their awful blunder. But then, all they can do is sew a few fig leaves together.

Now the serpent was more subtil than any beast of the field which the LORD God had made. And he said unto the woman, Yea, hath God said, Ye shall not eat of every tree of the garden? And the woman said unto the serpent, We may eat of the fruit of the trees of the garden: But of the fruit of the tree which is in the midst of the garden, God hath said, Ye shall not eat of it, neither shall ye touch it, lest ye die. And the serpent said unto the woman, Ye shall not surely die: For God doth know that in the day ye eat thereof, then your eyes shall be opened, and ye shall be as gods, knowing good and evil. And when the woman saw that the tree was good for food, and that it was pleasant to the eyes, and a tree to be desired to make one wise, she took of the fruit thereof, and did eat, and gave also unto her husband with her; and he did eat. And the eyes of them both were opened, and they knew that they were naked; and they sewed fig leaves together, and made themselves aprons. (Genesis 3:1–7, King James Version)

The man descended, he arrived. He arrived, and the homestead was already burned down, the dishes were broken. He beat them, that man killed them, and then he was alone. He remained there, milking that eland.

The story has ended, it has ended.

Notes

1. J. R. R. Tolkien, *"Beowulf*: The Monsters and the Critics," *The Beowulf Poet, A Collection of Critical Essays*, ed. Donald K. Fry (Englewood Cliffs, NJ: Prentice-Hall, 1968), 23.

2. Tolkien argues, however, that *"Beowulf* is not an 'epic,' not even a magnified 'lay'" (38).

3. E. E. Evans-Pritchard, *The Zande Trickster* (Oxford: Clarendon Press, 1967).

4. Evans-Pritchard, *The Zande Trickster.*

5. Prospero:

> Our revels now are ended. These our actors,
> As I foretold you, were all spirits, and
> Are melted into air, into thin air:
> And like the baseless fabric of this vision,
> The cloud-capp'd tow'rs, the gorgeous palaces,
> The solemn temples, the great globe itself,
> Yea, all which it inherit, shall dissolve,
> And, like this insubstantial pageant faded,
> Leave not a rack behind. We are such stuff
> As dreams are made on; and our little life
> Is rounded with a sleep. (*The Tempest*, Act 4, scene 1, 148–158)

6. The performance was by a Hlubi woman, about fifty years old, in a home in Nyaniso Location, Matatiele District, the Transkei. The date was November 8, 1967, and the time, about 11 am. The audience consisted of fifteen women and five children. Number 1739 in Harold Scheub's collection. The first part of this story appeared in Harold Scheub, *The Xhosa Ntsomi* (Oxford: Oxford University Press, 1975), 25–27.

7. The performance took place on November 9, 1967, at about 3 pm, in a home in Nyaniso Location, Matatiele District, the Transkei. The storyteller was a Hlubi woman, about forty years old. Thirty women, three men, and twenty children made up the audience. The performer evoked her somewhat bawdy narrative with a studied nonchalance, a straight face, and a businesslike delivery—and her demeanor was half the fun. The feces is included in the story as just another character, treated as such by the performer, and Trickster Hlakanyana's increasing frustration is developed by means of nonverbal actions

alone. Effective vocal dramatics and gesturing, and excellent relations with the audience mark this performance. Number 1808 in Harold Scheub's collection.

8. J. Tom Brown, *Among the Bantu Nomads* (Philadelphia: J. B. Lippincott, 1926), 181–85. A "fold" is a fenced enclosure.

9. R. S. Rattray, ed., *Akan-Ashanti Folk-Tales* (Oxford: Clarendon Press, 1930), 132–37.

10. Sigismund Wilhelm Koelle, *Outlines of a Grammar of the Vei Language* (London: Church Missionary House, 1854), 69–72.

11. Lit., a lie-sickness.

12. John Ciardi and Miller Williams, *How Does a Poem Mean?* (Boston: Houghton Mifflin, 1975), 4. Ciardi wrote, "The concern is not to arrive at a definition and to close the book, but to arrive at an experience" (2). And in response to W. B. Yeats's poetic query, "How can we know the dancer from the dance?" ("Among School Children," W. B. Yeats, *The Collected Poems of W. B. Yeats* [New York: Macmillan, 1956]), Ciardi said, "What the poem is, is inseparable from its own performance of itself. The dance is in the dancer and the dancer is in the dance." He argued, "Above all else, poetry is a performance" (4).

13. Dorothea Bleek, ed., "The Mantis and the Korotwiten" in *The Mantis and His Friends*, collected by W. H. I. Bleek and Lucy C. Lloyd (Cape Town: T. M. Miller; London and Oxford: B. Blackwell [1924]), 50–54.

14. The storyteller comments, "One man anoints another, putting his hands under his armpits into the perspiration. And the other gets it onto his face, where the first man anoints him, that he may become like the first man" (50).

15. Bleek, "The Mantis and the Cat," in *The Mantis and His Friends*, 19–21.

16. Bleek, "The Mantis and Kutegaua," in *The Mantis and His Friends*, 54–57.

17. Bleek, "The Mantis Takes Away the Ticks' Sheep" and "The Mantis and the All-devourer" in *The Mantis and His Friends*, 30–40.

18. Garvey Nkonki, "The Traditional Prose Literature of the Ngqika," M.A. [African Studies], University of South Africa, n.d., 52–53.

19. Notes by Dorothea Bleek, in the introduction to *The Mantis and His Friends*.

20. Bleek, "The Mantis Makes an Eland," in *The Mantis and His Friends*, 30–40.

21. See Nongenile Masithathu Zenani, "Sikhuluma," in *African Folklore*, ed. Richard M. Dorson (Garden City, NY: Anchor Books, 1972), 523–61.

22. Melville J. Herskovits and Frances S. Herskovits, *Dahomean Narrative* (Evanston: Northwestern University Press, 1958), 124.

23. Herskovits and Herskovits, "How Legba Became Guardian of Men and Gods: Why the Dog Is Respected," in *Dahomean Narrative*, 142–48.

24. Legba is spokesman for the gods; his role corresponds to the Fon political official known as "linguist."

25. Paul Radin, *The Trickster: A Study in American Indian Mythology* (New York: Bell, 1956), 63–91.

26. R. Becker, "Conte d'Ibonia: Essai de traduction et d'interprétation d'après l'édition Dahle de 1877," *Mémoires de l'Académie Malagache* 30 (1939): 33–35.

27. From James Sibree, Jr., "Malagasy Folk-tales," *Folk-Lore Journal* 2 (1884): 49–55. The Malagasy live on the island of Madagascar, off the southeastern coast of Africa.

28. These comments are taken from Harold Scheub, *The African Storyteller* (Dubuque: Kendall/Hunt Publishing, 1990), 258–59.

29. See Rhys Carpenter, *Folktale, Fiction and Saga in the Homeric Epics* (Berkeley: University of California Press, 1946).

30. John Gardner, *Grendel* (London: Gollancz, 1971).

31. Joseph Campbell, *The Hero with a Thousand Faces* (Princeton: Princeton University Press, 1972), 3–46.

32. This analysis is derived from Harold Scheub, review of Daniel Biebuyck, *Hero and Chief: Epic Literature from the Banyanga (Zaire Republic)*, in *Ba Shiru* 12, 1 (1985): 105–25.

33. C. M. Bowra, *Heroic Poetry* (London: Macmillan, 1964; original edition, 1952), 9–12, 123.

34. Daniel Biebuyck, *Hero and Chief: Epic Literature from the Banyanga (Zaire Republic)* (Berkeley: University of California Press, 1978), ix. Hereafter, quotations from *Hero and Chief* are cited in text. Biebuyck is referring to Finnegan's 1970 comment, "All in all, epic poetry does not seem to be a typical African form." It "seems to be of remarkably little significance in African oral poetry, and the a priori assumption that epic is the natural form for many non-literate peoples turns out here to have little support" (Ruth Finnegan, *Oral Literature in Africa* [Oxford: Clarendon Press, 1970], 110). See also Finnegan's article, "Studying the Oral Literatures of Africa in the 1960s and Today," *Journal des africanistes* 80, 1/2 (2010): 15–28. See also John William Johnson, "Yes, Virginia, There Is an Epic in Africa," *Research in African Literatures* 11, 3 (1980): 308–26.

35. R. Becker, "Conte d'Ibonia: Essai de traduction et d'interprétation d'après l'édition Dahle de 1877," *Memoires de l'Académie Malagache* 30 (1939): 1–136.

36. Bowra, *Heroic Poetry*, 9.

37. Gordon Innes, *Sunjata: Three Mandinka Versions* (London: School of Oriental and African Studies, University of London, 1974); Djibril T. Niane, *Soundjata, ou l'épopée mandingue* (Paris: Présence Africaine, 1960).

38. John Pepper Clark, *The Ozidi Saga* (collected and translated from the Ijo of Okabou Ojobolo) (Ibadan: Ibadan University Press 1977). Phonograph recordings and a film of this epic are also available.

39. For Rwanda and Zaire see, for example, A. Coupez and Th. Kamanzi, *Littérature de cour au Rwanda* (Oxford: Clarendon Press, 1970); A. de Rop, *Lianja: L'épopée des Mongo* (Brussels: Académie royale des Sciences d'Outre-Mer, 1964); John Jacobs and Jan Vansina, "Nsong Atoot: Her Konninklijk epos der Bushong," *Kongo-Overzee* 22 (1956): 1–39; Alexis Kagame, *La poésie dynastique au Rwanda* (Brussels: Institut Royal Colonial Beige, 1951). For the Soninke see, for example, Claude Meillassoux, Lassana Doucoure, and Diaowé Simagha, *Légende de la dispersion des kusa (Épopée soninké)* (Dakar: IFAN, 1967). For the Swahili see, for example, Lyndon Harries, *Swahili Poetry* (Oxford: Clarendon Press, 1962); Jan Knappert, *Four Swahili Epics* (Leiden: Drukkerij "Luctor et Emergo," 1964). For the Adangme see, for example, D. A. Puplampu, "The National Epic of the Adangme," *African Affairs* 1 (1951): 236–41. For the Fang see, for example, Herbert Pepper, *Un mvet de Zwe Nguema: Chant épique Fang*, collected by Herbert Pepper, edited by Paul de Wolf and Paule de Wolf (Paris: Armand Colin, 1972). For the Xhosa see, for example, Harold Scheub, "Performance of Oral Narrative," in *Frontiers of Folklore*, ed. William R. Bascom (Boulder: Westview Press, Inc., 1977), 69–73.

40. Of interest is the material he provides regarding the hero, the chief, and heroism, although he is conservative and descriptive rather than provocative and analytical in his judgments; the material that he has assembled gives him many opportunities to be the latter.

41. Daniel Biebuyck and Kahombo C. Mateene, eds., *The Mwindo Epic: From the Banyanga (Congo Republic)* (Berkeley: University of California Press, 1969), 14. Hereafter, quotations from *The Mwindo Epic* are cited in text.

42. Daniel Biebuyck, "The Epic as a Genre in Congo Oral Literature," in *African Folklore*, ed. Richard M. Dorson (Garden City, NY: Anchor Books, 1972), 267.

43. Carpenter, *Folk Tale, Fiction and Saga in the Homeric Epics*, 165, 182.

44. Denys Page, *Folktales in Homer's Odyssey* (Cambridge, MA.: Harvard University Press, 1973), 4.

45. Tinguidji, *Silâmaka et Poullôri*, ed. Christiane Seydou (Paris: Armand Colin, 1972), 55. "One can recognize a judicious use of theatrical technique as well as that of the tale, the story, skillfully combined. . . . If this epic begins as a story in which the antagonistic characters are presented in a situation that carries the seeds of the final outcome—once the images are in place, the storytelling technique is bit by bit replaced with that of theater, with the scene of combat against the serpent."

46. Biebuyck, "The Epic as a Genre in Congo Oral Literature," 261.

47. ‖Kábbo, "The Mantis Takes Away the Ticks' Sheep" and "The Mantis and the All-devourer," in *The Mantis and His Friends*, 30–40.

48. Thomas Mofolo, *Chaka* (Morija: Morija Sesuto Book Depot, 1957), originally published in 1925. For an English translation, see Thomas Mofolo, *Chaka: An Historical Romance*, trans. F. H. Dutton (London: Oxford University Press, 1931).

49. Shé-kárjsj Candi Rureke, *The Mwindo Epic*, in Biebuyck and Kahombo, *The Mwindo Epic: From the Banyanga*. This analysis is derived from Harold Scheub, "Narrative Patterning in Oral Performances," *Ba Shiru* 7, 2 (1976): 19–28.

50. William Blake (1757–1827), "The Tiger," in *The Oxford Book of English Verse*, ed. Arthur Quiller-Couch (Oxford: Clarendon Press, 1919), 489.

51. *The Epic of Gilgamesh*, an English version with an introduction by N. K. Sandars (Baltimore: Penguin Books, 1970), 7. Hereafter, quotations from *Gilgamesh* are cited in text.

52. *Beowulf*, a prose translation with an introduction by David Wright (Baltimore: Penguin Books, 1970). Hereafter, quotations from *Beowulf* are cited in text.

53. When Thetis dipped her son, Achilles, into the river Styx, she meant to make him invulnerable. But his heel was not covered by the water, and he was killed when an arrow struck his heel.

54. For African examples, see Hans Abrahamsson, *The Origin of Death: Studies in African Mythology* (Uppsala: Studia Ethnographica Upsaliensia, III, 1951).

55. *Njal's Saga*, translated with an introduction by Magnus Magnusson and Harmann Palsson (Baltimore: Penguin Books, 1970).

56. In Nadine Gordimer, *Face to Face* (Johannesburg: Silver Leaf Books, 1949), 9–15. See Epilogue.

57. The performance took place on November 16, 1967, at about 10:30 am, in a home in Bubesi Location, Matatiele District, the Transkei. The performer, a Hlubi woman, about fifty years old, narrated the story in Xhosa before an audience of fifteen children, fifteen women, and ten teenagers. Number 2056 in Harold Scheub's collection.

Bibliography

Abrahamsson, Hans. *The Origin of Death: Studies in African Mythology*. Uppsala: Studia Ethnographlca Upsaliensia, III, 1951.

Achebe, Chinua. *Things Fall Apart*. London: William Heinemann, 1958.

Becker, R. "Conte d'Ibonia: Essai de traduction et d'interprétation d'après l'édition Dahle de 1877." *Memoires de l'Académie Malagache* 30 (1939): 1–136.

Beowulf. A prose translation with an introduction by David Wright. Baltimore: Penguin Books, 1970.

Biebuyck, Daniel. "The Epic as a Genre in Congo Oral Literature." In *African Folklore*. Edited by Richard M. Dorson, 257–74. Garden City, NY: Anchor Books, 1972.

Biebuyck, Daniel. *Hero and Chief: Epic Literature from the Banyanga (Zaire Republic)*. Berkeley: University of California Press, 1978.

Biebuyck, Daniel, and Kahombo C. Mateene, eds. *The Mwindo Epic: From the Banyanga (Congo Republic)*. Berkeley: University of California Press, 1969.

Blake, William. "The Tiger." In *The Oxford Book of English Verse*. Edited by Arthur Quiller-Couch, 489. Oxford: Clarendon Press, 1919.

Bleek, Dorothea, ed. *The Mantis and His Friends*. Collected by W. H. I. Bleek and Lucy C. Lloyd. Cape Town: T. M. Miller; London and Oxford: B. Blackwell, 1923.

Bleek, W. H. I., and Lucy C. Lloyd. *Specimens of Bushman Folklore*. London: G. Allen, 1911.

Bowra, C. M. *Heroic Poetry*. London: Macmillan and Co., 1964. Original edition, 1952.

Brown, J. Tom. *Among the Bantu Nomads*. Philadelphia: J. B. Lippincott, 1926.

Campbell, Joseph. *The Hero with a Thousand Faces*. Princeton: Princeton University Press, 1972.

Carpenter, Rhys. *Folk Tale, Fiction and Saga in the Homeric Epics*. Berkeley: University of California Press, 1946.

Ciardi, John, and Miller Williams. *How Does a Poem Mean?* Boston: Houghton Mifflin, 1975.

Clark, John Pepper. *The Ozidi Saga*. Collected and translated from the Ijo of Okabou Ojobolo. Ibadan: Ibadan University Press 1977.

213

Coupez, A., and Th. Kamanzi. *Littérature de cour au Rwanda*. Oxford: Clarendon Press, 1970.

de Rop, A. *Lianja: L'épopée des Mongo*. Brussels: Académic royale des Sciences d'Outre-Mer, 1964.

Doke, Clement M., ed. "The Story of Mr. Lion-child and Mr. Cow-child." In *Lamba Folklore*. Collected by Clement M. Doke, 14–29. New York: American Folk-lore Society, 1927.

Evans-Pritchard, E. E. *The Zande Trickster*. Oxford: Clarendon Press, 1967.

Finnegan, Ruth. *Oral Literature in Africa*. Oxford: Clarendon Press, 1970.

Finnegan, Ruth. "Studying the Oral Literatures of Africa in the 1960s and Today." *Journal des africanistes* 80, 1/2 (2010): 15–28.

Gardner, John. *Grendel*. London: Gollancz, 1971.

Gilgamesh, The Epic of. An English version with an introduction by N. K. Sandars. Baltimore: Penguin Books, 1970.

Gordimer, Nadine. *Face to Face*. Johannesburg: Silver Leaf Books, 1949.

Harries, Lyndon. *Swahili Poetry*. Oxford: Clarendon Press, 1962.

Herskovits, Melville J., and Frances S. Herskovits. *Dahomean Narrative*. Evanston: Northwestern University Press, 1958.

Hyde, Lewis. *Trickster Makes This World: Mischief, Myth, and Art*. New York: Farrar, Straus and Giroux, 1998.

Innes, Gordon. *Sunjata: Three Mandinka Versions*. London: School of Oriental and African Studies, 1974.

Jacobs, John, and Jan Vansina. "Nsong Atoot: Her Konninklijk epos der Bushong." *Kongo-Overzee* 22 (1956): 1–39.

Johnson, John William. "Yes, Virginia, There Is an Epic in Africa." *Research in African Literatures* 11, 3 (1980): 308–26.

||Kábbo. "The Mantis Takes Away the Ticks' Sheep" and "The Mantis and the All-devourer." In *The Mantis and His Friends: Bushman Folklore*. Collected by W. H. I. Bleek and Lucy C. Lloyd; edited by Dorothea F. Bleek, 30–40. Cape Town: T. Maskew Miller, 1923.

Kagame, Alexis. *La poésie dynastique au Rwanda*. Brussels: Institut Royal Colonial Beige, 1951.

Knappert, Jan. *Four Swahili Epics*. Leiden: Drukkerij "Luctor et Emergo," 1964.

Koelle, Sigismund Wilhelm. *Outlines of a Grammar of the Vei Language*. London: Church Missionary House, 1854.

Mahabharata, The. An abridged translation by John D. Smith. New York: Penguin, 2009.

Meillassoux, Claude, Lassana Doucoure, and Diaowé Simagha. *Légende de la dispersion des kusa (Épopée soninké)*. Dakar: IFAN, 1967.

Mofolo, Thomas. *Chaka*. Morija: Morija Sesuto Book Depot, 1957. Originally published, 1925.

Mofolo, Thomas. *Chaka: An Historical Romance*. Translated from the original Sesuto by F. H. Dutton. London: Oxford University Press, 1931.

Niane, Djibril T. *Soundjata, ou l'épopée mandingue*. Paris: Présence Africaine, 1960.

Njal's Saga. Translated with an introduction by Magnus Magnusson and Harmann Palsson. Baltimore: Penguin Books, 1970.

Nkonki, Garvey. "The Traditional Prose Literature of the Ngqika." M. A. (African Studies). University of South Africa, n.d.

Page, Denys. *Folktales in Homer's Odyssey*. Cambridge: Harvard University Press, 1973.

Pelton, Robert D. *The Trickster in West Africa: A Study of Mythic Irony and Sacred Delight*. Berkeley: University of California Press, 1980.

Pepper, Herbert. *Un mvet de Zwe Nguema: Chant épique Fang*. Collected by Herbert Pepper; edited by Paul de Wolf and Paule de Wolf. Paris: Armand Colin, 1972.

Puplampu, D. A. "The National Epic of the Adangme." *African Affairs* 1 (1951): 236–41.

Radin, Paul. *The Trickster: A Study in American Indian Mythology*. New York: Bell, 1956.

Rattray, R. S., ed. *Akan-Ashanti Folk-Tales*. Oxford: Clarendon Press, 1930.

Raum,. J., ed. "Das Märchen von Mrile." *Versuch einer Grammatik der Dschaggasprache (Moachi-Dialekt)*. Berlin: 1909; reprinted Ridgewood, N.J.: Gregg Press, 1964.

Scheub, Harold. *The African Storyteller*. Dubuque: Kendall/Hunt Publishing, 1990.

Scheub, Harold. "Narrative Patterning in Oral Performances." *Ba Shiru* 7, 2 (1976): 19–28.

Scheub, Harold. "Performance of Oral Narrative." In *Frontiers of Folklore*. Edited by William R. Bascom, 69–73. Boulder: Westview Press, Inc., 1977.

Scheub, Harold. Review of *Hero and Chief: Epic Literature from the Banyanga (Zaire Republic)* by Daniel Biebuyck. *Ba Shiru* 12, 1 (1985): 105–25.

Sibree, James, Jr. "Magalasy Folk-tales." *Folk-Lore Journal* 2 (1884): 49–55.

Tinguidji. *Silâmaka et Poullôri*. Edited by Christiane Seydou. Paris: Armand Colin, 1972.

Tolkien, J. R. R. "*Beowulf*: The Monsters and the Critics." In *The Beowulf Poet: A Collection of Critical Essays*. Edited by Donald K. Fry, 8–56. Englewood Cliffs, NJ: Prentice-Hall, 1968.

Yeats, W. B. *The Collected Poems of W. B. Yeats*. New York: Macmillan, 1956.

Zenani, Nongenile Masithathu. "Sikhuluma." In *African Folklore*. Edited by Richard M. Dorson, 523–61. Garden City, NY: Anchor Books, 1972.

Index